Economic Sense and Nonsense

ANTHONY DE JASAY

Economic Sense and Nonsense

REFLECTIONS FROM EUROPE

2008–2012

Anthony de Jasay

Edited by

HARTMUT KLIEMT

LIBERTY FUND

Indianapolis

This book is published by Liberty Fund, Inc.,
a foundation established to encourage study of the
ideal of a society of free and responsible individuals.

𒂼𒄀

The cuneiform inscription that serves as our logo and
as the design motif for our endpapers is the earliest-known
written appearance of the word "freedom" (*amagi*), or "liberty."
It is taken from a clay document written about 2300 B.C.
in the Sumerian city-state of Lagash.

C   10 9 8 7 6 5 4 3 2 1
P   10 9 8 7 6 5 4 3 2 1

Library of Congress Cataloging-in-Publication Data
De Jasay, Anthony, 1925–
[Essays. Selections.]
Economic sense and nonsense: reflections from Europe, 2008–2012 /
Anthony de Jasay; edited by Hartmut Kliemt.
pages cm.—([The collected papers of Anthony de Jasay])
Includes bibliographical references and index.
ISBN 978-0-86597-878-2 (hardcover: alk. paper)
ISBN 978-0-86597-879-9 (pbk.: alk. paper)
1. Europe—Economic conditions—21st century.
2. Europe—Economic policy—21st century.
I. Kliemt, Hartmut, 1949–   II. Title
HC240.D365 2014
330.94'0561—dc23   2013050073

LIBERTY FUND, INC.
8335 Allison Pointe Trail, Suite 300
Indianapolis, Indiana 46250-1684

CONTENTS

PREFACE

This volume, companion to *Social Justice and the Indian Rope Trick*, in my Collected Papers, contains sixty monthly essays written for my column in The Library of Economics and Liberty website of Liberty Fund over the years 2008 to 2012. Those five years were something of a shambles in most of the Western economies, and their intellectual climate was not really pleasant. My five dozen essays, grouped roughly by subject, are contending with this climate and seek to defend what I believe is valid economics and the liberal thought which such economics supports. It is odd that it should require a defense. Prior to 2007, it was the accepted orthodoxy, the Washington consensus of reasonably free markets, free trade, flexible exchange rates, and decreasing regulation. In the changed climate of the past five years, this orthodoxy has been partly or wholly rejected. Whose fault is it?

In our era of fast technological change, transport and communications technologies advance fastest of all. Modern transport technology brought us globalization by transforming a vast range of products that used to move only a few miles into tradeable goods moving with ease from one continent to another. This long-distance trade lifted a billion or so of the Asian poor out of abject misery and was mostly a good thing in other respects. The same is hardly true of communications technology. Ideas that used to move fairly slowly from place to place, being filtered and tested a bit on the way, now are perceived with the speed of light all over the world, where the internet and the so-called social networks hold sway. This is far from always being a good thing. It is the enabling condition of what I call, with unconcealed ill will, *parrot talk*. It is my chosen adversary in this book. It rises when some authority launches an idea, a departure from the old, which is easily plausible and responds to an anxiety or a need for putting the blame on some scapegoat for things not going as they should. The idea is picked up by the media and, deplorably enough, by the lesser lights in our universities and is repeated, parrotlike, until it becomes the generally accepted new orthodoxy.

The time of troubles had a small beginning. In mid-2007 it became common knowledge that about 400 billion dollars of so-called subprime American residential mortgages, sponsored by a "socially" inspired government and accepted by bankers of subprime intelligence, were in fact duds. It was close to nonsense to suppose that such a paltry sum, spread over a multitude of banks in the vast North Atlantic financial system, could not be digested without major upset. However, with no apparent reason for thinking that it would be helpful, two of the highest officials of the world monetary system then announced that the economy was about to crash into the worst depression since 1930. The parrot choir took up this self-fulfilling prophecy with almost hysterical shrillness. Interbank trust, indispensable for a fractional reserve system to function, was shaken, though often for no good reason.

As events passed by the corpse of Lehman Brothers and the comatose bodies of the Royal Bank of Scotland, AIG, and Citigroup, the regulators felt it a good idea to pour oil on the fire and to ratchet up the solvency ratios the banks had urgently to attain. These rules in Basel I, II, and III successively gave everyone to understand that the regulators again and again judged the solvency of the banks insufficient—surely the right way to cement mutual distrust and frighten off interbank lending. An equally unintended and even more damaging consequence was that under Basel III, the banks had to shrink their balance sheets and starve small businesses, dependent on the banks, of the credit they needed in overcoming the recession.

To appreciate the regulatory zeal, one may add that the American banking system was going to be put to rights by the 32,000 pages of the Dodd-Frank Act and its appendixes and by having two lawyers looking over the shoulder of every banker to see that what is being done is really legal. The ideal seemed to be to have a system consisting of cozy little Main Street banks as pictured in the *Saturday Evening Post* of bygone days.

Parrot talk now takes it as settled truth that prior to the troubles that have been besetting the economy since 2008, business was underregulated and was left too much to have its own way. Economic sense tells us that the system was and still is a hybrid one, neither fish nor fowl, and there is no quick and offhand way for telling whether regulating it any further would do better or worse. In the long run, most if not all regulation is a drag on the market and an obstacle to achieving the marginal equivalences at which factor allocation and consumer satisfaction are at their best.

In these essays, given the times when they were first offered to the reader, I could not nor did I want to avoid politics. One area where politics and economics merge is, of course, the sovereign debt. Electoral exigencies have always pushed democratic governments to spending money they did not have. As ill luck would have it, the rising burden of their debt relative to their GDP has reached the dangerous zone for many nations just at the wrong time, when they were also trying to cope with the upheaval in their banking system. For the eleven (later increased to seventeen) European states that in 1999 caught themselves in the trap of a common currency and deprived themselves of the use of a powerful and relatively painless means of adjustment, the flexible rate of exchange, the discomfort was doubly acute. For reasons which look rather like economic nonsense, it became the accepted wisdom that dissolution of the Eurozone would be an unspeakable catastrophe. Even the exit of one of the smallest and quite absurdly indebted member states, Greece, would threaten the survival of the whole zone. "Saving" Ireland and Portugal and Cyprus, but above all "saving" Greece became the subject of an almost daily television soap opera of these years. One school of thought would give the member states access to Germany's checkbook. Failing that, federalism must be promoted so that the budgets of the member states should be subjected to agreement in Brussels and, in case of excess, the guilty state should be subjected to sanction. Economic sense tells us loud and clear that the sanction would be a wagging finger and the sorrowful sigh of "naughty, naughty child."

Where parrot talk is really coming into its windy and woolly own is the ethics of the "system," which must be replaced by a "new model" that is both more rational, in better control of mercurial markets, and above all more devoted to human well-being than to selfish greed. There is today a near-unanimous condemnation of the very existence of a risk-ridden system. "Security" has come to be a supreme value in both halves of what this book calls Euramerica. "Security" has no price and must be pursued regardless of costs. Deliberately accepting risk is close to immoral; "speculation" is only a little less loathesome than child abuse. The condemnation of speculation and particularly of one of its techniques, short-selling, is a fascinating feature of the moral confusion and economic nonsense of our day. In fact, shaving off price peaks by selling and filling in price troughs by buying, which the speculator must do to succeed, is a contribution to the stability we are all supposed to desire, and it should be rewarded by a medal if not by a nice subsidy.

We should have learned from Adam Smith, if we did not know it already, that it is thanks to the selfish greed of "butcher, baker, and brewer"—and, yes, of banker—that we have our dinner on the table. It is an easily grasped theorem of economics that it is by firm striving to maximize the present value of profits that the best allocation of productive factors among alternative uses is approximated. It is truly frightening to think of what would happen if firms, listening to parrot talk, really tried to "meet human needs" instead of greedily maximizing profits. We are, thank heaven, in no imminent danger of this bizarre prospect.

Anthony de Jasay

PART 1

To Spend or Not to Spend?

1. TO SPEND OR NOT TO SPEND?

To spend or not to spend, that is the question that has lately faced many an economic Hamlet. There are pressing short-term reasons that say "spend" to alleviate the recession that has already begun or to avert the depression that many commentators profess to see looming on the horizon. There are longer-term reasons that do not all point the same way. Indeed, most would rather advise not to spend. Apart from the short vs. long term divide, there is divided counsel, too, about the proper role of government in the economy.

The immediate question for economic policy revolves around the fiscal stimulus, if any, that should be administered to offset the downward drag that is now manifest in every economy worth the name. Two things need first to be borne in mind.

First, the recession (in the best case) or slump (in the worst) is almost completely self-started. It has no "objective" cause such as an oil embargo or grave balance-of-payments trouble. Discounting the trigger effect of the subprime losses suffered by the banking system in 2007—at about $600 billion a fleabite to the world financial structure—the damage to our economies came from the snowballing loss of confidence by which everybody frightened everybody else to behave like wary hedgehogs.

The second preliminary that the makers of policy have to bear in mind is that 2008 has marked the end of the mentality of "buy now, pay later" that has characterised American, British, and to a lesser extent other societies. In the modern Anglo-American type of economy, it was the accepted thing to finance consumption by credit card and other debt, household saving hovered around zero as homeowners reckoned that the rising property market was doing their saving for them. The high-spending lifestyle is clearly going out of fashion and looks like it is being replaced by a more Teutonic culture of caution

First published by Liberty Fund, Inc., at www.econlib.org on January 5, 2009. Reprinted by permission.

3

and thrift. Until very recently, using a credit card was considered by Germans as rather flashy and lightweight. It is now becoming just a bit daring everywhere else.

If household saving recovers and corporate investment is frightened off by all the talk about the coming "crisis," a gap opens up between capacity and demand, and it is this gap that public opinion urgently wants governments to fill by fiscal means. In Europe, the Maastricht rule of government deficits not exceeding 3 percent of GDP has been explicitly suspended. Had it not been, it would be violated regardless. Various stimulus "packages" have been announced and may well be increased in the coming year. The British package contains a large dose of reduced taxation on consumer expenditure and smaller doses of extra public spending, the whole amounting to nearly 4 percent of GDP. The public sector deficit will rise to over 8 percent in 2009. Smaller fiscal stimuli have been announced by most major European countries, the total amounting to about 1.5 percent of European GDP. Some of this is as yet vague and ill-defined, and the part to be devoted to public infrastructure investment can only be spent slowly as projects are approved and work gets going. (Europe's projected fiscal stimulus of 1.5 percent of GDP compares with the 2 percent of U.S. GDP that the Obama administration is thinking of spending on public infrastructure, though it could hardly do all or most of that within a twelve-month period.)

The European public spending plans would raise the budget deficits of the respective countries by between 1 and 5 percent of GDP. The British deficit would be brushing banana republic levels. Arguably, Britain can afford it, for its public debt is "only" 45 percent of its GDP. This compares with about 38 percent for the U.S.A. and Spain, 62 percent for Germany, 66 percent for France, and 104 percent for Italy.

It is on the level of the national debt that short- and long-term arguments about public spending clash against one another. It is plainly a waste to lose 300 billion euros of potential output in Europe (and a comparable sum in America) in a one-year recession, and if near-reckless public spending can avoid this, more glory to it. Contrary to eighteenth- and nineteenth-century beliefs that budget deficits are not only immoral but also practically impossible except sporadically, we now know that there is no technical obstacle to running high deficits if we take care of the balance of payments and national insolvency by import and capital controls. Obviously, such closing of the economy entails severe efficiency losses, but this is the price one must pay for a free hand on the budget. We now know all about the last-resort potential of the printing press and the docility of bond markets.

Against this slightly cynical view, the long-term argument is that if you run deficits even of 3 percent of GDP, let alone much more, year after year, while your GDP grows by only 1 or 2 percent, let alone less, year after year, you are in deep trouble before you know where you are. Of course you do not plan to remain profligate year after year, but like drug-taking, it is easier to start than to stop running high deficits. Inflation can boost the growth of GDP in nominal terms and thus helps ease the weight of the national debt, but it is an incubator of long-term ills; nor is it easier to cure than drug-taking. Nearly all European states are embarking on fiscal stimulation to save the short term, and nearly all are scolding Germany for refusing to do so. The fear is that Germany is free-riding on their programs. Their domestic stimulus generates a spillover into the German economy, but there will be no spillover of German demand into their economy. Germany has so far remained unmoved, with eyes fixed on the long-term fitness of the German export machine. Since 2005 Berlin has put its fiscal house in order and corrected the worst features of its labor legislation. It is reluctant to throw away these achievements. With its biggest and strongest economy playing odd man out, European anti-recession "coordination" remains the empty slogan it was always destined to be, but that is hardly a matter for great concern. It is easy to forget, too, that without German conservatism and stubbornness, the euro would not be excessively firm as it now clearly is, but would be sliding down the slippery slope (as the pound sterling is doing even though the British program of spend, spend, spend has not even begun). In this regard, it is indeed hard to tell who is free-riding on whom, Germany on the rest of Europe, or the other way round.

Nor is it sure that it is wrong to accept short-term pain as the price of long-term fitness, or at least the hope of it.

After decades of Thatcherism, Reaganomics, and "supply-side" emphasis, the dysfunctioning of a hybrid system of finance and the chill wind of recession have sent the makers of opinion and of policy in the Anglo-American sphere scurrying back to Keynesian certainties.

However, for all its admirable originality and inner consistency the Keynesian system has notorious faults. Perhaps the principal one is that it holds out an open invitation to lesser Keynesians to treat the economy as a complex machine made of rigid Meccano parts whose mechanical properties are fixed and known. There is the propensity to consume, the marginal efficiency of capital, liquidity preference and so forth, great impersonal data that make the whole economy move in certain ways when they move—but why do they move? It is all macro and no micro. It is too easy to forget that the data are the sums of human decisions subject to human expectations and they change as expectations change. The eminent Polish economist and statesman Leszek Balcerovicz holds that the authors of fiscal stimulus packages must be taking people for Pavlov's dogs who react predictably to signals because they live by conditioned reflexes and not by calculating reason. He cites studies showing that when national indebtedness is already high, government spending by further borrowing has no or negative effect on private consumption and investment. Not to spend more, but let the economy freely to find its own way, is a better policy. The best of all policies may well be one that has as few policies as possible.

A generation ago it was fashionable to detect regular cyclical movements in economic activity like the rhythm of strong and weak tides or the predictable seventh wave. Statisticians discovered long Kondratiev cycles, ten-year cycles and forty-month cycles. The numbers patiently conformed to the findings. Somewhat similar discoveries, though not based on the complicity of numbers, are sometimes made in political history. The political scientist Francis Fukuyama, who earned world fame with his claim that the onset of "liberal democracy" marks the end of great ideological confrontations, has lately found that there is a swinging pendulum that takes us from extreme interventionism to extreme free market practice and back again. He considers that the pendulum is now on its way toward more dirigisme and less reliance on free markets. (He does not go so far as to say that the pendulum is taking us from capitalism to socialism.) He may well be right, at least regarding the immediate future, for when a movement is clearly discernible, it is a safe guess that it will go on until it stops. The pity is that talk of a swinging pendulum makes a back-and-forth pattern seem inexorable, a Hegelian historical necessity that is destined to sweep all before it. Since theories of history, let alone of historical necessity, have a habit of being falsified by events, let us trust that this minor bit of theory of the policy pendulum will also turn out to be false. It depends on us whether it will.

2. WHO IS AFRAID OF THE NATIONAL DEBT?

With government and compulsory social insurance deficits running over 12 percent of gross national product in Britain, over 8 percent in France and over 7 percent in Germany in 2009, with 2010 promising to repeat much the same, Europe's economy seems to be wading along knee-deep in red ink. Most commentators profess to be scared by the prospect, not so much because of the 2009 and 2010 numbers, but because of what they portend for the years of normalcy that must follow the exceptional emergency from which we are just emerging. Others, a defiant minority, call this "deficit hysteria." Sir Samuel Brittan, the senior columnist of the *Financial Times*, explains that if recovery comes, it will soak up the deficit and reduce the debt, while if it does not come soon, it won't neither ought it to. Keynes might not have put it differently.

Much of the Keynes-bashing of recent decades was a reaction to the adulation surrounding a rather deformed and naïve image of Keynes in the decades following the Second World War. Without going into the subtleties of what Keynes really meant and how he was misinterpreted, one might usefully separate Keynesian economics from Keynesian mechanics. The latter at least is incontrovertible, resting as it does on the proposition that like all accounts, the national accounts always balance. They may balance at high or low levels of total income. An intended change in one item of the account is either accommodated by intended changes of the opposite sign in other items, or the intentions must be frustrated by a lower (or, subject to physical constraints, a higher) level of total income at which intentions are revised and mutually accommodated.

One might, for argument's sake, envisage that people in an Anglo-American style economy, who have been getting ever deeper into debt in the last ten years, decide to mend their ways and reshape their bud-

First published by Liberty Fund, Inc., at www.econlib.org on November 2, 2009. Reprinted by permission.

gets, so that intended net household saving moves from around 0 to 5–7 percent of disposable income. A simultaneous increase in net government dissaving (roughly, the budget deficit) by an extra 4 percent or so would offset this. Assuming that nothing else changed, a fall in private debt would simply be balanced by a matching increase in public debt. Of course, corporate net saving or dissaving and net exports may all change at the same time, and in 2008–09, the sum of all these changes was such that gross national product was reduced by 2.5 percent. None of this is meant to indicate the direction of causation nor the policy that, adopted in timely fashion, might have altered the course of these variables. All that is meant is that a rise in the net national debt *may* be mechanically offset by a fall in private debt. Another way to describe this is that the issue of government bonds is taken up by private savers. Does this mean that nothing much is wrong, for as the saying goes, "We owe the national debt to ourselves"?

Everyday plodding rather than emotion is needed in approaching this problem. To begin with, the debt is in part owed to ourselves, but in part we owe it to foreign (mainly Chinese, Japanese, and Gulf Arab) institutions and individuals whose saving covers the part of government dissaving not offset by our own domestic saving. In the accounts, this appears as negative net exports or capital imports. Our own net wealth decreases and some of our gross worth comes to be owned by foreign savers. In an age of globalization, this is not a catastrophe. It does mean, though, that our future balance of payments will be forever burdened with the service of this debt and if net exports continue to be negative, the burden will continue to increase year after year. It must be discharged or it will be added to the existing debt and thus augment the annual burden to be discharged. Ultimately, this must put the competitiveness of our economy to an increasingly severe test.

This is not a matter for despair, for the competitiveness of an economy can undergo a vast sea change in a mere decade or two. The United States was hugely competitive in the 1950s and 1960s and Europe was groaning under a "dollar shortage," but no later than 1971 President Nixon felt compelled to abandon the gold exchange standard and introduce an "interest equalization tax" to protect the U.S. foreign capital account. Be that as it may, the seeds of a problem are being sown in Europe and we must not be too surprised if they grow into big and ugly weeds.

However, whether or not "we owe it to ourselves," the root of the matter is that we owe it. If the national debt is a constant percentage of national income, the burden of servicing it is also constant and whether the service charge accrues to foreign or domestic savers, the economy will in due course adjust to it and remain in balance. But if the debt as a percentage of GDP keeps rising, it eventually becomes too big to support and a stop must be put to it one way or another.

Britain in 2000 had a national debt of 30 percent of GDP. "New Labour," elected after twelve years of Conservative rule in 1997, was by then in full swing to increase government expenditure. It reconciled this spending spree with the dictates of fiscal prudence by calling the extra money devoted to the National Health Service, education, and the police "investment" which it is not irresponsible to finance by borrowing. By 2007, the national debt had rocketed up from 30 to 60 percent of GDP. This percentage was still below the French 65 and the German just over 60, let alone Italy's over 110 percent. Its level was perfectly tolerable, but its rate of increase was not. Then came the so-called "crisis," a medium-sized financial accident that started with American residential mortgages and was blown up into panic proportions mainly by the self-fulfilling prophecies of official and media Cassandras. A world banking system that by the very nature of banking depended on confidence was loudly and shrilly declared to be teetering on the brink of collapse. As a result, it did slide to the brink and was there rescued from falling off by emergency capital injections and guarantees of the American and all major European governments.

Emergency measures leave a mark after the emergency has passed. Britain's current-year deficit of 12.4 percent of GDP will not automatically fall to 0. The Treasury's latest scenario foresees a gradual reduction to 5.5 percent in 2013–14, raising the ratio of debt to GDP to 76 percent, only a little above the Western European average. It is not made explicit how the deficit reduction is to be achieved—spending cuts are no doubt tacitly assumed—except that the growth rate of the economy is supposed to rise spectacularly to 3.25 percent from 2011 onwards. If the average interest rate on the debt were to settle at 5 percent, the interest cost on the projected 76 percent of GDP would be 3.8 percent of GDP, a percentage point more than at present. To accommodate this and still achieve a reduction of the deficit to 5.5 percent, non-interest spending would have to be squeezed by 7.9 percent of GDP. Anyone who believes that this will be done has never understood democracy.

In his major pre-election speech, Britain's probable future chancellor promised Churchillian blood, sweat, and tears for the next five-year Parliament. He announced specific spending cuts that sound highly unpleasant for all except the lowest income groups. Even so, the total of these measures would save only 0.6 percent of GDP, hardly worth the political cost.

Simple arithmetic is sending a bitter message. As long as the budget deficit (and never mind the "primary deficit") as a percentage of GDP exceeds the growth rate of GDP, its ratio to GDP must go on rising. In a recent very serious study by a former high Treasury official, the ratio of debt to GDP is slated to reach 120 percent of GDP by 2017. Making room for the interest charge on this debt, even if it were really "owed to ourselves," would necessitate spending cuts that no elected government would survive. Because the debt ratio would nevertheless go on rising, the spending cuts would have to grow in a vicious circle, a prospect simply not worth entertaining.

There is always a solution to every dilemma, though often it is a bad one. If in a democratic society the debt problem generates a vicious circle that has no solution under price stability, price stability will go out of the window. After World War II, the national debt in Britain hovered around 150 percent in an environment of gradually rising inflation. By the 1970s, usefully helped by the 1973 oil price shock, inflation accelerated. With the agony of the Labour government prior to the 1979 election of Margaret Thatcher, inflation peaked at 25 percent. The vicious circle was broken by a brutal reduction of the national debt in real terms. From its much deflated level, further reduction during the Thatcher years became feasible. Before the New Labour government started "investing" in public services at the turn of the century, the debt ratio looked quite safe at 30 percent. Double that level and

Putting things in absurdly comic terms may highlight their truth more than serious argument ever could. Frédéric Bastiat's mock advocacy of a "negative railway" made the idea of protecting horse-drawn transport from the advance of technology unforgettably laughable. The notion of a "negative factor productivity," applied to the state as a supposed factor of production, could be similarly enlightening, though far less funny.

The politics of economy is always accompanied by the background noise of commentary, advice, and more or less dire prediction by journalists, economists, and gurus of all persuasions. This noise has risen to thundering force since the surprise 2008–09 financial upset and recession broke the run of the previous fifteen Goldilocks years and has shaken confidence in the "Washington consensus" of freer trade, light regulation, and less onerous direct taxation. In the noise, we hear two main themes. One deals with great matters of the secular future and when it reaches crescendo, it shrieks "Death to Capitalism," though among its many variations some are more soberly analytical than the radical "it's the greed that done it" type. The emphasis is on describing the structure as one that was bound to collapse, and on some albeit smudgy blueprint of a "new order" that would be immune to disorder, aimlessness, and social injustice. The other main theme deals with the short term, the immediate problem of "What Is to Be Done?"[1] to get the economy back on to a steady upward course, avoid the dreaded 2011 Double Dip, prevent the disintegration of the 16-country Eurozone and the bankruptcy that threatens four or five of them within five years at most if their public finances stay on anything like their present trajectory.

First published by Liberty Fund, Inc., at www.econlib.org on August 2, 2010. Reprinted by permission.

1. This was the title of Lenin's famous pamphlet, which he wrote in 1902 on strategies for the Russian communist movement.

Much of the systemic and secular theme starts from the widely shared impression that the 2008 mayhem was due to the inability of free markets to stay in equilibrium, or to regain it when once lost. The contrary view, namely that it was due to the markets not being free enough, having been interfered with, for instance, by strong government sponsorship of mortgage lending to insolvent first-time house buyers, is not given much of a hearing. If markets are by their very nature unstable—and too many people from George Soros down to village schoolteachers are sure that they are—self-regulation cannot be trusted. A consensual welcome mat is laid out for a boundless procession of new regulations, mostly in the financial services area where markets are the most sensitive because transactions costs are the lowest.[2]

In recent gropings for a "new order" to replace the banker-ridden greedy capitalism, two items have stood out in a somewhat startling fashion: the "battle to defeat the market" and the Greek incident as a forerunner of the sovereign default threats that will rattle the Eurozone and that, for no very evident reason, must at all costs be resisted "to save Europe."

On the first of these headings, the German government has repeatedly cast the financial market in the role of a hostile force that upsets stability. Instability must not be tolerated; the politics of the democratic state must fight the dark forces of the market. It must, and will, defeat them. The first step to this end is to drive back "speculation." Hence the German interdiction of short selling, of sovereign debt securities, and of "naked" speculation. These are puerile measures showing an appalling lack of common sense. Fortunately, they are ineffective, for a transaction banned in Frankfurt can migrate to London. Should London succumb to moral browbeating about European solidarity— a most unlikely prospect—the transaction could move to Singapore or any other place whose computers can talk to those in the rest of the world. However, the general failure in continental Europe to grasp

---

2. Like Cato the Elder, who seldom failed to add to a speech that "by the way, Carthage ought to be destroyed," French and German political leaders seldom miss an occasion for urgently demanding the adoption of a worldwide "Tobin tax" to increase transactions costs. Fortunately, other G20 governments simply shrug off this proposal as being almost too silly to be discussed.

the true role and effect of speculation is symptomatic of the counter-productive mindset that dominates policy-making in the area.

How did speculation "against" Greek government bonds work? If it was successful at all, it must have sold Greek bonds before they crashed and bought them back after they crashed. By selling high and buying low, speculators damped down the high price to some extent, and shored up the low price to some extent, reducing each way the volatility that would have prevailed if the speculators had not specu-lated it down. Frau Merkel, the German chancellor, spoke as if it had been the speculators who had made Greece crash. Obviously, they did nothing of the sort and could not have done so if they had tried. The market for Greek government debt collapsed because it realized, much too late in the day, that Greek public finances looked hopeless even in their window-dressed form. Like shock-absorbers, the speculative "short" position opened up at the outset and closed again after the event had softened the impact of what was becoming apparent, i.e., that the Greek state was rushing headlong towards default. It was not by "combating the speculators" that it could be stopped and reversed.

Why, however, was it so important to reverse it? Why would the "new order" of tightly regulated and neutered capitalism, with markets obedient to the will of governments, offer better results?

It was proclaimed as axiomatic that Greece must be saved, and it was "saved" by European governments, the Commission, and the IMF jointly putting up 110 billion euros to ensure the redemption of Greek state debts for an initial three years. As far as one can see, this gesture "saved" the European banks and the diaspora of Greek shipping mag-nates from losing the money they rashly and thoughtlessly invested in Greek bonds. It did not "save" the Greek economy from anything worse than reverting from the euro to the drachma on a devalued basis, thus making the competitive position of the country a little less hopeless. It did not "save" the Eurozone from its basic weakness, namely that member countries with different cost structures have to live with the same currency—like a fixed exchange rate graven in granite—and the same central bank discount rate. Postponing Greek default by three or five years will cost the rescuer governments a substantial percentage of 110 billion euros which they will lose when Greek sovereign debt will inevitably be "restructured."

It is also treated as axiomatic that if Greece defaults, Portugal, Spain, perhaps Italy and even others will follow suit "by contagion." But there is nothing contagious about a country failing to balance its books. Though bandying about meaningless words like "contagion" and "toxic" is not particularly helpful to sentiment, it does not cause sovereign default to spread from one country to another if such default was not written on the wall to start with. Default by California would not cause Illinois to default; it is the state of the public finances of Illinois that would cause it.

Misunderstanding, the loss of common sense, the thoughtless swallowing of populist rhetoric and pompous pseudo-expertise seem to be guiding the great enterprise of remodelling capitalism and liberating us from the cruel dictatorship of markets that will fail and fail again unless held tightly under control. Perhaps there was a case for a sharp look at the rules, constraints, and distorted incentives without which the mayhem of 2008 could not have happened. What the great enterprise of renewing and reforming is about to do instead is to find ways and means for cluttering up the economy worse than it ever was. Fortunately, like the patient who survives intensive medical treatment, the European economy will not stop in its tracks even if it is shot in the foot by its caring but bemused political masters.

4. TWO CHEERS FOR FISCAL AUSTERITY: PART 2

Policy-makers, commentators, and gurus are neatly divided in two over the immediate and pressing question of what to do about the economy in the face of truly frightening budget deficits when the economy seems to be crying out for an expansionary fiscal policy. The division is perhaps deepest in Europe where the economic recovery looks less vigorous and the deficits more intractable than anywhere else among major economies.

One school of thought is holding on to what is irrefutable, almost truistic in Keynesian economics. If demand is for a lesser output than capacity would permit, additional demand by government will be met by additional output. Government demand can therefore be increased up to the limit of output capacity. Some of the extra demand injected by the government will "leak" into imports, increasing the output of foreign countries, but the rest will be met by additional output in the home country. Sacrificing this extra output on the ground that it takes a budget deficit to call it forth is sheer waste and is inexcusable. There is a domestic multiplier by which the extra income generated by filling the output gap engenders the amount of domestic saving needed to equate saving to investment, or what comes to the same thing, to dissaving. The accounting identity that total household and corporate saving must equal domestic investment, net exports and government dissaving, is not in dispute. It is one of the strong attractions of the Keynesian system in which macroeconomic subtotals are linked together mechanically by impersonal constants and variables, so that moving one leads to predetermined changes in all the others. However, once the economy is not conceived as a great Meccano set, easy to understand and manipulate, but as a locus of individuals' responses to their expectations and perceived incentives, the tempting Keynesian conclusion of filling the output gap by fearless recourse to

First published by Liberty Fund, Inc., at www.econlib.org on September 6, 2010. Reprinted by permission.

budget deficits that are never too large as long as the output gap is still open starts to become more and more dubious.

The opposing school that advocates austerity instead of fearless deficit financing thinks that it has a knockdown argument. It is one of good housekeeping, serious husbandry: it is that you cannot for long spend more than you earn.

Taken strictly, this is not true. You can go on forever spending more than your income (hence getting ever deeper into debt) as long as the cumulative total of excess spending (i.e., the national debt) increases at a rate no higher than the rate of increase of national income. If national income stops rising, the national debt cannot be allowed to rise much further. Counterintuitively, this condition is harder to satisfy when the national debt is only 25 percent of national income (the case, roughly, of Rumania) than when it is 80 percent (the case of France in 2010). Supposing a year when the two economies both stagnate at zero growth and their deficit is at the Maastricht maximum limit of 3 percent of GDP, the Rumanian debt ratio would jump to 28 percent of GDP and the French would creep to 83 percent, a rate of increase of 12 percent for the former and 3.75 percent for the latter. Like in the race of the hare and the tortoise, despite the more rapid rise of the Rumanian debt, it would be the French one that first reaches a ratio of GDP at which its burden becomes a millstone around the country's neck because the annual interest charge it imposed would bring about a distribution of incomes that penalizes both labor and enterprise to an ever greater degree. The effect would bear some resemblance, though on a less fatal scale to the "demographic time bomb" menacing most European economies that will in coming decades have to maintain an ever larger pensioner class in the style it is accustomed to from the labors of an ever smaller active population.

Evidently, the higher the annual growth of GDP, the higher will be the deficit that can be supported without an increase in the national debt ratio. Here is the nub of the current controversy between orthodox Keynesians and Good Housekeepers about the right fiscal policy to escape the recession. The orthodox Keynesians say that deficit-cutting austerity under present circumstances is sheer masochism. If anything, the deficit should even be increased so as to exploit the output gap, produce more income and more employment. The Good Housekeepers say that deficits are already at the danger level beyond which the debt burden becomes unsustainable. Given the political obstacles to reducing welfare expenditures, and given that failing sharp deficit reduction, the annual service charge of the debt will be increasing, the economy will be caught in a vicious downward spiral of deficits increasing the debt burden which engenders greater deficits until sovereign default in some form finally interrupts the process. Therefore, as Mrs. Thatcher famously said, "There is no alternative." Austerity must prevail over Keynesian orthodoxy.

Between April 2010 when the Greek "crisis" peaked and July 2010, three of the major European countries, Germany, Britain, and France, as well as other, supposedly less creditworthy ones, have in various forms signaled that they have opted for budgetary austerity. Each has made symbolic gestures ranging from voluntary reductions in ministerial salaries and the laying off of ten thousand official cars and their chauffeurs to the cancellation of state hunts and garden parties. More significantly, a few albeit timid cuts were made in some welfare entitlements, with promises of more to come. The amounts saved are as yet near to negligible, but the fact that social welfare, the most sacred and untouchable of the services governments are elected to provide, is now being cut, is of truly historic importance. Ever since the early post-war years, governments and their oppositions have been engaged in a bidding contest, offering innovations and extensions of welfare services in a fierce competition for tenure. As a result, the share of central and local government spending as a percentage of national income kept creeping ever upward from the mid-twenties in the 1950s to the mid-forties by the turn of the century and in some countries touching 60 percent in 2009. The "ratchet effect" became the first empirical law of democracy: under majority rule, welfare entitlements are either maintained or increased, but cannot be reduced.

As was to be expected, the competitive bidding in offering an ever more complete and more expensive welfare state to the electorate has generated its own ideological justification. "Social justice," meaning whatever a democratic government did to change the distribution of wealth, income, and privileges in favor of particular groups or classes, came to be regarded as self-evidently righteous. Inequalities were understood to be self-evidently unjust. Capitalism was tolerated on the tacit understanding that it does not challenge the social democratic governments of both Left and Right and acquiesces in the extensive redistribution involved in rising welfare entitlements and the targeted provision of public goods.

Accepted political theory teaches that by creating law and order, protecting property, and enforcing contracts, the state organizes society out of the state of nature. In doing so, it functions as a factor of production, complementary to labor and capital just as the latter are complementary to each other. It would not be totally outlandish to speak of three factors of production, labor, capital, and the state, and attempt by regression analysis to estimate the productivity of each separately. We may quantify the factor (state) by the share of public expenditure in total GDP.

This is a Panglossian and even an angelic view of the state that can be badly shaken by doing what the economist worth his salt normally does, that is, to look at what happens at the margin. If you increase labor with capital remaining unchanged, the marginal product of labor will presumably diminish and in some rather contrived circumstances might decline to nought. Likewise, by piling on more and more capital to be used by an unchanged labor force, the marginal product of capital will eventually be reduced and might even settle at zero. Imagination, however, has a hard time in conceiving of either labor or capital having negative marginal productivity. It is harder to think of negative factor productivity than of Frédéric Bastiat's negative railway.

However, if the state is understood as a factor of production, one of a complementary threesome with capital and labor, the possibility of negative marginal productivity springs to mind as a matter of course. Providing law and order and protecting property and contract (and leaving national defense on one side as too indeterminate to account for in abstract theory) are in peacetime not very costly. Devoting to them 5 percent of GDP might do the job. In this single-digit zone, the marginal product of the state is probably very high. Though doing so is sheer guesswork, we might suppose that its marginal product is still respectable when state spending reaches 15 to 25 percent of GDP. But it is more likely than not to be in a declining phase. At what level of state spending it sinks into negative territory is partly a question of the good sense of government, the character and civic culture of the people, the prevalence of corruption and pointless waste, the effect of a social safety net on the work ethic, the effect of taxation on initiative and above-average performance, and so forth. Pages and pages would be needed to list all the factors likely to have some influence. Any conclusion would always be somewhat speculative, perhaps swayed by ideology and prejudice. What matters as much as the elusive objective truth, however, is that large numbers of workers, professional men, and entrepreneurs are viscerally convinced that the fully developed welfare state is crowding out parts of the private sector and feels like a millstone about their own necks. Believing this, they act accordingly and make their belief come true.

If so, then two cheers for austerity and two cheers even for the somewhat uncertain promise of it. Two cheers, in other words, for the unexpected and very salutary prospect that the negatively productive factor may at last have some of its depressive margin trimmed.

5. WHAT BECAME OF THE LIQUIDITY TRAP?

Over half a century ago at Oxford, when along with my research appointment I was also doing some teaching, I had an Indian student who was a graduate of an Indian university but, for reasons of prestige, came to read an undergraduate course. Once I gave him an essay to do on the Natural Rate of Interest. At his next tutorial, he read aloud an immensely complicated and confused text that I did not comprehend and I was sure that he did not either. I gathered all my forces of didactic persuasion and explained to him, or I thought I had, where he had gone astray and how the problem can be reduced to its essentials. Then, exhausted, I sat back, proud of myself and full of admiration for the quality of Oxford teaching of which I had just shown such a glowing example.

My pupil looked at me darkly and resentfully and blurted out: "I did not come to Oxford to have problems simplified!"

Recalling this sobering episode, I begin to suspect that my Indian student was wiser than I and wiser than he knew. Perhaps the clean logic and elegant simplicity of the Keynesian system, in which all Western economists now alive have been brought up, has misled us to see the economy as an elementary contraption made of a handful of Meccano pieces we can move around by just a handful of levers. All advanced economies are at present suffering from two very serious ills. One is an alarming year-by-year rise in the public debt at a rate faster, in some countries much faster, than the rise of national income which is supposed to assure its service. The terminal form of this malady is where everyone's income is entirely absorbed by paying interest on the national debt, and everyone's sole source of income is the interest he gets on the savings he had lent to build up the national debt. For this to work, all income from labor and capital must be taxed at a 100 percent, yet people must still be willing to work and invest.

First published by Liberty Fund, Inc., at www.econlib.org on June 6, 2011. Reprinted by permission.

The other grave ill common to advanced countries is chronic unemployment, especially of the young, at a rate high enough to drive to despair those who genuinely want to earn their living.

A very high fiscal deficit and very high and persistent unemployment are not absolutely incompatible in the Keynesian system. At a stretch, they could occur together, but they look strange and do not fit into our habits of thought. This is probably why the policy advice coming from experts and politicians on how to deal with these ills is breaking down into two contradictory streams: one wants to take a cure of fiscal austerity to slow down the accumulation of public debt, while the other, pointing to the "output gap" that shows the tens or hundreds of billions by which the economy is running below its capacity, argues that fiscal austerity is absurd waste when so many human resources are left idling on the dole. The two ills seem to call for mutually contradictory cures.

In the Keynesian economy, severe unemployment due to insufficient demand for goods and services is potentially a stable equilibrium. Investment is what it is because its marginal yield is decreasing and if more resources were invested, their yield would fall below the relevant rate of interest. Actual investment is matched by actual saving; hence the investment will generate a level of aggregate income which, in turn, will induce the amount of saving that matches the investment. The higher the share of marginal income that goes into saving instead of consumption, the lower will be the increment of aggregate income generated by incremental investment. (Economists call the inverse of this ratio the "multiplier.") The resulting suboptimal equilibrium with its "output gap" is ascribed to over-saving. To remedy it, the consumer is exhorted to go out and put his credit card to work. Additionally, the government is very willing to do its bit and spend more, letting its debt rise a bit faster. As long as resources are left unemployed, piling on more debt can supposedly do no real harm. Some governments have been taking this medicine intermittently for decades, and all have gone on overdose since 2007. Orthodox Keynesians are rubbing their eyes in disbelief that such massive fiscal stimulus, never before seen in peacetime, is doing so little to reduce unemployment and narrow the "output gap."

If the economy fails to respond to the fiscal push, can recourse to more liquidity float it off the sandbank? A cardinal assumption of Keynesian theory is that the demand to hold money becomes infinitely elastic at some low but still positive rate of interest. This rate is the "liquidity trap." Old-style central bankers may be spinning in their graves at the noise of "quantitative easing" as more and more debt securities are sucked up by the central bank and are replaced with more liquid money and near-money, yet the interest rate relevant to capital investment will not go any lower. Hence, no matter whether the economy is splashing ankle-deep or knee-deep in liquidity, investment will remain inadequate to dent unemployment. However, as we look at real numbers in money and capital markets since 2007, we are left wondering about what has become of the "liquidity trap." The interest rate at the short end of the yield curve is as near zero as not to matter, and even at the long end it looks negligibly low if the riskless rate of just over 3 percent is deflated by the probable rate of future inflation which, too, should hover near or above the 3 percent level. In other words, if the risk-free real rate is in fact at about zero, there is in fact no such thing as the liquidity trap, and at least for the present, it cannot be blamed for the economy idling along at the lower edge of the output gap.

The upshot of all this is that much as the simplicity of a Meccano or Lego construction is pleasing to the mind that looks for clarity and order, the clarity we need in economics is not found in Meccanomics or Legonomics. The orthodox Keynesian full employment recipe of "fine tuning" by monetary and fiscal policy that was practiced with much confidence and some occasional success in the first few post-war decades has been losing credibility since the 1970s and looks very doubtful at present. The bucket and the axe are replacing the tuning fork as the policy tools governments are trying to wield today.

One can only wish them success in whatever they attempt to achieve by these policies; but one wishes that they would listen to the little voice of doubt that whispers more and more persistently that the best policy of all might well be to have less policy altogether.

6. THE ARCHBISHOP AND THE ACCOUNTANTS

In a finite world of known resources, with none left unclaimed by a putative owner, nothing can be given to somebody without taking it from somebody else. This is true whether the transfer is voluntary, mutually agreed on, or imposed by brute force or by recognized authority. The identity of the given and the taken is shown up in double-entry accounting. Its practice may be the manifestation of a vulgar truism, but it is nonetheless a clear indicator of where we stand and a safeguard against foolish thinking. It is a pity that its lesson is so often forgotten or ignored, sometimes deliberately and sometimes inadvertently. Ambitious theories of what their avid readers are pleased to call "distributive justice" or "social justice" deal with resources as manna falling from heaven, as a cake that got baked in some unexplained fashion by little green men and is now ready for us to slice and share out as justice demands, or as the product of the "laws of economics" to be distributed "as society chooses." Politicians who promote some wholly laudable broadening of the social safety net or the extension of a highly useful public service, and who meet with resistance on grounds of unaffordable cost, contemptuously dismiss the objectors as petty "bean-counters." Ordinary people, both the selfish and the altruistic, are tempted by the promise of collective benefits and regularly fail to connect them to the burden that must fall upon the likes of them if the benefit is to be provided. Manifestly, not all people think like accountants. Some think like Rowan Williams, the archbishop of Canterbury. But no one else speaks with the authority of his office.

In the June 9, 2011, issue of the *New Statesman,* the voice for three generations past of the soft-Left intelligentsia of Great Britain, the archbishop wrote an article castigating the u.k.'s center-Right government for its radical deficit-cutting stance. He leaned as far left as anyone could without totally losing his balance. Admittedly, it is not the first

First published by Liberty Fund, Inc., at www.econlib.org on July 12, 2011. Reprinted by permission.

25

time that the holder of his office descends in the political arena and attacks always the same one of the two contending teams; Archbishop Ramsey did so when he turned his ire on Mrs. Thatcher a quarter century ago. Even if not unprecedented, rank partisanship by the leading cleric of the established church in a fundamentally decent, civilized country is wrong and is not doing either religious or lay institutions any good.

In the avalanche of comments triggered by the article, many defend it by claiming that the archbishop has no less a right to express his views on matters of common interest than any ordinary citizen, and he was in fact writing in that capacity. This, of course, is arrant nonsense. A high dignitary in a sensitive position remains a high dignitary and cannot help being regarded as such no matter how loudly he claims that he is writing just "as an ordinary citizen." In fairness to the archbishop, it is not he who pretends to such an impossibility but his eager defenders.

He does, however, advance far more serious and destructive propositions. I shall call the first "California Democracy," the second "St. Augustine's Plea." In both, the archbishop argues as if accountants had nothing to say about reality.

He finds that the British people are filled with fear of the impending pain the harsh long-term deficit-cutting policies of the present center-Right government will inflict upon them—policies for which they did not vote. This, he suggests, is a denial of democracy, though he protests that he is not advocating a proliferation of plebiscites. It seems, though, that he must be advocating just that. Otherwise, how could people vote for or against particular policies? Not spelling this out, but in effect denying it, must cast doubt on the logic or sincerity (or both) of the archbishop's complaint. This reads rather like a barely disguised incitation not to submit to the sovereignty of Parliament.

Under the form of democracy prevalent in the U.K., people vote for representatives and vest certain powers in them. Most of the representatives belong to parties which either govern or oppose the government. In this system, constant adversarial debate from one election to the next is designed to inform the electorate about the rights and wrongs of the policies either party proposes to follow if given the chance. Obviously, blanks must remain, all promises may not be fulfilled, and circumstances may alter cases. However, to say that the electorate "has not voted for" major policies is to blame the Cameron government for practicing representative rather than direct democracy.

The archbishop is implicitly demanding a hybrid between the representative and the direct, which we may for simplicity label "Californian Democracy." In such a hybrid system, there is a machinery for asking the electorate whether they wish to adopt some new policy or amend an old one so as better to serve the public as well as to raise some state tax to a similarly benign effect. The electorate fairly reliably answers that yes, they do want the new measure that will make something better, and no, they do not want the tax to be raised. California, enjoying this enhanced form of democracy, has duly arrived to the brink of bankruptcy and has been blundering along it for many years thanks to the grace that protects drunks, but at least nobody can seriously say that "they have not voted" for it. To be sure, the Swiss practice a somewhat similar system that works better, but then in Switzerland everything works better.

Taking office in 1997 and earning respect for fiscal restraint and prudence, the Labour government between 2000 and 2007 went on a spectacular spending spree, reassuringly calling it "investment" in health and education. The result has been at best mixed in the National Health Service and dismal in education (which does not necessarily confirm but at least does not contradict the suggestion made a while ago in this column about the negative productivity of government). The upshot was that Britain entered the 2007–09 stormy years greatly weakened and emerged from them a fiscal wreck. In the 2010 general election, the incumbent Labour party offered to halve the deficit by 2015, the center-Right coalition to eliminate it wholly by the same date, making it very clear that most of the reduction must be achieved by severe spending cuts and only a smaller part by higher taxes. The electorate could have been under no illusions about the pain to come when it voted for this program.

A minor but highly interesting detail of the article is the accusation that the present British government is resuscitating the distinction between the "deserving and the undeserving poor." Whether it is doing this, and whether doing so is sinful, harmful, or both, must be open to informed judgment. In this, it is quite unlike murder, torture, or willful humiliation, which we must reject as sinful and harmful without arguing for or against them. The present column would strongly argue that bringing back the distinction would be morally right and also sound policy, but it is perfectly legitimate to judge the matter differently. However, the archbishop presents the making of the distinction as obviously beyond the pale like murder, torture, or perhaps child pornography, about which there is no room for argument. By a linguistic sleight of hand, it has been made into a shameful wrong that we all condemn.

The crucial point of the article, however, is that the deficit-cutting program inspires anxiety and is wrong because it does not guarantee "cast-iron standards" of health, education, and other "strategic priorities." In the plainer English that used to be required at Cambridge and Oxford when the archbishop was there as a young man, everything could not be a priority at the same time, let alone a "strategic" one. Even in the trendier and woollier language he now uses, deficit-reduction is not a priority, though everything else may well be. It comes after all the "priorities" have been taken care of under "cast-iron guarantees." When will that be?

The answer is in St. Augustine's much-mocked prayer to God: "Give me chastity and continency—but not yet."

The accountants, if asked, would point out that as long as all the highly desirable "priorities" are met, the non-priority items, such as the fiscal balance, will reflect the fact. The deficit will not stop; indeed, for all we can tell, it may actually worsen, since this is what it means to say that the "cast-iron standards" have priority. Whatever the present generation is given over and above what it earns, is an increase in the burden of the debt the next generation must carry. Within reason, it is our policies that decide how great the burden of the children shall be. They have no say in the matter. Perhaps there are arguments, having to do with such metaphysics as the "utility" of inter-generational income that could justify this, though I hope that few would fall for them. In any event, before trying to justify the fact, it should be frankly recognized that it is a fact because the accounts must balance by definition. No one, not even a high authority, should get away with acting as if it weren't so.

7. TWO WAYS, BUT WHERE TO?

Having for a pulpit a regular column in the *New York Times,* Paul Krugman speaks to us as one who is really sure about what is what. He is also thoroughly exasperated by the pigheaded blindness of those of us who have their hands on the levers of policy and are responsible for the astronomical waste and needless pain inflicted on the economies on both sides of the Atlantic and especially on the Eurozone. His thesis is that we are actually in a state of genuine depression, involving a loss of potential output that hardly bears thinking about. The depression is of our own making and is unnecessary, serving no purpose. It ought to be and could be terminated forthwith.

Its cause is the misguided attempt by the majority of Eurozone states to tackle their indebtedness by reducing the rate at which it has been increasing as a proportion of GDP for the last two or three decades. For the average Eurozone state, this proportion rose from 30 to 90 percent of GDP. It is now rising each year at 3.5 or 4 percentage points for Italy and France and at 8 percentage points for Spain—to speak only of the countries that are not on intensive care like Greece, Portugal, and Ireland, nor in reasonable health like the Teutonic group. All seventeen states signed up to the Golden Rule that would limit their "structural" budget deficit to 0.5 percent of GDP, but it is far from evident that all will succeed or even genuinely try to achieve this in the foreseeable future. The agreement they signed, though not yet ratified, provides for "sanctions" by the European Court of Justice, but serious sanctions cannot realistically be applied. Meanwhile, the order of the day is austerity, mostly by cutting expenditure as in Spain, increasing taxation as in France, and curbing tax evasion as in Italy.

Many economists, with Paul Krugman and Joseph Stiglitz in the lead, argue that dealing with indebtedness by austerity, though a common-sense remedy for a household, is self-defeating at the level of an entire

First published by Liberty Fund, Inc., at www.econlib.org on July 2, 2012. Reprinted by permission.

economy, for austerity stifles economic growth; hence it reduces tax revenues and worsens the budget deficit that the austerity was meant to improve. The argument is enthusiastically seconded by politicians who expect to win votes by promising maintained or increased government spending on welfare, subsidies, and other popular items, some of which may even have genuine merit, but cannot be afforded.

Krugman's mantra is "my spending is your income." If I spend more, your income rises; hence, you spend more and the money I have spent comes back to me. We are both better off. It is simply foolish not to see that this is the obvious and wide-open way out of the depression that austerity has brought about.

Austerity, to be sure, operates by a variety of measures, some of which are dictated by the laws of least resistance and are inefficient or harmful. They are biased to raising taxation rather than reducing spending, and also to multiplying the bewildering tangle of regulatory and fiscal interventions, each of which was designed to serve some good purpose but whose aggregate is oppressive and strangles the normally expansionary impulse in the economy. How good an alternative is the Krugman way?

The "my spending is your income" mantra is true enough in a closed economy, but false in an open one. You may not spend the income you receive from me on what I have for sale, but rather on what a Taiwanese manufacturer of electronic gadgets has for sale. Your extra income does not flow back to me, but "leaks" into inputs. It is not surprising, then, that Krugmanites often show some more or less disguised sympathy for protectionism in some fig-leaf–covered form. Worse than the leakage into imports is the effect on both the willingness to invest and consumer confidence. David Ricardo saw that government debt depressed private demand as business and consumers take account of the future taxes they will be made to pay to service the debt. A similar but wider effect of increasing government debt is that it brings closer the day when the threat of sovereign default simply forces the adoption of the most cruel austerity. It is as if the Keynesian multiplier took on a negative value, decreasing aggregate demand when government dissaves and increasing it when government saves.

Consider a scenario where three not-so-solid Eurozone countries, France, Italy, and Spain, decide to take the Krugman way out of the stagnant or gently declining economic conditions the present austerity creates for them. Tentatively, though with limited confidence, we may suppose that if they open the valves of government spending their annual deficit rises to 7 percent of GDP for France and Italy and 9 percent of GDP for Spain; that this deficit is maintained for three years; and that at the end of this period, the economies of these countries enter into such a growth phase that they can without austerity obey the Golden Rule and run a balanced budget. (Ignore the strong likelihood that in a democracy, a balanced budget would provoke a pressing demand for more welfare, more subsidies, and lower taxes that the government would find electorally impossible to resist.) Under these assumptions, by the time reasonable growth began, the proportion of debt to GDP of the three countries would be roughly 22 to 28 percentage points higher than at the outset. At unchanged interest rates, the service charge on the national debt could require an extra 1 to 1.5 percent of GDP forever after, a handicap whose weight looks easy when seen from afar but a heavy servitude when it is borne year after year.

This handicap may perhaps be brushed aside as bearable. There is, however, a far more disturbing implication of the putative return to growth via higher government spending. In fact, apart from the assumption that it lifts the economy out of depression, it is impossible to tell where the Krugman way would lead it. One possible arrival point would be highly dangerous. Uplift by easy government spending and easy times would leave these economies as inefficient and inflexible at the end of three years as they were at the outset. However, growing at 2.5 percent they would certainly import more and may well export less than at a growth rate of 0 or 0.5. Their current balance of payments, already negative, could become dramatically weak. The semi-permanent sovereign debt "crisis" they now live with would become a mother of all balance of payments crisis. There are currently persistent demands for Germany to take on the sovereign debt crisis on the transparent pretext that as separate national currencies have been replaced by the euro, separate national debt obligations must now be replaced by a mutual common obligation, the Eurobond. Germany has up to now declined the honor of supporting a Eurobond, and is very unlikely to accept the honor of supporting the Latin countries' balance of payments deficits. One alternative is the breakup of the euro, a reversion to the

the obstacles that contort the economy. Burning all but a few of the three thousand pages of a code of labor law would do wonders for job creation at the expense of job protection. It would be ironic but poetic justice if, by a desperate but bold change of course, austerity would finally bring back more prosperity for all in a more liberal order that majorities love to hate and vilify.

8. THE PLATINUM RULE

Platinum is worth more than gold. Though the best should not act as the enemy of the good, it is a bad mistake to lose sight of the platinum once, if by great efforts, the gold has been gained.

After watching for two years the tragic-comic Greek drama, the vicious downward spiral sucking a country into a black hole despite one futile effort after another to "rescue" it, many European governments are telling themselves (though staunchly denying it to the world): "There, but for the grace of God, go I." Softened up by this awful example, twenty-five of the twenty-seven member states of the European Union (EU) have agreed to conclude treaties with one another to observe the golden rule of a balanced budget allowing only a minute deficit, and to adopt the domestic legislation, including a constitutional amendment if necessary, to implement it. True to form, Great Britain and the Czech Republic begged to be excused (which prevented the radical move of putting the Golden Rule directly into the EU treaties). The passage of the Golden Rule through twenty-five legislatures is hardly assured, but even the intention of making it the established European fiscal standard merits a look at its logical foundations.

MODES OF SELF-DENIAL

There is a set of fairly universal rules of conduct that comes about spontaneously as a matter of everybody behaving in his or her best interest by treating others the way they wish others to treat them. A rational person will refrain from stealing the property of others in the expectation of others not stealing his, rather than he and the others all stealing from each other. Technically, these rules are conventions which are adhered to out of self-interest and by and large enforced by the threat of retaliation.

First published by Liberty Fund, Inc., at www.econlib.org on March 5, 2012. Reprinted by permission.

Beyond these conventions of right conduct, there are particular occasions to undertake acts in self-denial. They involve the suppression of what Hume called a "passion" in favor of some less palpable and more distant interest that on consideration seems superior, but whose dominance must be reinforced by some explicit undertaking. Such undertakings follow one of three modes:

The Contract

You promise to provide a good or a service of value to another party if he or she promises to provide value in exchange. If the performance of the two promises is simultaneous, you get what you value as and when you give what you value less, while if you do not give, you do not get. There is no conflict between interest and "passion." However, if the other party performs first, you have got what you wanted, and it takes a measure of self-denial to perform your part of the bargain. Contract is the instrument of such self-denial. It is enforced by retaliation, the "shadow of the future" (if you default on this contract, you will have trouble finding parties to contract with you in the future), or by a formal judiciary process. Thus, a contract binds you to do what in certain circumstances you would rather not do.

The Unilateral Promise

You promise to another party, or indeed to the world at large, to do something or conduct yourself in a certain manner without your fulfillment of the promise being conditional on some quid pro quo. Legal doctrine is very firm in holding that this is not a contract. The Geneva Convention on war and prisoners of war is such a promise, as is your word to your wife that you will do the washing up three days a week forever. Such promises are not enforceable except informally by the risk of retaliation and the loss of reputation, a risk contingent on circumstances and not always high.

The Vow

The vow is a promise of self-denial given to yourself that you will not yield to certain "passions," e.g., will not gamble, smoke, drink to excess, or take drugs. Enforcement is more problematical than for the unilateral promise. If you do not honor your vow, you may lose reputation and self-respect, but the force of these deterrents is seldom overwhelming. Above all, they might not penetrate the thick skin of the state at all. Thomas Schelling with admirable conciseness called a constitution "a vow" by the state. In its constitution, the latter promises to make certain kinds of social choices and not to make other kinds— for example, regarding fiscal policy, the manner of treating judges, or more generally, the rules it will apply in the making of decisions about the freedoms and resources of its subjects. If it violates an article of this vow, the enforcement problem is paradoxical: how clear is the picture of the state both intimidating the judges and protecting their independence, or vowing fiscal rectitude while borrowing up to 10 percent of the national product year in year out, whether it rains or shines? How plausible is the idea of the state punishing itself if it transgresses the limits it has set on the exercise of its power—limits that classical liberals still fondly believe to act as a barrier to protect individuals from the encroachment of collective choice?

GOVERNMENT LIFESTYLES

A political Parkinson's Law lays it down that "Entitlement spending expands to push the budget deficit to the limit just short of bankruptcy." It expands driven by electoral rivalry, and for the same reason it is very hard, sometimes politically suicidal, to shrink it. This law plays a part in the choice of a government's "lifestyle":

Spend-and-borrow

This has been the predominant type of Western-style democracies in the last three or four decades. Notable exceptions were Canada and Sweden, both having succeeded in reversing the expansion of their welfare state without too much political drama, and Germany, where Chancellor Gerhard Schroeder (1998–2005) pushed through a labor market reform which set the German economy, sluggish like much of the rest of Europe prior to his reforms, on a vigorous upward course that cost him his political life. Elsewhere, spend-and-borrow continued to predominate until 2008 when every government got a big fright but nevertheless continued with this policy because the momentum was hard to stop and the fraught years after 2008 did not seem the best time to change direction.

Spend-and-tax

This is the rage that naturally follows when spend-and-borrow has been pushed to the limit and the rise in the national debt becomes really frightening. At this stage, governments scramble to shut tax loopholes and to raise taxes on the rich, on incomes from capital and enterprise—measures that pay political dividends but do too little to tackle the deficit. They also crank up value-added taxes which are "antisocial," hitting the poor and the middle class, but which have a big enough effect on the deficit.

It is worth noting that spend-and-tax is the "lifestyle" that most easily satisfies the Golden Rule; the latter does not prohibit high spending provided taxes are set high enough for revenue to cover it fully. Most economists would condemn this way of satisfying the rule. However, in the short and medium term there may be no other way. The Golden Rule is partly a unilateral promise by which a country in the Eurozone seeks to reassure its fellow members in the zone that it will not upset the common currency applecart, and partly a vow to bite the bullet for its own good. As such, it has only very weak enforceability. Neither unilateral promise nor vows are easily enforceable. The idea that the European Union will somehow sanction a breach of the Golden Rule is wishful thinking by Berlin and grown-ups do not take it seriously. Nevertheless, if against the odds the Golden Rule were adopted and by and large respected, it would be a force for good, because it would make governments and the electorates face the realities of scarce resources instead of the dream of cloud-cuckoo land, where the money is always there to back any measure that seems a good idea at the time.

Curb spending and raise taxes

In an extreme version, this is the shock therapy that must be adopted when the state finds itself in the danger zone where the national debt is nearing 90 percent of the national income, let alone more, and the interest on the debt is about to rise sharply at the margin because successive tranches of it that fall due for renewal can only be refinanced at escalating rates. Britain in 2010 seemed to be going for such shock therapy. The therapy will only be accepted by the public when it is sufficiently frightened and interest groups ease up on the merry-go-round of protecting themselves at each other's expense. In its mild form, curbing spending by offsetting its basic propensity to rise, and gently intensifying the fiscal pressure along the lines of least resistance, is the fairly typical medium-term way of life of most states. It combines political survival with minimal economic growth.

Curb spending and reduce taxes

There is, if courage and a bit of luck lead to it, a possible path for the economy that converges toward the Golden Rule. Along this path, growth lifts revenues sufficiently for the rate of the deficit to be smaller than the rate of real growth plus the rate of inflation. National debt falls in total and falls even more as a proportion of national income; a virtuous cycle operates. Thanks to compound interest, the national debt as a share of national income shrinks faster than you would think, and finally a balance is reached where even a bit of bad luck, such as an adverse turn in the world economy, can be safely resisted. When the path of the economy reaches this benign stretch, we could say that beyond the Golden Rule, a Platinum Rule has been satisfied.

THERE COULD BE MORE GROWTH

When most men and women need to make some effort to survive and to better themselves, there will be economic growth unless sufficient causes frustrate it. There is, in other words, a presumption of growth; it is not positive stimuli that are really needed to establish it as the normal state of affairs, but rather the removal of the obstacles we put in its way.

The unemployment rate in Spain has long been at least 20 percent and currently it is 23 percent. For under-25s, it is double that rate. The majority of the employed have legal job protection of such force, including judicial review of the "fairness" of dismissal, that employing someone on other than a short fixed-term contract is to give him lifetime ownership of the job. In France and Italy, the risk of hiring a person and having to live with him whether he is suitable or whether he is still needed is only a little smaller. A French industrial company puts the average cost of dismissing an engineer at one hundred thousand euros. There is a 9.8 percent unemployment rate in France and a six-figure vacancy for artisans and other skilled workers. The educational establishment loathes apprenticeships which "condemn" the young to manual labor and stop them from going to university. There are one hundred thousand apprentices in France and six hundred thousand in Germany. Germany has an export surplus of 170 billion euros, France an import surplus of 70 billion. The annual cost of complying with all regulations and doing the paperwork involved in the United States is estimated at $10,600 per employee. New banking regulations in Europe are forcing banks to starve perfectly sound small enterprises of working capital. And so on. Officious regulation and well-meaning but destructive income redistribution are the obstacles that keep growth below what it could otherwise be.

There is a rough-and-ready correlation between the weight of these obstructions and interferences—a heterogeneous jumble that cannot be expressed as a single index number—and the share of national income pre-empted for purposes decided by the collectivity, such as the cost of running the state and the local authorities, entitlements, and "social" insurance. In 2011, out of one hundred euros of value the average Frenchman added to the national income, fifty-seven were pre-empted by the state for these purposes, leaving him forty-three. This is too little to the point of being absurd. The individual may try to get out from under by borrowing from the next generation, i.e., voting for deficit financing. This could be prevented by sticking to the Golden Rule. But in either event growth would be stifled.

There is no indisputable level that would satisfy the Platinum Rule as well as the Golden one, but it is obvious that any marginal rise in the share left to individuals' own choices would have a positive marginal effect. The Promised Land may begin at sixty or more for the individual, forty or less for collective choice. It would be reassuring to know that after the bitter experiences suffered since 2008, European states are on the path towards it.

9. A FISCAL CURB TO TAME THE STATE?

The world is wallowing in a comfortably lukewarm sea of monetary and fiscal ease. Budget deficits are at levels hardly ever seen in peacetime. In 2009, Germany's budget deficit will reach about 8 percent of gross national product, France's may top 9 percent, and both Great Britain and the United States will have deficits of around 12 percent. Only ballpark forecasts can be made for 2010, depending on the vigor of the economic recovery the year should bring, but deficits are more likely than not to remain dizzyingly high. Keynes, if he saw the numbers, might feel that his modern-day disciples have learned their lesson almost too well.

In this environment, a serious attempt to end deficits by the force of law is truly sensational and deserves more attention than it has received. The two houses of the German federal legislature have enacted a constitutional amendment that limits the combined deficits of the federal and state governments from 2016 onward to an average of 0.35 percent of national income.

"Average," in this context, means "over the whole of the economic cycle." In other words, the German government does not violate its constitution if it runs a deficit of 2, 3, or even 5 percent of GDP in the down phase of the cycle provided that it runs a surplus of 2, 3, or 5 percent in the up phase. This presents an awkward problem of identifying the phases of the cycle while they are happening rather than after they have happened. (Mr. Greenspan found the same problem with "bubbles." It is easy enough to say that the Federal Reserve should have pierced the 1929 stock market bubble, the 2001 dot-com bubble, or the 2007 house price bubble before they went too far, but one does not necessarily see that a bubble is a bubble before it has gone too far.) Future German governments will always be under pressure to relax the 0.35 percent rule to meet the threat of a possible recession and to

First published by Liberty Fund, Inc., at www.econlib.org on August 3, 2009. Reprinted by permission.

40

move to a sizeable deficit, but they will also come under pressure not to run a surplus for fear of aborting the recovery. Will future German governments ride roughshod over the rule or circumvent it either overtly or by accounting subterfuges and definitional fudge?

A constitutional rule that bars a monarch, a representative government, or the majority will of a society from doing what it very much wants to do is a logical curiosity. It is not unlike this conundrum: "The king decreed that the king must not do X, and that if he does do X, the king must undo it and punish the king for disobeying the king." (For "king," you may read "the administration" or "the sovereign people" without getting any nearer to resolving the logical problem.) Thomas Schelling, one of the acutest minds of our age, said it all when he called the constitution a *vow*. It is like a promise to oneself and one's near and dear to stop smoking or taking drugs; the difference is that it is rather more solemn and more awkward to break openly than an ordinary promise. In any case, however, keeping or breaking it is up to him who has made the vow. The separation-of-powers argument disguises this simple truth. It is functions, not powers, which are divided between the legislative, the executive, and the judiciary branches of government. Its power is undivided.

Let us, however, give Germany the benefit of the doubt. If there is a people that genuinely wishes such a constitutional rule to work and would accept a modicum of austerity to allow it to work, it is the German. Let us suppose, admittedly against the odds, that a constitutional rule limiting the budget deficit to an annual average of next to nothing does really work as an effective curb in Germany or somewhere else. What would be the likely consequences?

The democratic pressure on the government to do good, to help this or that activity and to make the welfare state ever more caring and ever more complete, would continue unabated. The basic reason, of course, is that the hopeful beneficiaries of each and every such measure would expect to bear only a fraction of its cost, the rest being borne by everyone else. Many of the beneficiaries would indeed expect to bear none of the cost, or better still, would simply assume that the cost would be met by some bottomless cornucopia of the state. The government could yield to the electorally most vital of these pressures and spend the necessary sums, but only by increasing total taxation by the same amount, since borrowing from the future would be banned by the constitutional curb.

The politically most feasible targets for levying more revenue would be corporation taxes and personal income and estate taxes on the top slice of income-receivers. However, both these sources are quickly exhausted. Corporations are mobile and cannot very well be stopped from removing themselves or their profits to fiscally less hostile places. Individuals are less mobile, but at high marginal rates of tax are apt to shift their efforts from the making of money to rescuing it from the taxman. Experience proves that even when the distribution of income is very unequal, the real scope for capturing the top slice turns out to be disappointingly small. For really large increases in tax revenues, the government must turn to excise sales or value added taxes. These are politically less easy targets. They are regressive, hitting the poor and the middle strata more than proportionally. If each round of higher government expenditure is regularly accompanied by a round of higher consumption taxes, even the more obtuse kind of voters will soon get wise to the fact that they are paying the price of every "gift" the government hands them.

The upshot, it seems, is that the share of GDP the state can pre-empt for its expenditures hits a ceiling. The ceiling may be high or low depending on a society's culture, and may change over the long run. But in any case, there is a ceiling. Putting it in other words, if government is really prevented from mortgaging the future, it becomes genuinely *limited*, though it may not be *small*.

Classical liberal thought has always held that government must be limited, but has never given plausible reasons why it should choose to limit itself, nor why society would choose to limit it. Friedrich Hayek was and is still admired for his constitutional theory which tacitly assumes that sweet reasonableness will make everyone opt for liberty and prosperity. It would be wonderful if a piece of legislation, such as the German 0.35 percent fiscal curb inspired by a dread of abysmal deficits, proved to be a step towards bringing such a wishful ideal closer to reality.

10. CAN SOVEREIGN BORROWING
BE A CRIMINAL OFFENSE?

There is a winding path in our contemporary history from the Keynesian multiplier through the double-dip recession, majority rule, and sovereign debt default, to the penal responsibility of a former Hungarian socialist premier for the excessive budget deficit of his country—a path whose twists and switchbacks it is perhaps instructive to survey.

Three generations of economists have been brought up on the Keynesian mechanism of the economy. They think in the terms John Maynard Keynes formulated to describe the Meccano construction he put up—the propensity to consume, the saving-investment identity, liquidity preference, the marginal efficiency of capital—even when they are in substantive disagreement with Keynes about what these levers really do and how they ought to be pulled to get certain results. The domination of Keynes's model is not undeserved. It is clearer, less ambiguous than its predecessors; it is far easier to teach to students and more convincing to the man in the street because it holds out the prospect of simple remedies against the ills of unemployment on the downside and overheating on the upside that a market economy is apparently so apt to catch.

Over the three years 2008–10, most governments in Europe and America have been knowingly swallowing big doses of the Keynesian remedies to pull their economies out of recession. Some did so as a matter of deliberate choice; the u.s.a. is the clearest example. Others, of which France is the most typical, merely allowed their vast welfare overhang to act as an automatic stabilizer. With well over 50 percent of GDP absorbed by government spending and independent of market demand, and with the oncoming recession actually stimulating govern-

First published by Liberty Fund, Inc., at www.econlib.org on September 5, 2011. Reprinted by permission.

ment spending on unemployment benefits while government income falls as tax receipts fall, the French-style modern welfare state generates the rising dissaving needed to offset the falling private investment and consumption. This big government is supposed to act as its own stabilizer. In fact, during the grim years of 2008 and 2009, France's GDP fell noticeably less than the Western European average, and the country's mostly left-leaning intelligentsia had much satisfaction in pointing out that a model biased toward "social protection" is proving to be more stable and resistant to shocks than one biased toward unfettered free markets.

However, the automatic stabilizer effect of the welfare state involves an equally automatic swelling of government debt, for the stabilization operates through additional government dissaving. A rough measure of this dissaving is the budget deficit. Whether the deficit rises thanks to automatic shortfalls in tax revenues and costlier social protection, or because governments deliberately pump up anti-crisis spending programs, the effect is the same. Over the three years 2008–10, the sovereign debt (roughly, the cumulative budget deficit) of the European states as well as of the United States rose by 20 to 30 percentage points of their GDP, reaching 85 percent in France and 100 in the United Kingdom and also in the United States. Current economic consensus holds that the 90 percent level is critical and once beyond it, it is inordinately painful if not impractical to work it down again. A fundamental and almost sacrilegious question then arises: does the Keynesian mechanism work as it was supposed to do? Do the stabilizers really stabilize? Could it be that while the deficit ought to stimulate output and employment through the effect of the Keynesian multiplier, the rising level of the national debt acts as a kind of negative anti-multiplier that offsets the stimulus?

If it had gone by the book, the recovery that started in the second half of 2009 should have been gaining speed and roaring ahead full blast in 2011. Instead, in most of Western Europe and the U.S.A., it has slowed down to near stalling speed and stock markets are dramatically signaling the coming of the second dip of a double-dip recession soon.

We may soon be witnessing the coming in the journals and textbooks of a "new paradigm" in which macroeconomic activity is governed not by one multiplier but by two. One is the old and familiar

Keynesian one in which incremental government dissaving increases aggregate demand by an amount greater than itself. The other—call it the counter-multiplier—kicks in when the level of sovereign debt approaches the worrying level. Some countries may start worrying at 60 percent of GDP (which they have agreed to do in the late lamented Maastricht treaty that no one took seriously), while others, like Italy today, keep a poker face with sovereign debt at 120 percent. But once at the worry level, any incremental sovereign indebtedness will actually decrease aggregate demand as industry gets frightened and cuts investment and employment, and as households try to reduce credit card and mortgage debt.

If this "new paradigm" of the two multipliers is at all right, it brings a silver lining with the black clouds. While massive increases in the deficit and monetary "easing" of unheard-of proportions fail to stimulate the recovery and may in fact suffocate it, deficit-cutting may, contrary to orthodox beliefs, act as a stimulant: a negative change in government deficit multiplied by the negative multiplier would then produce rising aggregate demand. If only protestations of fiscal rectitude and promises of balanced budgets could be believed!

Under the "new paradigm," there is no countercyclical excuse for the deficit. It is plainly bad not only for the next generation, which does not count for much in democracies, but also for the present one, which is usually quite ready to vote for it and shoot itself in the foot. In Hungary, which has been known to invent some original ideas in the past, the question has now been raised: Can a government or its head be held responsible, and perhaps criminally responsible, for running the national debt? The present center-Right government of Viktor Orban is waiting for the courts to rule whether legislation to this effect is constitutionally admissible.

In Hungary, over two four-year terms of a socialist government from 2002 to 2010, the national debt was run up from 53 to 80 percent of GDP. With the sales of the "family silver," i.e., state assets mainly to foreign buyers, and with inadequate maintenance of the capital stock, national impoverishment was greater than this. Profligacy peaked in 2006. The government of the ex-communist billionaire Ferenc Gyurcsany looked like it was losing the general election, but with some bold promises of an extra month of payments to all pensioners and other gestures of social generosity, he "bought" re-election. (Soon afterwards in a surreptitiously recorded closed-door speech to party cadres he admitted to have "lied morning, noon and night."[1]) Buying an election by taking the money from the electorate's own poorly lined pocket is perhaps not a felony. Perhaps it is not even an indictable offence. But then what is it? Unless Hungary were to legislate differently, it is nothing at all, it is just normal practice under majority rule.

Politically correct Western European opinion never forgave Hungary for giving Mr. Orban's center-Right a two-thirds majority in the 2010 election. The language barrier is so impenetrable that news agencies and foreign correspondents rely for information and interpretation on a small soft-Left core of Hungarian intellectuals well versed in the jargon of political correctness. The very idea of making a head of government like Ferenc Gyurcsany in some manner accountable for using deficit finance to get himself re-elected turned in Western European media to an appalling symptom of the anti-democratic leanings of the Hungarian center-Right. Even the elite press, from the *Economist* and the *Financial Times* downwards, condemned it as authoritarian. An editorial in the latter declared that such matters should be left to the courts—which is what the Orban government has done by referring it to the constitutional court even before benefiting from the advice of the *Financial Times* editorial.[2]

Chances are that no legislation that would make it an indictable offense to use the nation's credit and to steal money from the electorate to bribe it and get oneself re-elected will get on to the Hungarian statute book. The evidence the prosecution could ever muster would always be equivocal. This is a great pity, for such a law is, to put it no higher, an urgent necessity, and not in Hungary alone.

1. See "Excerpts, Hungarian 'Lies' Speech," BBC News, September 19, 2006. See also Balazs Koranyi, "'We Lied Morning, Noon and Night'—PM's Tape That Left Nation on Brink," *Scotsman,* September 20, 2006.

2. See Neil Buckley, "Orban Drags Hungary through Rapid Change," *Financial Times,* February 7, 2011.

PART 2

The Third Way to Stability?

1. GREED, NEED, RISK, AND REGULATION

Accusations of every kind of devilry are raining down on capitalism as never before—not that it has ever been much in popular esteem. Now it is condemned as immoral, selfish, greedy, imprudent, and unstable. Its crazed pursuit of profit rides roughshod over decency, civic spirit, and social justice. It produces in response to the lure of dollars, not to satisfy real needs. It generates glaring inequalities and provokes bitterness and class hatred. Last but not least, it is unable to correct its own inherent excesses.

The heat of these charges makes it urgent to understand at long last that what goes by the name of capitalism in ordinary language is a hybrid system crossbred from liberalism and social democracy, where the freedom of contract is allowed to work in some respects but is stymied in others and where perverse incentives springing from taxation and regulation are mixed with the profit motive that drives competitive markets. It is the performance of this hybrid that draws every man's hostility. But even if it were fully realized that the economy we live by is a brew of freedom and regulatory constraint, market and government, who can really tell whether it tastes bitter by too much market or too much government?

I think that much needless strife could be avoided by identifying the irreducible core content of capitalism, stripped of comic book images of the cigar-smoking moneybag with half-clad bunny girls sitting on each knee and the half-starved laborer staggering under a cruel load. Every economic system puts some labor and some capital in double harness. What distinguishes capitalism from pre-capitalist and putatively socialist systems is that in capitalism, the two factors—labor and capital—are furnished by separate sets of persons who are linked together contractually in a node by firms. The latter are personified by entrepreneurs who may own some of the capital and bear more of

First published by Liberty Fund, Inc., at www.econlib.org on July 6, 2009. Reprinted by permission.

the risk, or boards of managers who own little of the capital, bear little of the risk, and are the agents of the owners. Some theorists consider that entrepreneurs and managers furnish a third factor of production besides labor and capital, namely, organization of the cooperation of the two other factors.

In a first rough approximation, the share of each factor in the jointly added value is the result of a bargain between each factor and the firm. An indefinite number of bargaining solutions are conceivable. However, only one equilibrium solution is plausible. Under it, the firm pays workers the marginal value-product of their labor and pays capital the marginal return on investment. If workers were paid less, the firm would gain by hiring more, and if they were paid more, it would gain by shedding some labor. The firm is similarly incited to attract more capital if its yield exceeds its cost and to repay debt or buy back its own shares in the contrary case.

This plain yet superbly adapted balancing mechanism, driven by what its enemies are pleased to call "greed," is absent, or present only in embryonic form, in pre-capitalist systems. In idealized socialism, where all labor and all capital is owned by one single entity, "the people," the mechanism is a shadow of that under real capitalism just as prices are the shadows of real prices struck in real bargains between opposing interests of buyers and sellers.

Bearing all this in mind, I will review some of the evergreen and also some of the merely fashionable criticisms of capitalism, such as:

Capitalism is socially irresponsible.
Capitalism panders to greed instead of meeting need.
Capitalism is unstable and so the strong hand of the state must
    hold it on course.
Capitalism fosters reckless risk-taking.
Capitalism needs re-regulation to survive.

My object will be to see how well the core concept itself, rather than its passing warts and blotches, stands up to the barrage of passionate attacks of our day.

CAPITALISM IS SOCIALLY IRRESPONSIBLE

Several charges fall under this claim. One is that acting solely in re-sponse to the profit motive, the firm ignores the multitude of interested parties who are one way or another affected by its actions. They include its customers; its suppliers; the home town; and all who are harmed by any externalities by which the firm spoils the environment, aesthetic and cultural values, and the social climate of its community. In the language of political correctness, this is summed up in the phrase that the firm must consider its "stakeholders" and not just its shareholders.

In an owner-operated firm, a relative rarity in modern capitalism, the owner has the freedom to decide how much profit, if any, he will devote to the well-being of his customers, to easing the problems of his suppliers, to community development, good works, and any other altruistic purpose beside reinvestment and his own consumption. Some of these uses of his profit may actually enhance his future profit by generating goodwill, some may flatter his vanity, and some may sat-isfy his sense of charity. Little of this concerns the nature of capitalism. Most are moral questions which men face whether they are "capital-ists" or not.

The case of the modern corporation, owned by shareholders and managed by paid managers, is totally different. The management may justify spending some of the profit, or indeed forgo the making of some, to benefit "stakeholders" if doing so enhances future profit. But it must not do so otherwise. Doing so in order to look good or to sat-isfy the managers' own altruism is stealing the shareholders' money and betraying their mandate. Such breaking of elementary rules of what belongs to whom is wrong even if we ignore the damage that devia-tion from the objective of profit maximization will do to economic effi-ciency. This is a detail that the "stakeholder" argument grandly over-looks.

A somewhat different but related charge accuses the capitalist firm of social irresponsibility because profit-maximization serves the inter-ests of capital only but would, if it could, squeeze labor to the point of inhumanity. The apparent bias against labor is mostly an optical illu-sion due to the fact that adversarial bargaining over wages and condi-tions is highly visible, while no such adversarial bargaining surfaces in the firm's recourse to its shareholders or to the capital market. However, in reality the profit-maximizing firm is unbiased toward either labor or capital. Towards either, its attitude must be one of striving to equate marginal value product to factor price, whichever of the factors it may prefer.

What does it really mean to abandon this rule of profit maximization in favor of the sort of ostensible "social responsibility" in the shape of an employment policy that makes managers popular? Here, of course, we must deal with a pro-labor policy that goes beyond enlightened self-interest and beyond what makes workers more productive by enhancing loyalty, stability, and health.

It is obvious enough that the firm makes a mistake when it underpays its employees relative to their marginal product. But what if it overpays them—which it is supposed to do, at least occasionally if not permanently, in the name of social responsibility? It would be making a mistake, as the decline and fall of General Motors testifies (though the latter overpaid and overcommitted itself to future benefits not because it wanted to be socially responsible, but because its management was soft rather than greedy).

Since value added would not be increased by paying labor over the odds, the immediate effect would be its redistribution from capital to labor and a signal to the firm to reduce the labor force and also to decrease the capital it employs. The ultimate effect is difficult to predict and would depend, among many other things, on whether the firm obeyed the signal and reduced sail or not. However, the gift made to the overpaid workers would have to be paid for one way or another by the rest of society, a kind of hidden taxation its members may not recognize but may not agree to if they did. If there must be redistribution, let it be done overtly and frankly by legislation and not by falsifying the function of capitalism as a mechanism of efficient resource allocation.

CAPITALISM PANDERS TO GREED INSTEAD
OF MEETING NEED

In any type of organization, the top dogs are greedy and can exploit for personal gain any latitude they can get away with. This is likely to be as true of feudal lords and party central committee members as of entrepreneurs and corporate executives. The blame lies not with capitalism, but with the wide range of human characters.

In reality, the grievance is that the capitalist firm responds to wants expressed by dollar bills laid on counters. The well-to-do have more dollar bills than the needy. Hence capitalism accommodates inequality.

How otherwise could need express itself? People might make periodic declarations listing their needs. The political authority could add up the lists, charging designated enterprises with producing the required quantities by using resources in labor, capital, and materials provided by "society" as a whole in some fashion. Socialism that gives "to each according to his needs" must be imagined along such lines.

The sin of capitalism, then, is not so much that it panders to greed and ignores need, but that it is not socialism. If socialism were ever realized, its hopeless inefficiency at meeting needs and its unresponsiveness to wants would no doubt be blamed on its not being capitalism. Any system is liable to be censured for not being another. This is perhaps no great matter and we can live with it. The real mischief is done by asking a system to be both itself and another.

CAPITALISM IS UNSTABLE AND SO THE STRONG HAND OF THE STATE MUST HOLD IT ON COURSE

The world economy has of course never moved along on a ruler-straight course. Nothing permits us to say that its changes of direction and rhythm, some of it relatively severe and painful, have been due to its capitalist type of organization, the less so as it exhibited some such lurches in pre-capitalist times as well. One could with equal likelihood assert that far from needing more government for running straight, the economic system is unstable precisely because it is, and has always been, a hybrid rendered unstable by incompatibilities between its contractual and its regulatory components.

Only the settled judgment of economic history can provide a plausible answer to this question, and economic historians as a whole have not yet reached a settled judgment. However, even a single economic variable can move so as to raise strong suspicion about government interventions as a stabilizer.

Consider thrift. One factor in the vulnerability of the economy to the shock it received in the latter part of 2008 was high indebtedness. It is fair to say that its major cause was government policy. Debt interest is, but the cost of equity is not, deductible from company tax in most countries, which depresses corporate saving below what it would otherwise be. Compulsory "social" insurance and state provision for health care and old age pension weakens the precautionary motive for saving by households. Democratic politics, where the electorate likes to vote for more spending and fewer taxes, raises government dissaving. Highly developed low-saving welfare states are a "soft touch" for the strongly export-oriented emerging economies, notably China, and the result is a very lopsided international balance of payments and indebtedness.

Looking at other important economic variables closely enough would relieve perverse effects of government presence that may be only a little less malignant than the effect on debt. Accounting rules are one case of moot point; job-protecting regulations are another.

It is strongly asserted, particularly in Germany and France, that "Anglo-Saxon" capitalism is more unstable and socially destructive than the "Rhenanian" type prevalent in Continental Europe. The latter is less harsh, more consensual and collegial; it gives management more autonomy from shareholders, and unions more influence on both management and government. Above all, it is more stable (or Krisenfest) and less vulnerable to business downturns.

Two reasons are cited. One is that European capitalism is not as "financial" or "speculative" as the American one (Great Britain counts as an honorary non-European). This reason appeals to the economically illiterate, but is mostly false, for speculation is parasitic on volatility and, if at all successful, eats up some of the instability that would otherwise prevail.

The other reason for crediting "Rhenanian" economies with greater resistance to fluctuations is that they are welfare states, with public expenditure pre-empting one half or more of GDP. When private demand collapses, public demand is upheld or increased, and only less than half of GDP suffers a downturn. High-tax, high-deficit, and high-spending welfare states grow more slowly in normal times, but offer stability and protection on bumpy stretches of the road.

This argument has some force, but not enough. The latest (June 2009) forecast of the OECD projects a fall of 2.8 percent for the United

States and 4.8 percent for the Eurozone in 2009. In 2010, the United States should have growth of 0.9 percent and the Eurozone none. Unemployment figures show no less unfavorable comparisons for "Rhenanian," ungreedy, etatist capitalism.

It is not unfair to add that where state involvement in the economy has been intense, national debt as a share of GDP tends to become uncomfortably high. In such economies—France, Italy, Belgium, and Greece spring to mind—the government finds its hands tied when a sharp downturn would call for strong fiscal stimulus and open-handed spending.

CAPITALISM FOSTERS RECKLESS RISK-TAKING

It is not hard to fathom that the more developed an economy is, the more instruments it has that both facilitate the taking of risks and the transfer of these risks to those more willing to bear them than those who had previously taken them. Securitization that makes debts marketable, futures trading of commodities and securities that permits both risk-taking and hedging, and derivatives that do both in turbo-charged forms advance the technology of risk-taking as well as its least-cost distribution among potential risk-bearers. Their economic function is valuable. But is the risk-taking they facilitate really reckless, and if so, why?

Because of the recognition that owners are not necessarily the best managers and may be wise to entrust their assets to others who show expertise in the art and science of making the assets work, the principal-agent problem increasingly penetrates the capitalist economy. The problem is serious and has no ideal solution, for as the agent and the principal are typically motivated by a different set of incentives, the actions of the former will only imperfectly serve the interests of the latter. The intrinsic conflict of interest can at best be attenuated.

The main way capitalist practice found to do this is to pay corporate executives in leaving the firm bonuses and stock options that are contingent on results achieved by the executive, his team or department, or the whole corporation.

In the last couple of decades, the scale of these bonuses and options has expanded to reach levels that in many cases, particularly in banking and the law, but also in mass manufacturing and high technology, have come to be regarded by public opinion as unjustifiably excessive and indeed obscene.

This is undeniably a case of market failure. Overpayment of apparent or real executive talent and reputation is thought to exist for a variety of reasons, one being that the "product" is not standardized and that those who buy it, namely other corporate executives and board members, are engaged in reciprocal back-scratching. If they overpay others, others will return the favor and overpay them. The game, fueled by both greed and vanity, leads to an absurd level of bonuses and options. Even in structurally very imperfect markets, absurdities in due course produce their own remedies. One could, for example, hazard the guess that some compensation consultants, instead of playing the game of the boards that retain them for advice, will find it more profitable to serve shareholder groups and even to ally themselves with proxy solicitors to help form such groups.

However, even if the average level of bonuses and options were eventually deflated, the bias the system imparts to recklessness would remain. It is a system of "heads I win, tails I do not lose." If results are poor, bonuses, albeit reduced, are still paid, and if options do not rise in value, at least they can never fall to a negative level. It is worth taking large risks even at long odds, because the expected value of the bet will always be positive.

The obvious remedy is to stop granting options that are in fact "long" calls (that either work or expire valueless), and grant combinations of "long" calls and "short" puts (which are exercised against the holder if the outcome is negative, i.e., if his company's shares fall below the option level when it expires). The call and the put have to be accepted or rejected together. To make the option attractive while still retaining its deterrent effect against reckless risk-taking, the put may be smaller than the call and any loss it yields could be chargeable against profits on the calls but not otherwise payable. These details may be left to bargaining as long as the principle of "heads I win, tails I lose" is preserved.

CAPITALISM NEEDS RE-REGULATION TO SURVIVE

Industry and commerce deal with property in tangible assets and the matching liabilities. Finance deals with intangible rights in property and the derivatives of such rights. The difference lies among others in the fact that tangibles cannot, but intangibles can, be created at the stroke of a pen at the will of two consenting parties. In other words, the quantity of financial assets and liabilities is in theory infinitely elastic, and is limited by one or both of two things: confidence and regulation. This is no doubt why financial regulation is treated as different in kind from any other, and why, after each crisis of confidence, it is felt to be inadequate and in urgent need of radical reform.

Let it never be forgotten, though, that the latest crisis was triggered in August 2007 by the sudden recognition that with U.S. real estate prices on the decline, subprime mortgages of about $600 billion were no longer worth their nominal values. This was a paltry sum for a major banking system. It should have been shrugged off with a pained grimace and a reasonable fraction of it written off. Instead, voices of highly placed authorities, including the head of the IMF and Britain's Chancellor of the Exchequer, cried "Fire!"—a self-fulfilling prophecy by those who should have known better. A stampede started for the exit, lashed on by the media that responded naturally to the perverse incentive that panic-mongering sells more newspapers. The end result was a very nasty world recession that need not have happened.

It is tempting to think that more and cleverer regulation would have prevented this outcome. But if the Basel II solvency rules had been twice as severe as they were, many banks would still have carried liabilities of ten or more times their own capital. In an earthquake of confidence, being leveraged ten times is just as bad as twenty or thirty. The most draconian regulation cannot remove risk from leverage, and removing leverage altogether would be to put the economy back in the Dark Ages.

Financial innovation can produce quirks that make the desire for more regulation excusable enough. Credit default swaps (CDS) are very clever insurance instruments. However, they permit any number of parties to insure the same credit against default. A loan or bond of $10 million may well be insured a hundred times for a total of $1 billion.

Grave conflicts of interest could arise. Sooner or later, the free market would have developed remedies by organizing an exchange that imposed collateral to limit counterparty risk and would have provided information on "open interest." But it is understandable that a nervous public wants regulation at once.

Regulation can at best be imperfect and cannot help being a drag on the economy's growth potential even if it were capable of protecting it from shocks. Its great vice is that it is a fount of illusions, making people believe that if a thing is regulated, one need not handle it with care.

Thus in conclusion, the above review of common criticisms of capitalism—that it is socially irresponsible, that it panders to greed not need, that it is inherently unstable and needs to be regulated by government, that it fosters reckless risk-taking, and that it needs to be re-regulated by government to survive—must be viewed in the present-day context that what goes by the name of capitalism in ordinary language is a hybrid system crossbred from liberalism and social democracy. It is not therefore surprising that the performance of this hybrid draws criticism from every direction. But even if it were better realized by commentators and regulators alike that the economy we live in is a potent brew of freedom and regulatory constraint, market and government, who can really tell whether it tastes bitter because of too much market or too much government?

2. TRUDGING DOWN THE THIRD WAY

Some of us hold that there is a presumption in favor of freedom and that the burden of proof lies on those who would violate it. Interference with the freedom of contract, to name but one important freedom, is presumptuous and requires cast-iron justification. Failing it or when in doubt, freedom must prevail. Others, no doubt the majority, feel on the contrary that freedom needs justification. They find it in its consequences, in the growing material well-being that the freedom of contract tends to bring about. The freedom of contract is good if its consequences are good. If they are not, it is not.

It is this consequentialist stand that has now turned resolutely against freedom, at least in the economic domain. It is blamed for financial mayhem in 2007, a stock market crash and the onset of recession in 2008, and who knows what, perhaps another Great Depression. Since the media all say that the latter is indeed a possibility, business pulls in its horns, which is the surest way to bring it about. In the nature of things, democratic electorates order their governments, "Don't just stand there, do something!" Governments, understandably enough, get busy doing it. We are off, trudging down the Third Way.

Joseph Stiglitz, whose economics nowadays is two parts scholarship, three parts catchy demagogy, tells us that 2008 is nothing less than the 1989 of capitalism. The historical equivalence of the fall of the Berlin Wall and the bankruptcy of Lehman Brothers puts paid to two equally sickly systems. Neither will do; we must have something better.

No one will dispute that it is always better to have something *better*. Liberalism ("classical liberalism" in American English), capitalist free-for-all, and deregulation proved bad; re-regulation and dirigisme must be better.

This is a conclusion that majority opinion in most of Europe has always been longing to hear. "Unfettered" capitalism has never been

First published by Liberty Fund, Inc., at www.econlib.org on December 1, 2008. Reprinted by permission.

congenial to the German ethos that prefers cozy corporatism, frowns on feverish competition, and wants an economy that is both "market" and "social." France's two dominant modes of thought, obsessive egalitarianism and awestruck respect for a big and powerful dirigiste state, both generate hostility to free markets and capitalist enterprise (or, as they put it, "financial capitalism"). Throughout, but particularly in Southern Europe, the religious culture affirms that "social" justice has a distinct meaning and that capitalism undermines it.

All in all, the consensus now is that just as socialism had discredited itself in 1989, capitalism lost credibility in 2008. Neither is good enough. One needs a new system that takes what is good in each: a well-regulated free market, vigorous growth, and stability; the firm hand of the state on the tiller, fair competition, and just rewards for all.

Even before dismissing this conclusion as pathetically naïve, we should question one of the consequentialist premises on which it rests. Are the falls of the Berlin Wall and of Lehman Brothers equivalent evidence of failure? No sensible consequentialist needed the Berlin Wall to fall before noticing that "real existing" socialism and all its works were an appalling failure from beginning to end. On the other hand, sensible consequentialists had realized that the gradual loosening of administrative controls, the dismantling of trade barriers and the shift from (progressive) income to (regressive) consumption taxes since 1945 were accompanied by (or perhaps actually caused) six decades of albeit bumpy but historically unprecedented growth of wealth and redeemed the world's poorest from abject misery. This performance, spectacular by the standards of the past, has earned forgiveness for capitalism in the eyes of many who by instinct and woolly ideas would have felt more at home in a mildly socialist and dirigiste climate. Withdrawing this forgiveness at the sight of what may or may not prove to be the first major bump in the road since 1992 does look rather hasty. Nor need one bow a penitent head at the charge that the 2007 financial mayhem was the fault of insufficient regulation coupled with the irresponsibility of greedy bankers. There was much regulation, all apparently of the wrong sort. But we only know after the event what the right sort would have been. It is a fact that the American overlending on credit-unworthy, no-recourse mortgages was at least in part the result of official urging to help the poor own their homes, and to the facilities offered by Fannie Mae and Freddie Mac. It is also a fact that obliging banks to mark down collaterized securities to the price they would fetch in a panic-stricken market, combined with their desperate need to show respectable Basel II solvency ratios to more and more nervous depositors and call money lenders, was a regulation-made recipe for setting up unmanageable vicious circles. The plain truth is that while there is no denying the blind silliness of many bankers, the real culprit was a hybrid system that was neither really free nor a fully automatic machine and whose component parts have unsurprisingly proved incompatible.

Needled on by strident anger and blame for all that went wrong, and guided by experts determined to fight and win the last war while believing that they are preventing the next one, politicians are getting ready for what is likely to be a protracted campaign of re-regulation. In the first round, the central target will be the financial sphere. Banking supervision will be tightened and banks will have to please their regulators before they please their customers. Securitization may be restricted, and banks that transform loans into marketable securities may well be required to retain a proportion in their own portfolio or otherwise assume the credit risk. Credit default insurance is likely to be limited by strong margin requirements. All such measures will be aimed at reducing system risk, though what they will in fact do is to reduce the transferability of risk. The cost of credit will have to increase and the efficiency of capital markets must decrease, though it may be that the resulting more sluggish and less efficient system will enjoy easier public acceptance. Bankers will be a little less like wizards and more like post office clerks.

One objective of putting a stop to the "free-for-all" will be to make stock, bond, and commodity markets more stable. The Third Way is actually paved with potential schemes to achieve this. They start at the curbing of speculation and end with state marketing boards and the closure of auction markets. It is ironic that speculation is the pet target of public opinion that takes it to be both immoral and sterile. In addition, there is a belief that "bear" speculation (short selling) makes prices go down. Any economics student whose instructors are worth their salaries knows that all successful speculation reduces price volatility below what it would be if there were no such speculation. The reason is simply that in order to succeed, the "bull" must buy low and sell high and the "bear" must sell high and buy back low, with each of these trades moving the price in the direction opposite to where it would otherwise go; i.e., they smooth out volatility. Never mind the economics—speculation must and probably will be curbed if the dirigistes have their way.

From finance, the swell of enthusiasm for more dirigisme is almost bound to spill over to commerce and industry. "Incomes policies" and fiscal devices to make income distribution more equal are also a popular means to a "better, more stable, and more just" order cleansed of the "extremes" of Left and Right. We are probably committed, and condemned, to trudge down the Third Way for a while. It is a great pity, but there is always the hope that we will come out wiser from the experience.

3. OPEN SEASON ON THE
CAPITALIST FREE-FOR-ALL

They always hated what they called the capitalist free-for-all. Op-ed journalists, freelance commentators, and left-leaning economists always resented the trust the Thatcher-Reagan iconoclasts had placed in deregulation, self-correcting mechanisms, and the "blind forces" of the market. They did so partly because, to their mind, this meant the rejection of rational, well-informed and hence benign policy-making for which they felt specially qualified, and partly because the free-for-all rode roughshod over notions of "social justice" in which they firmly believed. Belief in what passes for social justice, one of the strongest threads in the tissue of opinion, deserves a separate discussion if not a separate shelf of books, and I hope to devote a column to it shortly.

Regarding the efficiency of market mechanisms, however, the anti-capitalists used mostly to confine themselves to cautious sniping, for a full frontal attack was awkward to mount while this system was delivering unprecedented material progress for the last half-century and was lifting a billion and a half people out of abject poverty.

Now, at long last, it is open season. Shooting up the free-for-all has the enthusiastic support of public opinion because it is supposed to have grievously failed. In its place, recourse is to be had to the strong arm and helping hand of the state to undo the trillions of dollars worth of damage wrought by stampeding bankers.

Public opinion holds deep beliefs, received from the media and from resentful economists, about how and why great events happen. It is absolutely convinced that Roosevelt beat the Great Depression. The judgment of many reputable economic historians that the New Deal actually retarded the recovery is almost totally ignored. Likewise, the current economic downturn is ascribed to the pernicious practices

First published by Liberty Fund, Inc., at www.econlib.org on February 2, 2009. Reprinted by permission.

of laissez faire. It is a fair bet that the coming generation of economic historians will refute this belief, too. For it is already clear that what undermined the banking system (and through it, indirectly, industry and trade as well) was not the lack of regulation, but rather the hybrid nature of the regulations in force, made up of mutually incompatible rules. Imposing fixed solvency ratios on the banks was rather like ruling that you must always have at least €100 in your pocket. Since you must never use it, it is as if you did not have it at all. Once the need arises, you must sell the shirt off your back before using it. Combine this solvency rule with the "mark to market" rule that forced banks to write off to near-nothing the collateralized debt obligations they held once the media started shrieking that they were "toxic! toxic!" and their market temporarily disappeared—in part because nobody could use their last €100. Taken together, the two regulations were strong enough to ruin almost any banking system.

Another spectacular example of the vanity of belief in regulation is the recent Madoff fraud. Acting under the eagle eye of the Securities and Exchange Commission, and with his accounts audited by a firm hardly fit to audit the corner grocery, Madoff could attract several tens of billions for his fraudulent scheme from investors who might have been more careful if they had not been reassured by SEC supervision and audit. Regulation imparts a virtual stamp of approval that is really, well, "toxic! toxic!" if regulators are incompetent or corrupt. It is an open question whether regulation by fallible human beings is not more dangerous than the much-maligned free-for-all where people must watch their step.

It is no use saying that what we need is *better* regulation. We should always take something better than whatever we have, but it is infantile to think that we always can and that saying so will make it so.

The supposed free-for-all may now be fair game, but then so must be the hunter. It is high time to return fire rather than duck or cower penitently under the punishment.

The whole controversy must be seen from a broader perspective. Is the free-for-all both viable and self-correcting? Respectable general equilibrium theory says it is. Empirical proof is not conclusive, for there is not, nor has there ever been, a pure enough free-for-all to provide a copper-bottomed thesis. Is socialism viable and self-correcting?

Economics and psychology say that on the whole it is not. No contrary evidence exists. Even though pure socialism has occurred no more than pure capitalism, mankind's experience with Russian, Chinese, Indian, and African attempts at socialism was sufficiently disastrous to make the answer an incontrovertible "no." There is, then, the hybrid system (or rather spectrum of systems) that unfolds as we advance along the Third Way, the "new, moral, sensibly controlled" ideal mix of elements borrowed from purebred capitalism and socialism and fitted together in the hope that it will work better than either of its two purebred parents.

Advocates of the Third Way claim that it would preserve the virtues of free markets while curbing their vices. It is strange to hear talk of free markets in countries where between 40 and 55 percent (soon to rise to between 45 and 60 percent) of the national product is disposed of by government bodies and compulsory social insurance. Directly or at one remove, deliberately or inadvertently, government influence must be all-pervasive and dominant in those countries.

A typical hybrid economy conjures up the image of a walking patient with multicolored plastic tubes snaking in and out of every orifice of his body. The tubes infuse and evacuate fluids of all sorts that nourish, stimulate, restrain, and neutralize the effects of other fluids. They supplement, redirect, and override the body's own autonomous circuits. Each tube turns out, after a little while, to need strengthening, offsetting, correcting by one or more new tubes, each of the new tubes turning out to need even newer, cleverer supplementary tubes. Every single tube adds something better, an improvement in safety, efficiency, and, why not, moral uplift to the body's own innate equipment. There is every hope of ever-better results. There is no end result, for the assembly of tubes is never final, but keeps evolving and getting more complicated. Little by little, however, the patient starts looking less and less like a potential athlete, and more like a real invalid. Could it be that the plastic tubes and the body's own circuits do not mix so well?

4. COLLECTIVE CHOICE AT WORK

At one time or another, most of you have seen in the street the warning sign "Danger: Men at Work." None of you have seen a danger sign warning "Danger: Collective Choice at Work." This is probably a great mistake, for collective choice has an immense destructive potential, ranging from corrosion to explosion, and the fiction that the social contract makes it all right and all benign is at best a half truth and at least a half lie. The present article looks at what tends to happen when collective choice is at work where men are at work and are paid wages for it.

The knee-jerk understanding of collective choice is "democracy," where its rough-and-ready meaning is one-man, one-vote majority rule circumscribed by constitutional limits on what the majority may and may not do, with these limits being fixed by the majority itself in some higher, constitutional incarnation. The gaps between this ideal and the ways it works out in practice are well known. In any case, the democratic ideal is only a very special case of the form collective choice may take. In its general form, it is the solution of a "game" by which the decisions of some members of society are accepted by most or all as binding. The former rule and gain the outcomes they seek, the latter are ruled by habit, passive acquiescence, the threat of raw power or, at the limit, because of defeat in war or insurrection. Each of these "games" may be formalized, and its solution reached at the lowest cost, for society is persuaded to adopt a rule of choice-making (e.g., "The dictator's word shall have the force of law," or "Majority vote by secret ballot shall be decisive").

All this looks very abstract and far removed from the prosaic contingencies of industrial relations, the labor market, and the scandalous malfunction of the contemporary economy on far too many countries where unemployment ranges from 8 to 25 percent of the active popu-

First published by Liberty Fund, Inc., at www.econlib.org on December 3, 2012. Reprinted by permission.

lation. In fact, however, the way from abstract generalization to prosaic misery is short and direct. The French code of labor law currently runs to 3,200 pages. Its rate of growth, if that is the right word to use about the number of its pages, puts to shame the rate of growth of the economy. It promises a spurt of expansion in 2013, when the "historic" negotiations between the Patronat (the employers' association) and the labor unions about reforming the labor market, that have been going nowhere for three months, will have reached their deadline and the government will step in with fresh legislation. Meanwhile, unemployment has passed the 10 percent mark and seems inexorably headed for 11 percent by mid-2013.

Unemployment has a number of major causes and each of these is in its turn caused by many minor ones. Overshadowing all, especially in France but also in Spain and Italy, is the modern labor law.

A French employer can terminate a labor contract of indefinite duration for a number of obvious and fairly evenhanded reasons, but not because he judges it to serve his own best interest (e.g., because he wants to replace an employee with a more suitable candidate). The widest category authorizing him to dismiss an employee is "economic redundancy." Unsurprisingly, the law is unable to define "economic" without much ambiguity. The employee can seek juridical remedy from the courts, arguing that his dismissal was not economically necessary. The courts, massively encouraged by the media and the government, with the latter being threatened with protest strikes and attacks in the legislative chamber, often disallow the dismissal because they judge the economic justification not strong enough. The employer may be forced to reinstate the employee because its business is not loss making, or because, though running at a loss, it is the subsidiary of a multinational group that is not running at a loss. The ringside public is greatly excited and puts forward a remarkable version of the science of economics — for instance, that the employer can well afford to retain the employee because its sales are more than sufficient to pay the wages. The employer, if it is a public company, is often accused of seeking to cut its payroll to please the stock market, a place well known to be a temple of greed and sin. For redundancies of more than nine persons, the employer must propose a "social plan" that may include offers of alternative employment, vocational training, and severance payments over and above the legal minimum. The government may not approve the "social plan" and the matter may finally end in the courts after a fight that may take years.

The obstacles in the path of redundancy, including union and government opposition, bad public relations, and a protracted court fight, may in most cases be bought off by generous severance payments that in some celebrated cases have reached two or more years of salary.

The rational employer will under these circumstances only hire an additional employee if the latter's expected marginal product over a given period is greater than his wages and payroll taxes for the period plus probability-weighted cost of overcoming the legal and institutional job protection, should the necessity for closing down the job arise. The employer, a busy manager, may not actually make this detailed and pseudo-precise calculation, but will simply conclude that he would just as well not face the job protection by the unions backed by the state and the media, should the need arise to cancel the job he is considering creating today. He will instead just stay put, not create the new job or fill it with a fixed-term employee whose contract automatically terminates in a short while. The net result is a rise in temporary employees, fairly high job security for the "ins" who are on indefinite contracts, and a very bleak outlook for the "outs," particularly the young. Unemployment of 10 percent or more is becoming the standard, blithely blamed on the "crisis," the banks, the "speculators," and the Chinese. In France, the "Anglo-Saxon" liberal globalizers will be found even more blameworthy.

The French case gives a special edge to the malignant role of collective choice in the workplace. French labor unions have a negligible membership outside the public service providers, such as the tax offices and the state railways. They are maintained by mostly covert state subsidies. The influence and the salaries of the union hierarchy depend not on the service they render to their members, but on the image they manage to project as the frontline defenders of the working class. They proclaim branch- or industry-wide collective bargaining, the security of employment, and payroll-financed social services as sacred taboos and are ready to incite their members to strike action whose cost they do not even indirectly bear. In terms of collective choice, they are the rulers; the wage-earners are the ruled who persist in believing, despite the mounting evidence to the contrary, that the decision-making rules work to their advantage, and the unemployed are the helpless victims of it all. In the "historic dialogue" now going on between the Patronat and the unions, the government in an oblique and apologetic manner is asking the unions to give up some job security in exchange for some job creation. These negotiations are making no noticeable headway and should end presently by the government taking over. Everybody's incentives will remain exactly the same as before.

Hope, such as it is, lies in the gradual return of individual choices into the play, and their intrusion into what is now the reserved domain of collective choice. Collective bargaining, for one, must lose its sacrosanct monopoly and so must the exclusive right of unions to represent workers and be accepted as their sole agent. Labor law must cease to be the expression of what collective choice deems to work in its favor, such as the recruiting of allies and the harvesting of votes, and must instead find its bases in what the parties directly concerned can most easily accept. It would be wonderful indeed if the trimming of collective choice would lead to the rediscovery of the freedom of contract.

5. INSTINCTIVE BLUNDERS: JOB PROTECTION AND REDISTRIBUTION

Man has some instinctive reactions to events that shake one's belief in genetically selected behavior being favorable for the survival of the species. When caught by a storm in open country, his instinct is to seek cover under a tree, which is precisely the thing he must not do if he is weighing one outcome against the chance of a much worse one. Would he rather get wet or be struck by lightning? Experience over countless millennia should have taught him the way lightning mostly strikes, but apparently his instincts have not learned the lesson. Likewise, when he is pushed, man's reaction is to push back, though his best defense would be to pull the pusher on and use his very momentum to bring about his downfall. To say man learns this by taking judo lessons, if he learns it at all, is only part of the answer. Perhaps genetic selection of the best behavior for survival should have taught him over countless millennia to use judo to defend himself. While the individual's instincts seem to lead him to blunder some of the time, government's "instincts" lead it to blunder much of the time. One very grave blunder it never avoids—a blunder denounced in this column more than once over the past few years—is to tighten the labor code and pile on ever more draconian job protection measures when unemployment is high and looks like staying high.

There are two rival views about what a job is and ought to be. One is liberal and symmetrical, seeing labor as a service that is freely bought and sold as a matter of contract between the provider and the user of the service. The other is social and sees labor as a particular relation in which the employer becomes responsible for the employee who, in turn, owes him some service. The relation is not symmetric; the employer has fewer rights and more responsibilities than the employee,

First published by Liberty Fund, Inc., at www.econlib.org on September 3, 2012. Reprinted by permission.

and this is only just because the two parties are unequal in resources and needs.

The liberal contract provides for an indefinitely repeated series of services by the one and payments by the other party. Either party has the same freedom to terminate the contract, usually after due notice. For a variety of reasons, including paternalism, genuine sympathy for all but especially for long-service employees, and as a matter of sound business practice that values the fostering of loyalty and good will, the liberal employer will often do for his employees more than the contract obliges him to do, and such generosity is the more likely to be repaid as it is not a contractual requirement but an expression of decency and generosity. The social labor contract is more inclusive than the liberal one and imposes obligations on the employer that under the liberal contract he might or might not undertake voluntarily. Fringe benefits being contractual, they do not generate loyalty and good industrial relations as they do when they are given voluntarily. Moreover, the legislator intrudes so massively into the employer-employee relation that the contract becomes a three-party one. Vital aspects are not mutually agreed, but fixed by the government in its eagerness to protect the employee. Fixing the minimum wage, the "legal" work week, and the "legal" retirement age are such aspects. They are popular for being "socially just" but they do the same kind of harm to the economy as the legislated rigidity of any price. They harm it to a greater degree because they are among the most important of all prices.

However, no government participation in the fixing of the terms between employer and employee is as destructive of jobs as job protection. The idea that the employer is somehow responsible for the future of his employee—the notion that underlies the rule of lifetime employment by the same employer—implies that hiring and firing are not symmetrical. The pain and damage that firing does to the employee must be compensated by such bounties as the severance payment, the extended period of notice, the securing of alternative employment, and under some legislations even the subjection of the firing to the approval of a labor court. The severance payment may vary widely over and above a "legal" minimum.

It has been estimated that the cost of firing an employee may average two years' wages of a semi-skilled male factory worker. Michel Sapin, the minister of labor in the new socialist government of France, has recently promised "to make firing so expensive that it will be as good as prohibiting it."

Accepting this figure, for want of a more precise average, as the cost of discharging his responsibility for his employee's future, an employer must reckon that hiring a person for an indeterminate and uncertain period would cost him this person's wages for any given period plus severance equal to two years' wages divided by the probability of the eventual need to fire the person at the end of that given period. The sooner the need may arise, the more expensive it is to hire him. This expense would be attenuated if the severance payable would vary inversely with the length of service, but in any case it would be a tough obstacle to taking on a new employee. The sensible thing would be to hang on to all old employees until they retire voluntarily, and to hire nobody afresh. The net effect of job protection would then be great job security for those entrenched in their jobs and no jobs for those, mainly young people, who are looking on from the outside.

This goes some way towards explaining both of the most depressing features of the European employment picture: a persistently high average unemployment rate (hovering just under 10 percent, a historically exceptional level), and within this an even more exceptional youth unemployment rate (ranging from 20 to near 50 percent, which is between the scandalous and the incredible and should drive young people to despair and destructive madness).

Fortunately, these unbelievable high rates of forced idleness need not be believed. In a recent book,[1] we learn that not counting in the under-24 young labor force those who are either at university, at training courses, or otherwise engaged, so that the number of actual job-seekers is reported as a percentage of those who either do or could search for a job because they are not otherwise busy, overstates the unemployed as a percentage of their age group. Correcting for the overstatement in this way, the young unemployed in Spain are not 49 percent, but only 19 percent—still scandalous, but not apocalyptic.

---

1. Steven Hill, *Europe's Promise: Why the European Way Is the Best Hope in an Insecure Age* (Berkeley: University of California Press, 2010).

Be that as it may, it is clear enough that if an employer must calculate his expected cost of employing an additional worker using not only the worker's wage and social insurance, but also a risk factor made up of the severance and other costs of getting rid of the additional worker should the need arise to do so, unemployment of both the young and of adults will be higher than it would be without job protection. Providing for the cost of overcoming job protection is an integral part of the expected cost of additional employment. The government's knee-jerk reaction of intensifying job protection when unemployment rises—an instinctive blunder—will only increase unemployment further and make it more persistent.

The other major instinctive blunder of government is more long-term and acts at a deeper level. When income inequality increases, as it has done in recent decades as hundreds of millions of East and South Asians were drawn into the labor market and their output into world trade, public opinion was shocked that profits were racing ahead while semi-skilled and unskilled wages at best stagnated. The knee-jerk reaction of governments was to "correct" by intensifying redistribution from rich to poor, notably by spending more on education and health care and by not defusing the pensions time bomb that would have required the ratcheting up of the pensionable age in line with rapidly rising life expectancy.

Without the rise of these various entitlements, after-tax profits and the top slice of "earned" incomes would rise faster, as would the share of saving compared to consumption. Capital accumulation would accelerate. Eventually, it would outpace the rise in the world labor force due to the rush of Asian villagers into urban factories. As infrastructure the world over improved and capital equipment per worker grew, the world income pendulum would be swinging back from profits to wages and from a very unequal income distribution towards a less unequal one. This, in effect, would be the strongest long-term mechanism for lifting the unskilled and the underemployed out of poverty. It is this spontaneous mechanism that is so perversely destroyed by the instinctive blunder of busily hurrying to redistribute income.

6. IN FANTASYLAND:
THE STRESSLESS ECONOMY

Europeans are now longing for a "new economic order" that would be stressless. If such a one were feasible, it would be hapless.

Back to Square One. After the post-war decades of slow and uneven but rewarding progress toward a better integrated world economy, less restrictive and red tape–ridden, allowing more freedom of contract and becoming more responsive to the ebb and flow of underlying change, it turns out that this was all a great mistake. The market "cannot regulate itself." Politicians and educated opinion, with the French out in front, are again decreeing the "end of laissez faire."

There are two distinct strands in this retreat to the past, or rather to the wishful image that is now made of it. One is technocratic, the other is popular and even frankly populist.

The technocratic view is that the dysfunction that was set off in August 2007 and has since grown to alarming proportions was due to reckless deregulation of the financial system and more generally to the withdrawal of governments from their controlling and safeguarding role. Since the invisible hand has proved to be unsafe, let us once again put our trust in the strong hands of the state and let us, without procrastination and horse-trading, build a new regulatory framework that will preserve the strengths of free markets while ensuring their smooth working and protecting them from wild stress and strain.

It should not surprise us if future historians were to conclude that this reasoning was a typical case of *post hoc, ergo propter hoc*—the troubles came after deregulation, therefore they were caused by deregulation. In fact, the chain of causation was probably less pat and simple. An exceptionally low real interest rate spectrum due primarily to the gigantic East Asian excess saving has generated a housing price bubble in the

First published by Liberty Fund, Inc., at www.econlib.org on June 1, 2009. Reprinted by permission.

United States, Britain, Spain, and Ireland. It is very doubtful whether the Federal Reserve could have resisted this even if it had wanted to. At least partly if not wholly as a result of stimulation by public policies favoring home ownership by very low income groups, there was much overlending on mortgages, risky even if house prices had remained at their inflated level and loss-making if they turned down—as they duly did. Fannie Mae and Freddie Mac could not hold off the degradation of mortgage portfolios. The physical capital represented by the mortgaged housing stock was not damaged, but the securities that had big batches of both prime and subprime mortgages as their collateral (and that bankers allegedly did not even understand) were damaged by a loss of confidence that temporarily froze them into illiquidity. There were many would-be sellers but only a few "vultures" would buy, and they only at near-absurd prices. Securities whose mortgage collateral may have become 30 percent nonperforming and that percentage, in turn, would all end in foreclosure and permit, within a year or so, no more than 50 percent of the mortgage debt to be recovered, would under these conditions have an intrinsic worth of roughly 85 percent of their par value (a loss of 50 percent on the 30 percent of defaulting mortgages, i.e., a 15 percent on all the mortgages). The "vultures" might buy some at 20 percent of the nominal value which very few banks would willingly accept. However, in that case under the "mark to market" rule, they had no choice but to devalue their mortgage-backed securities to 20 percent of the par value, declaring a truly frightening loss of 80 percent. This was the trigger of the panic.

From then on, the rest follows fairly easily. Credit default insurance losses are a multiple of the mortgage-based losses, although they are matched by the gains of counterparties. In fact, all purely financial losses are matched by gains or avoided losses, the whole being a zero-sum game that impacts the distribution of wealth, but not its total amount. However, at this point the effect on confidence enters the game. In particular, the influence of modern, aggressive media on partly-informed opinion becomes decisive. "Things are really not too bad" is not a good headline but "things are catastrophic" is. August authorities, including the head of the IMF, get into the headlines and the evening news by announcing that much, much worse is to come.

Such prophecies are self-fulfilling. Even the prudent customers who have no credit card debt will stop buying durable goods, and the financial mayhem infects the "real" economy. It is a perfectly open question whether more regulation could have prevented such an outcome. Quite possibly it might have aggravated it, and may yet make any recovery slow and awkward.

Be that as it may, the politicians and the technocrats will now pile regulation on regulation, making the economy more rigid and sluggish, because the groundswell of popular sentiment imperatively demands it. Reading of eleven-digit bank losses and trillion-dollar deficits, of crisis and meltdown, and trembling for their jobs, people are stressed and dream of a "new economic order," an escape from stressful and unpredictable capitalism. No matter that most of what they are told about such an order is hot air, they believe in it as they long for a world where they own their jobs and cannot be fired, where prices are "just" and do not fluctuate, where healthcare is free, pensions safe, and perhaps above all, nobody earns much more than they do. In most of Europe, the egalitarian obsession is becoming frenzied and a major source of stress.

The trouble is that a tolerably efficient economy generates stress and cannot be purged of it without going back to quasi-medieval and quasi-bolshevik ways. It is worth pausing a moment to see why this is so.

The defining feature of capitalism is not that workers are short-changed and speculators frolic with fashion models, though such things may occur as they would in any other conceivable order (as they did in the late socialist republics, too). Instead, it is that labor and capital are contributed to productive use by two different sets of persons. Talk of harmony, co-determination, and reasonableness will not alter the fact that one of the two sets of people wants a high share for labor in total factor income and the other wants a high share for capital. The resulting stress could be lifted if the provider of labor and capital were the same person. This was the case in medieval times when the artisan owned his tools, the merchant his stock-in-trade, and the serf or peasant farmer his draft animal. It was also supposed to be the case in Soviet Russia and Tito's Yugoslavia where workers were told that all capital belonged to them—a claim beneath notice. Either way, Fantasyland without capitalism would be desperately poor.

Moreover, a stressless economy would be altogether predictable. As prices would have to be "just" or "fair," they could not be allowed to go up and down and hence could not equate supply and demand. Producers, consumers, or both would be left frustrated. Probably they would feel stressed when seeing how their neighbor resorted to the black market. As the market would be prevented from emitting signals, investment would have to be decided on criteria set by central planners authorized to do such things. French experience shows that the result might be a superb network of TGV lines built at astronomical cost, admired by all but yielding only a minuscule return on the capital investment before the numbers are corrected by creative accounting. (The same goes for nuclear power stations whose future decommissioning cost, an utter unknown, is just not mentioned in polite company. French economic history is teeming with white elephants, dressed up as information technology or renewable energy, that help to explain the uninspiring performance of the economy despite its many favorable endowments.)

Admittedly, much stress results from people comparing their own mediocre destiny with the greater success, higher income, prettier wife, and cleverer children of a colleague or neighbor. Apparently, there is now hard medical evidence, showing up in tangible biochemical symptoms, that this is the case. It would be plausible anyway on a priori grounds.

Some of this stress-inducing inequality—such as unequal incomes, though hardly unequal wives—could perhaps be smoothed out by controls on salaries, bonuses, and professional fees as well as taxes. The smoothing out would have to be radical, for even small inequalities can generate just as much resentment, envy, and self-reproach as large ones. Hence egalitarian policies would have to be drastic to make Fantasyland stressless.

Too obviously, though, it would not and could not become stressless. The stress of living in a hapless, impoverished economy subjected to really radical equalizing policies hardly bears thinking about. But how to tell this to the masses clamoring to be led to Fantasyland?

7. THEY WANTED A NEW ORDER

For ages before the panicky recession of 2008–09, there has been a persistent anti-capitalist background noise all around us. It was loudest in France and Latin America, in the universities and the media all over the world. It was made up of the voices of socialists, professional politicians and union apparatchiks, cranks, "dealers in second-hand ideas," and resentful failures. Defense against them was not a very demanding task. While the dogs barked, the camels advanced. After all, in less than a century, the capitalist order made good the mad devastation of two world wars; beat and buried two mighty and nasty totalitarian systems, Nazism and Soviet socialism; and brought the standard of living of ordinary working people up to a level their grandparents never even dreamed of.

Admittedly, while its competitive and meritocratic features broke down the privileges of birth, it did generate much inequality, too (though no one has managed to show why inequality was a wrong). It abused the environment (though it was a good deal easier to spare the earth when it was populated by one and a half billion people than now when it carries over six billion). Last but not least, it made it easy and tempting for people to enjoy the material good and forget the spiritual (though the choice was not imposed, but left to them to make). Above all, unlike any other system ever tried, capitalism worked.

The shambles of 2008–09 has shaken this defense. Small defects snowballed into big avalanches. The self-fulfilling prophecies of expert commentators and high officials who should have known better have deflated confidence and made banks fall like ninepins. The screaming headlines spread the panicky mood, with obvious effects on both consumer and investment spending. The news of governments running up deficits of 8 to 10 percent and more of GDP, bailing out shaking banks, and printing money as fast as the presses would run, all in a des-

First published by Liberty Fund, Inc., at www.econlib.org on December 7, 2009. Reprinted by permission.

78

perate effort to save the economy from an even worse fate, was held up as proof that a free market system is inherently unstable, cannot run itself, and needs the strong hands of government to hold it on a tolerably even course. That deregulation did not seem to work in 2008 was promptly taken as proof that it never could and never will. (It was overlooked that the system as it stood was a hybrid with disparate elements of regulation broken up by bits and pieces of deregulation. No one can tell whether it was too much or too little of either that caused it to splutter and seize up in 2008.)

The background singsong of the usual choristers of anti-capitalism has, understandably enough, become stronger and more confident. Regrettably, many illustrious representatives of the establishment have also joined the choir. Two of the most eminent, the governor of the Bank of England and the chairman of the Financial Services Authority, have been wondering aloud about the "social usefulness" of a highly sophisticated financial system, sounding almost nostalgic for the good old post office savings bank that should be good enough for all socially useful purposes. (The unanswered question of how we tell what is and is not socially useful did not trouble them.) Both German and French opinion leans decidedly the same way and blames the "Anglo-Saxon liberal ideology" for the present hesitant and uncertain approach toward more regulation.

The twentieth anniversary of the fall of the Berlin Wall has now added a new theme to the anti-capitalist music, though it was already *allegro vivace* enough. It is now the ex-Soviet satellites that were let go by Russia in 1990 that are supposed to be disappointed and to chant, "We did not want this, we wanted a new system, a New Order."

It is perfectly true that large sections, perhaps the majority, of the ex-satellite peoples are disappointed. The contrary would be surprising. They had been convinced that only the Iron Curtain and the perversity of "real-existing socialism" kept them from the prosperity they knew to be commonplace in Western Europe. When the Iron Curtain was raised, real wages and standards of life did not jump by 150 percent overnight to catch up with the West. Some things started to improve, other things did not, or got worse. As the distribution of income became somewhat less equal, the unskilled and above all the pensioners suffered genuine hardship. Under socialism, housing was scarce and new construction of appalling quality, but rents were nominal. Electricity, gas, and public transport were almost free, as were education and an equally miserable health service. Jobs were dismal but secure and nobody had to work hard if he did not feel like it. Most of these charms of "real-existing socialism" have become a distant memory, embellished by man's usual bias in favor of the good old days when he was younger.

In the first decade of the post-Soviet era, a number of the liberated countries started doing well to very well; Hungary, Poland, and the Czech Republic were leading the pack, notching up growth rates of over 5 percent, and some smaller states, notably Slovenia, Slovakia, and the Baltic states, were riding faster still. In the new century, the record became patchy. Poland and the Czech Republic, where post-socialist reforms were fairly radical, have continued to do relatively well, while the Baltic states and Hungary were riding for a fall. The case of Hungary is characteristic. In 2002 the ex-Communist party regained power, and in 2006 managed to retain it, by "stealing" both elections with a sparkling spending spree, loose money, "generous" public sector wage and pension increases, and many of the bells and whistles of what has since been called a "premature welfare state." By 2007, the country was teetering on the edge of a cessation of payments, was saved by a gigantic $24 billion IMF and EU facility and is now on a bread-and-water diet, a 7 percent fall in GDP and no relief in sight before they work their budget and balance-of-payments deficits from low double- to low single-digit levels. For average opinion, this is not how they expected to fare under capitalism.

The East German disappointment is perhaps sadder still. For eighteen years after reunification, the West German lands have subsidized the East German ones to the tune of about 2 percent of total GDP. Output per head in the East started off at 40 percent of the Western level and has by now reached 70 percent. This is by all sober accounts a spectacular achievement. Despite much higher unemployment than in the Western part of the Federal Republic, the East as a whole has been well treated by capitalism and if it is much poorer than the West, there are half a dozen sound structural and sociological reasons why it should be. Despite this, there is widespread bitterness and self-pity in East Germany. It is amazing to hear them complain that according to the most educated guesses of the research institutes, it will take another forty to eighty years before the standard of living in the East finally catches up with that in the West. One must rub one's eyes and ask: but why on earth do you believe that, by rights, it must ever catch up?

The answer is loudly given by the ventriloquist left-wing intellectuals of the world's media who put words in the mouths of the East Germans, and indeed of all the post-Soviet peoples. They did not want this system; they did not willingly adopt capitalism; it invaded them, took them over; what they really wanted was a New Order, a regime not of greed and savage competition of man against man, but one of justice, freedom, and kindness. But they never had a chance to put it into effect; capitalism pre-empted the space.

If only we could be told what such a New Order means and how it can be installed, we would doubtless opt for it. Pending that bright day, let us not spoil the capitalism we have.

PART 3

The United States of Europe and America

1. THE FOOLISH QUEST FOR STABILITY

"Oh, what a tangled web we weave, when first we practice to deceive" ourselves that economic variables function best when they are fixed—or, isn't stability more desirable, more reassuring than volatility? If ups and downs cannot be suppressed altogether, at least let us control them by regulation rather than leaving them to the self-destructive gyrations of the market free-for-all.

It is now the established consensus that the 2007–09 financial upheaval was the fault of the self-destructive propensity of unregulated markets. The minority view, which the writer of this column has also argued, is that the system was a hybrid between freedom and regulation and each element undermined the possible virtues of the other. There is no telling what the outcome would have been with a system of more, less, or no regulation. The issue may be decided by a future generation of economic historians. Meanwhile, bygones are bygones and we are in for an ardent quest for more stability, more fixity of elements that are destined to move and change to adjust to a changing reality. The first batch of new regulations, the Volcker Rule and Basel III, is already with us. It may be claimed that it means to adapt the system to changed realities. In fact, it looks more like a rule book for fighting the last war, and the perverse effects of Basel III on banking and insurance are already becoming apparent.

The most fervent and excited of the current quests for fixity is in the Eurozone. When twelve of the fifty American states are technically bankrupt, nobody is predicting that the dollar will become worthless and the United States will fall apart in fragments. Such a fate, though, is supposed to await the euro and the EU if some of its tottering sovereign debtors are forced into default. It is not really obvious why this is so readily accepted as gospel truth, except perhaps because the media unanimously trumpet that it is so. Accordingly, after some angry pro-

First published by Liberty Fund, Inc., at www.econlib.org on February 7, 2011. Reprinted by permission.

tests by the German taxpayer who is the ultimate EU paymaster, Greece and Ireland received emergency transfusion in 2010. Portugal may only just get by in the next two years without being bailed out, but at a high cost; it had to pay 6.7 percent interest on new ten-year loans last month. The majority of Eurozone countries are suspect, most notably Spain, Italy, Belgium, and France (in that descending order). All have the same chronic ailment: their budget deficit is a higher percentage of their GDP than the rate of growth of the latter, so that their national debt is a steadily rising proportion of GDP. The London *Economist* calculates that by 2015 it will be 165 percent for Greece, 135 percent for Ireland, 100 percent for Portugal, and 85 percent for Spain (this relatively sober Spanish number is thanks to the thrifty Aznar years, just as the high French figure is due to the spendthrift Mitterrand and Chirac regimes). Evidently, the annual interest charge on the debt pre-empts a growing share of GDP, making the burden ever harder to bear. Adding insult to injury, much of the debt is not "owed to ourselves," but to foreigners. The corresponding percentages are 58 for Greece, 64 for Ireland, 66 for Portugal, and 39 for Spain. The service of this foreign-held debt is a charge on the balance of payments which may be literally impossible to meet by generating a surplus.

Instead of giving it up as a bad job and meeting the oncoming defaults by what is politely called "restructuring," the EU, after much heart-searching, has decided to throw good money after bad, redeem maturing private debt by loans from a new intergovernmental stability fund and preserve the status quo at least for the next few years. If, as it now looks likely, the arithmetic will get worse every year, such quest for stability will have proved to be a foolish one. The only realistic hope for a way out would be a rise in the inflation rate from 2 to 6 or 7 percent—in itself a dreaded element of instability—that would shrink the debt in real terms. Even that would only work for countries whose debt was mainly medium or long term, for the service charge of short-term debt promptly moves up in parallel with the inflation rate. France, for instance, would get less debt relief from inflation than Britain.

In focusing its current agenda on the unwelcome variability of exchange rates and commodity prices, the G20 is also off to a quest for stability. As the quest will exhaust itself in twenty bored delegations listening to each other's wishful thinking speeches in summit meetings and sending meaningless replies to each other's dreary memos, one might be tempted to ignore this attempt at world economic government. However, it does deserve some wary attention, for the loud rhetoric of the G20 promotes in the public mind the kind of fantasy economics that could in future years well be reflected in foolish policies.

Mr. Sarkozy, president pro tempore of the G20, is calling for it to adopt a "new monetary system" to replace the present vacuum. In practice, this means the re-introduction of fixed exchange rates. At present, only China operates with a fixed rate, one result of which is the accumulation of $2,600 billion of currency reserves which is of no conceivable use, present or future, for China has little chance of swinging into a massive trade deficit, and the United States of America into a massive trade surplus, that would enable these reserves to be spent on something useful. However, despite the widespread nostalgia for fixed rates, there is no danger of a "new monetary system" where the burden of adjustments now borne by exchange rates would have to be borne by other variables, such as employment, the price level, and taxes (all of which are also objects of the quest for stability). At worst, the G20 may resolve that the question "merits further study."

The other major point of the G20's agenda is the regulation of commodity prices. Nobody knows how this could achieve stability any more than how to make water flow upward, but everybody claims to know that speculation is the culprit and must be brought under tight control.

If there were no speculation, i.e., no adjustment to what the future is likely to bring, commodity stocks would always be at the minimum needed to conduct ordinary trade, for carrying more than hand-to-mouth stocks would tie up capital. Minimum stocks provoke high volatility of the price in response to any change in supply or demand. How does speculation, accused of causing more volatility, affect this mechanism?

When a speculator anticipates a price rise, he will seek to buy the commodity as a "future," i.e., for future delivery. If his demand is met by a "short seller" who promises future delivery, one ends up gaining, the other losing; they settle and nothing happens to stocks. If, on the other hand, no short seller is there to meet the demand of the long buyer, the "futures" price rises above the current "spot" price, the difference (called the "contango") making it worthwhile to buy the com-

2. EUROPEANS KNOW BETTER: THE ATLANTIC CLEAVAGE ON FINANCIAL REFORM

In German, they give the name *Besserwisser* to the man who always has all the answers and better than you or I. In English, one could call him Heknowsbetter. The financial and banking mess that started off in August 2007 with a relatively modest total of $600 billion of sub-prime mortgages on American homes turning out to be "nonperforming" and culminated a year later with Lehman Brothers collapsing, and such names as Citicorp, Royal Bank of Scotland, American International Group, UBS, Hypo Real Estate, and not a few others maintained on life support, roused all Heknowsbetters to frenzied activity. Some declared that capitalism has proved its own irredeemable rottenness, others that the "real" economy needed sheltering from the ravages of predatory finance, that deregulation has proved a disaster and global regulation was an urgent need. Many a German and French Heknowsbetter voiced the conviction that the real culprit was the cabal of "Anglo-Saxon" economists and bankers drunk on "neo-liberal" dogma and market fetishism, greed and reckless ignorance of risk.

The Europeans, with honorable exceptions, have always regarded the "Anglo-Saxon" theory and practice of finance with envious suspicion and unconcealed disapproval. Now that it stands there with egg on its face, European critics of it are sure of holding the moral and intellectual high ground. They are aggressively calling for a complete reconstruction of the financial system along characteristically European lines. Their proposals cluster around three main headings: the size and role of the banking system, its regulation, and bankers' pay, especially the bonus system that is to public opinion as a red rag is to a high-spirited bull.

Lord Turner, chairman of the U.K. regulatory authority whose intel-

First published by Liberty Fund, Inc., at www.econlib.org on October 5, 2009. Reprinted by permission.

ligence puts him in the very top rank of all the Heknowsbetters, has recently been wondering aloud that the British financial service sector might have grown too big for the good of the economy. It might then be salutary to make it shrink. (Amusingly, at about the same time Lloyd Blankstein, chief executive of Goldman Sachs and about the last person who ought to say such things without blushing, felt it advisable to say that many of Wall Street's new financial products may not be "economically and socially useful.")

How can we tell that an industry is too big for the good of the economy and its products are "socially" not useful? The market tells it and we hear what it tells when profitability is declining and the products will not sell. However, the contrary was the case for many years, and this is why the worldwide financial services industry grew so much faster than the world economy. Changes in financial techniques, notably the transformation of non-marketable mortgages and loans into marketable assets and the distribution of risks via derivatives, have promoted higher economic growth which in turn created further demand for these financial services. If, as many believe, these developments came to a natural end in 2008, and if the bank failures and forced writedowns are the market's way of saying so, let us by all means stand by and see it happen. If, on the contrary, the mayhem in 2008 was provoked by ill-conceived policy measures from which it was right and proper to rescue the banks, then it is odd to want to shrink them by a new round of policy measures that are already promising to do much damage.

One such measure is the "Tobin tax" on all financial transactions. Hitherto, it was mostly the alter-mondialist cranks and grampuses who were ranting in its favor. Now Lord Turner wants it considered, and Germany's socialist Finance Minister Peer Steinbruck wants it with a punitive rate that would truncate some types of useful dealings. The establishment in Paris is sighing for a way of imposing it without letting too many transactions escape to Singapore.

In any transaction, two parties, seller and buyer, lender and borrower gain or expect to, and there is some marginal gain for the whole economy. How the Heknowsbetters find that if the transaction is "financial," it should be punished, is unfathomable.

On both sides of the Atlantic, but particularly in Europe, a stricter regulation is demanded, above all to force banks to raise more capital to support their balance sheets. If there were no regulation at all, banks could choose between being strongly or weakly capitalized. Strong capitalization is costly, it dilutes the equity of existing shareholders, but it permits the bank to make riskier loans and to attract wholesale deposits at a cheaper rate of interest. Weaker capitalization forces the bank to make do with retail deposits and to avoid making risky loans, but it reduces the cost of capital. Their existing customer base, the wishes of their shareholders and the temperament of their management would make some banks go for stronger, others for weaker capitalization. Regulation of leverage and capital ratios means that the banks have no choice, "one size fits all" and Heknowsbetter determines the "size." One result is that many banks resort to off-balance-sheet devices, another that many try to shrink their balance sheets to avoid having to raise more capital. The latter result, in turn, produces the "credit crunch" that governments, business, and the general public plaintively reproach.

The Franco-German consensus diverges most sharply from the Anglo-American one in the matter of the remuneration of bankers. It believes that unlike pop singers and soccer players, bankers are paid far too much, which breeds a culture of greed, short-termism, and reckless risk-taking—quite unlike the dear old Post Office. The trading desks of banks that deal in securities, commodities, and derivatives for the bank's own account are hotbeds of immoral speculation, the traders manning the desks get obscenely high bonuses, and the whole activity lacks economic and social utility. There is much anger that the "Anglo-Saxons" do not agree to jointly limiting bankers' pay and in particular the traders' bonuses. The Europeans cannot go it alone.

Admittedly, it is hard to see any good reason why traders should get seven- and even eight-figure bonuses that enrage public opinion. However, there is no good reason either for fixing remunerations by public opinion poll. As to the "economic and social utility" of banks doing short-term trading for their own account, how can any Heknowsbetter tell that the trading produces none? Why, then, is it consistently profitable, sometimes (as in 2009) staggeringly so? Normally, useless trading at best breaks even over the years, and makes a net loss if the trader has to be paid. The only explanation for consistent though volatile profit-

3. OUR CHERISHED OPTIMUM CURRENCY AREA: ITS TRIALS AND TRIBULATIONS

It is just fifty years ago that Robert Mundell formulated the concept of the optimal currency area and set off an avalanche of theories that developed it and of empirical studies explaining why it mostly did not work and why it worked when it did. It is about two decades since the project of a common European currency began to gain ground and a dozen years since its flesh and blood reality.

When its adoption was decided, Milton Friedman gave it but a couple of years before it would collapse. His razor-sharp mind was convinced that a system of sovereign states with independent fiscal regimes, different legislation, and imperfectly integrated factor and product markets cannot operate a common currency without getting into an unholy mess that will bring about the breakup of the common currency area.

It is now an accepted fact of history that many of the early advocates of a common currency largely agreed with Friedman's prognosis. They were mostly Christian Democrats or right-leaning Social Democrats, meliorist, mildly corporatist (as Friedrich Hayek would put it, "constructivist"), no fervent believers in the nation-state, and also more than a little jealous of the U.S.A. whose power overshadowed the European mosaic of disunited countries. The French contingent of these centrist politicians and intellectuals also believed that if there was to be a united Europe, only the French could and would lead it, while the Germans, having lost two cataclysmic world wars and covered with shame for the Holocaust perpetrated in the second, sought forgetfulness and a fresh, non-national start in a united Europe. All had an overt objective: to enhance prosperity, to stimulate economic growth, to have the somewhat laggard Europe catch up with American performance. Joining together in a common currency area would help to achieve this.

First published by Liberty Fund, Inc., at www.econlib.org on May 2, 2011. Reprinted by permission.

Besides the overt purpose, however, the shrewdest among them also had a covert one. Like Friedman, they thought that a currency area without a high degree of economic integration was dysfunctional. Unlike Friedman, however, they did not expect this to lead to an early breakup. Instead, they believed the member countries would almost subconsciously and step by reluctant step move toward greater economic integration which, in turn, would almost imperceptibly bring about the political integration that was their real goal. As power drifted from national capitals to Brussels (and more recently also to the expensively feathered nest of demagogy at the European Assembly in Strasbourg), a federal but tightly united Europe would emerge.

The cack-handed attempt to accelerate this process by foisting on the member states a singularly inept and verbose European Constitution, a monument to mindless verbosity with the Social Charter apt to undermine the economic advantages of greater unity, was sunk by its defeat in the Dutch and French referendums that produced the right result for wrong reasons. Five years later the Lisbon Treaty, only a little less damaging, took its place and is causing only a manageable amount of pointless inconvenience. Meanwhile, economic integration is advancing, but the trials and tribulations of a common currency area, lacking anything like the optimum conditions, are outpacing them at what looks like menacing speed.

The exact conditions that warrant two or more (not necessarily contiguous) countries abandoning their separate currencies and adopting a common one have to do with the costs of alternative means of remedial adjustment when the economy of one country gets, so to speak, out of kilter with the other(s). The adjustment may take place automatically or be administered by government policy or, of course, a dose of each.

An underlying assumption of the optimum area theory is that the mere fact that two regions are using different currencies reduces trade between them to some significant amount below what it would be if they were in the same currency zone. This effect is due solely to transaction costs being higher if foreign exchange is involved. (It is reasonable to accept this assumption, but very difficult to assess it quantitatively. Some estimates have put the reduction of trade between two contiguous regions of the u.s. and Canada due solely to the two using two different currencies at 30 percent or more, a number that looks implausibly high.) If the region gets into balance of payments trouble, having a separate currency of its own can serve as a means of remedial adjustment either by an automatic decline in the exchange rate if it floats freely, or by devaluation if it is fixed. In either case, the region pays for the luxury of having its separate currency and the means of adjustment the currency provides, by incurring the loss of potentially higher trade—a permanent opportunity cost of currency independence.

The theory postulates that there are other means of adjustment, such as the level of output and employment; downward price and wage flexibility; mobility of capital and labor, both geographically and between sectors producing tradable and non-tradable goods and services; as well as shifts in taxes and transfers between regions subject to the same fiscal system. They may be subsumed under the heading of economic integration.

Broadly speaking, if remedial adjustment can be obtained by greater integration at a lower cost than by having a separate currency, a region can gain by giving up its own currency, joining a multi-country currency area and striving for ever greater integration with the rest of the area using the same common currency.

Summarily, this was the promise held out by the creation of the Eurozone, starting with twelve countries, expanded to seventeen at present and due to expand further as a few more candidate countries manage to satisfy some fairly easy conditions of entry. A good deal of integration was achieved by way of creating a single market in goods though not in services, and in mobility of capital though not of labor. Certain areas of integration, notably the establishment of a high-tax cartel politely called "fiscal harmonization," are still being fought over.

At its establishment, the euro area was promised durably to raise economic growth by 1 percent or more, a staggering acceleration destined to change the course of European history. Disappointingly, there is no evidence whatever that this has happened or is due to happen. We may note, with bittersweet irony, that instead of Europe becoming economically more like America, it is America that is straining to become more like Europe, piling on gigantic new welfare entitlements that, like Europe, it cannot or will not pay for and that, like Europe, it cannot stop from pre-empting an ever larger share of the national product.

Why is the optimum currency area failing to deliver the great good that seems implicit in the flawless logic of its theory? The reason, I suggest, is that the theory tacitly assumes that economic policy pursues the same objectives of maximizing an area's material well-being throughout. Plainly, however, a typical modern government depending for its continuing tenure on the favor of an electorate does not operate under the same constraints in a multicountry currency zone as under its own particular money that it shares with no other country (nor, we may add with a side glance at the U.S.A., when its own money is also the world's foremost common reserve currency).

When Mr. Mitterrand was elected president of France in 1981 and turned the country towards "the morrows that sing," socialism proved its generosity by showering new "social rights" and entitlements all round, raising public spending at a dizzying pace. The balance of payments duly weakened, the markets fled from the franc and the government in 1983 was forced into a spectacular U-turn, moderating its generous financial largesse. (It also blamed France's deficit on Germany's surplus and insisted that it is not the franc that must be devalued, but the deutschmark that must be revalued.)

No U-turn of sobriety and discipline is imposed by any one member government of the seventeen-nation "optimum currency area." The area is a characteristic public choice problem, offering to each of its members a free rider option. Each member government has a strong electoral interest to take the option and ride free in the sense of letting rip both its budget and its balance of payments deficit in order to win the next election. As the effect of one country's free riding is diluted over sixteen others, the offending country is not punished by the markets as France was after 1981, and is under no constraint to behave responsibly. The sanctions periodically thought up and brandished by Brussels have so far simply been ignored and continue to look naïve and unenforceable.

The rest, as the saying goes, is history. It is punctuated by "crises" such as the Greek rescue, the Irish rescue, and the Portuguese rescue. Whether more are to come, and whether rescuing to gain time before real decisions must at last be taken, is anybody's guess. The zone for now seems to be rearranging itself into two halves, the Latin and Catholic Club Med half and the Teutonic and Protestant-ethic Northern half, the latter carrying the former. Both halves cherish the "optimum currency area," the Club Med half for the protection from market forces and the free rider option it offers, the less happy-go-lucky Northern part, one suspects, mostly because it fears the unknown scenario of a breakup of the area and would rather muddle through than face that. If history teaches us something about the future, it is that it will not bring any clean-cut outcome, but a long succession of trials and tribulations, muddles and fudges.

4. EUROZONE: IT SEEMED A GOOD IDEA AT THE TIME

In the type of society we live in, two kinds of order are intertwined. One is driven by agreements, contracts, and custom resulting in exchanges between individuals exercising the freedom of choice that the circumstances of each permit. Their circumstances are partly a result of the past, partly of their own doing. The other kind of order is driven by command in the form of laws and ad hoc regulations and orders determining what society or its various groups and categories must and must not do. It thus produces collective choices to which individuals are forced to conform by the principle of submission leading to political obedience. Political obedience is considered legitimate because the collective choice rule on which it rests (for example, majority rule) is claimed to be of people's own choosing.

Collective choice where some, perhaps a majority but perhaps just a small and assertive group, decide for society as a whole, has the power to pre-empt or otherwise override the order based on freedom of exchange. They have obvious, identifiable incentives to do so. The response to incentives takes two major forms. One is redistribution; by collective choice, taxation on the revenue side and the provision of public goods and services on the expenditure side transfer resources from those who produce them to those who will consume them. The welfare state is the typical result, but a warlike state armed to the teeth could also be created in this way by collective choice.

Collective choice can, and all too often does, produce another and potentially quite vicious result. Friedrich Hayek, whose severe diagnosis of this result was his most valuable contribution to political philosophy, called it Constructivism.[1] Disrespectfully and suggestively, one might also call it "Toys for the Boys."

First published by Liberty Fund, Inc., at www.econlib.org on October 3, 2011. Reprinted by permission.
1. See Friedrich A. Hayek, "Reason and Evolution," *Rules and Order,* vol. 1, *Law,*

The Boys are usually well-educated, intelligent, and very ambitious men and women forming networks at or close to the centers of power. They are overrepresented in political parties, in the higher reaches of regulatory agencies, and in the better sort of print and audiovisual media. Their fertile minds keep producing good ideas, blueprints of new structures that, if duly constructed, should make the world a better place. For the Boys, such Toys promise a double boon. One is the satisfaction of being the champion of a good thing, of progress. The other, less easily avowed, is that as newly constructed institutions come with new job opportunities, exciting career prospects will beckon to the inventors and promoters of the new Toys.

A grand and ambitious one was being constructed module by module over four decades, starting with the Coal and Steel Community, continuing with the Common Market and then the European Union. In the crucial 1992 Maastricht Treaty, the member states undertook to respect certain rules of good fiscal behavior (an undertaking contemptuously ignored by both Germany in some years and France nearly all the time) and agreed to adopt a common currency, the euro. The Eurozone, intended by the more nationalistic and socialist of its sponsors "to look the dollar area in the face," became reality in 1999.

Its appeal was not only to Euro-idealism and anti-Americanism, but also to economic interest. It was confidently forecast to raise the area's growth rate by between 0.5 and 1 percent a year, a cumulative gain of astronomical proportions. It was also promised not to raise prices: two deutschmarks were to become one euro, but a two DM cup of coffee was not supposed to become a two euro cup. (Those who promised this have not learned of the "money illusion." The cup of coffee promptly rose to two euros—but this was the least of the euro's disappointments.) Perhaps the main economic effect of the common currency was that under its umbrella, staunchly held over them by the European Central Bank which in its early years acted as the spiritual heir of the highly conservative Bundesbank, the member states had a fairly free hand to run up budget deficits with little fear for the effect

Legislation and Liberty: A New Statement of the Liberal Principles of Justice and Political Economy (Chicago: University of Chicago Press, 1973), for a full description of this topic.

on their currency. The country that went the furthest out on this limb was Greece, and the Eurozone woke up to the weight of the sovereign debt pressing upon most of its other member states, too, when Greece was found to be facing almost imminent bankruptcy with its sovereign debt at about 160 percent of its modest GDP.

Two rescue plans and a lot of acute pain later, Greece is edging closer and closer to insolvency and the prevailing intention of the Eurozone powers-that-be is that they must keep throwing good money after bad, for Greece must be "saved" at all costs even if she preferred not to be saved. Extravagant calculations of the cost of quitting the euro are being floated: Greece would lose 40 percent of its GDP if it reverted to the drachma, while if Germany led a dissident group of the fiscally honest countries, Austria, Finland, and the Netherlands, into a separate currency area—as proposed by H. O. Henkel, one of Germany's most prestigious industrialists—she would lose 20 percent of her GDP straight away and 10 percent in subsequent years. The absurdity of these estimates is exceeded only by the childish credulity of their audience. The gravest forecasts of the Cassandras do not even have numbers attached: they simply say that if Greece went, Portugal, Ireland, Italy, and Spain, and maybe France, too, would "necessarily" follow and the consequences would be "incalculable." Therefore neither Greece nor any other country must leave the Eurozone. Q.E.D. With everybody busily engaged in frightening everybody else, and this in a modern economy with an advanced financial system that cannot function without a measure of confidence, the consequences may be "incalculable" indeed. It does seem a pity that freedom of speech comprises the freedom to spread panic on the back of half-baked scenarios and a refusal to lose face and admit honestly that the good idea was not such a good one after all.

It is hard to credit but sadly true that it has become a firmly held dogma that if Greece is not "saved," the whole Eurozone will fall apart by way of a cataclysmic chain reaction. Looking so marvelous and exciting in 1999, the great Toy looks fragile and a source of anguish in 2011. No one is courageous and skeptical enough to ask why default by a country accounting for a minuscule 3 percent of the zone's economy should fatally cause the whole zone to "explode." "Chain reaction" is the muttered answer. But is economics really the same as nuclear physics? The grim answer probably is that if enough people believe it, it may become rather like it.

Logically enough, the Boys, refusing to lose face over their currency area, are pinning new hope on another and more powerful new Toy, a real federal union with a centralized budget for the whole area— the sole realistic condition for converting the national debts of the member states into a common Euro debt for which all are jointly and severally responsible and that the "nasty speculators would not dare to attack." Much could and no doubt will be written about the whys and wherefores of such a budget and debt union, about sovereign nations willing to submit to it and about Germany accepting the role intended for her, namely that of guarantor of last resort and rich aunt. All this column can predict at this stage is that no folly is too great, and that we can look forward to many a future summit meeting just like the dozens that brightened the past.

5. STONE-AGE BANKING, ANTI-SPECULATION, AND RESCUING THE EURO

With healthcare reform in tatters, unemployment and the deficit blamed on the government, and foreign policy reaping a harvest of defiance and contempt by Israel, Iran, and the Afghans, President Obama sought consolation in the only area where he and popular emotions were still at one: in banker-bashing. Lest his proposed great banking reform should look too much like pandering to crass populism, he found a prestigious ally in the venerable Paul Volcker, a former Federal Reserve chairman of formidable reputation and what seems to be nostalgia for stone-age banking. The Obama plan has been launched as the Volcker Plan and is likely to fare better at the hands of Congress than any of the other great White House initiatives.

The Volcker Plan would restore the spirit if not the letter of the long defunct Glass-Steagall Act that used to forbid retail banks to engage in investment banking and vice versa. The intention is to make the former safe from the "speculative" risks of the latter. It would bar trading for their own account by retail banks and limit their size to a maximum to take care of the "too big to fail" syndrome. Mr. Volcker stated that the latter provision affects only five U.S. banks and another ten or so non-U.S. ones—the latter reflecting the habitual American assumption that U.S. law applies to German, Swiss, and French banks as a matter of course. It is amusing to note that the Volcker Plan sees the chief danger to the banking system the "speculative" trading of banks for their own account. Both the Controller of the Currency and the former chairman of the Securities and Exchange Commission have stated explicitly that such trading has not been a source of significant loss, and that the near-crash of the banks in 2007–08 was caused, not by "speculation," but by bad lending to credit-unworthy house owners

First published by Liberty Fund, Inc., at www.econlib.org on March 1, 2010. Reprinted by permission.

and credit card debtors on silly conditions. So-called "toxic" securities that turned out to be almost unmarketable were not made "toxic" by their intrinsic wickedness and rocket-science sophistication, but by the underlying loans that were nonperforming. The rest of the world banking upset was the snowball effect of lost confidence, flogged on by panic-mongering by those who should have known better.

Be the facts as they may, the common belief, incessantly repeated by self-appointed experts, remains unshaken: it was all caused by deregulation that allowed the greedy bankers, fund managers, and their ilk to engage in "speculation" instead of financing the "real" economy. There is an ineradicable belief that the shuffling of "paper assets" is divorced from the "real economy," or indeed harms it. Virtually everybody, including the regulatory authorities in both the United States and Europe, is sure that speculation is wicked and the harder it is trodden on, the better it is for the economy—besides making capitalism a little less immoral.

This is arrant nonsense on a par with voodoo. Nobody is very clear about what is and what is not speculation, but if pressed, most would say that speculation is the buying of securities and commodities with the sole object of rapid resale, or the selling of them with the sole object of rapid repurchase. It is wicked because it yields easy money and, as Mervyn King, the governor of the Bank of England, likes to say, it is "not socially useful." Some even think it is harmful to legitimate business and to stability. "Bear" speculation that starts with sale and ends with repurchase is thought to be particularly vicious and is heavily restricted; if the public had its way, it would be outlawed altogether.

A little horse sense suffices to see why this is absurd and why speculation is "socially" and in every other way eminently useful. If it makes money, it has bought low and sold high, or sold high and bought back low. In either case, it was a buyer at or near the trough and a seller at or near the peak of the fluctuating price of the asset or commodity the speculator "attacked." His "attack" lifted the price when it was low and lowered it when it was high. It reduced volatility, the amplitude of price movements, below what it would otherwise have been: it stabilized the unstable.

The much-hated speculation has just rendered an albeit indirect but useful service to economic stability in Europe by "attacking" (as the commentators put it) the euro and thus ringing the alarm bell about reckless government spending. For at least a decade, the Greek state has been running at a rapidly rising deficit without anyone paying much attention. Had Greece retained the drachma as its money, one or more devaluations would have taken place, but with the euro, the exchange rate no longer acted as a signal nor as a regulator of Athenian housekeeping. Creative accounting showed only half of the real deficit. When early this year it became public knowledge that the deficit was running at 12.7 percent of GDP, the euro started to fall in relation to the dollar and a "short" position in euro of $8 billion opened up in the forward exchange market. In relation to the volume of trade and payments in euros, this sum is hardly more than a rounding error, but its appearance raised the alarm about a speculative "attack" upon Fortress Europe through the Greek back door that was left ajar. Next April and May, $20 billion of Greek state debt is due for redemption and there seemed a real possibility that Athens would be unable to raise the means to pay it. There was much talk of speculators smelling blood, turning upon Portugal, Spain, and Italy once they drove Greece into bankruptcy and presumably out of the Eurozone. Though the actual volume of speculation was probably quite modest, public rumor and imagination magnified it and feared that it was due to grow much larger, toppling one Club Med country after another. Greek Premier Papandreou spoke darkly about a "battle between Europe and the market."

The question of how a modern state can go bankrupt deserves a moment's reflection. When the currency was all metallic and credit creation was confined to the discounting of short trade bills, a state could simply run out of money if its power to squeeze taxes out of its subjects fell short of its needs and ambitions. Charles II of England in 1672 had to go cap in hand to Parliament to be bailed out by extra taxes. With paper currency, whatever the nominal independence of the central bank, a state can always print the money it needs to pay off any debt provided it is denominated in its own currency. Moody's has been muttering lately that it will have to rethink the triple-A rating of U.S. government debt. This is childish talk: the United States may well owe a trillion dollars to Asian governments; it can always print one trillion dollars in fresh Treasury bills to pay it off. (It is truly laughable that the credit insurance premium on Unilever's five-year debt at 0.48 percent is actually lower than the credit insurance premium on five-year U.S. Treasury bonds at 0.64 percent.) The real problem is limited to debt in another state's currency that the debtor state cannot print. The ominously rising government debts of Greece, Portugal, Spain, and Italy are in euros and dollars, and they cannot print either of the two. The European Central Bank could give them euros against fresh debt obligations of their own, but should it do so if the latter are potentially worthless? If anyone in Europe has broad enough shoulders to take responsibility for such operations, it is Germany.

Joseph Stiglitz, the Nobel Laureate economist who has lately become the undisputed star commentator on every aspect of every nation's economy, has taken time off from calling for a radical enlargement of the Volcker Plan to put the banks in their place and from urging unemployment to be reduced, to condemn what he called "fiscal fetishism." It is only fiscal fetishism, a stone-age, superstitious fear of persistent deficits, that stands in the way of bailing out Greece or anyone else in need of it, and thus presents needless austerity and more unemployment.

Due in part to worries about the power of speculation (also it just smooths the way for fatal outcomes that are destined to happen anyway), Germany does not want to take on the burden of paying off Greek debt today and perhaps other Club Med debt tomorrow. Using Brussels as proxy, she is telling the Greeks to do what it takes to put their house in order, with mid-March being the deadline for them to show that they are doing so. The Greek response so far is that they have gone to the limit of austerity and if Brussels were to insist on more, Greece would collapse and bring down the euro with it. This is fairly obvious counter-bluff to neutralize the Brussels bluff. The euro will not unravel, Greece will not collapse but will be bailed out in a minor way while making moderate progress towards cleaning up its fiscal house. If speculation had not rung the alarm, things might have drifted further down.

6. BUTCHER, BREWER, BAKER, BANKER:
ALL MUST WORK BY THE GOLDEN RULE

The French outdo most other Europeans in many things. Not all are to their credit. They are apt to be volatile, grandiloquent, smug, articulate to the point of glibness, and willing to argue that white is black, if only to contradict you. They work hard, but it must be to their own palpable advantage. They have a persistent blind spot where other peoples have their instinctive understanding of elementary economics. Instead, they have either the traditional Catholic antipathy to profit, "speculation," and the "reign of an unbridled market," or more likely Marxist drivel hammered into them at high school and university. Most are convinced that "purchasing power" is not the counterpart of what they produce (so that each strike reduces it), but money the government keeps "blocked," letting the rich help themselves to it but refusing it to the poor, so that it must be frightened by strikes and mass demonstrations into "unblocking" it.

It must be seen and heard to be believed what feverish field days the public has been having in the last few months, especially those who make their voices heard and revel in listening to themselves (and the number of such in our electronic world is multiplying by the day). They drive home how and why the country is threatened with complete meltdown, how bankers are "given" billions of public money to replace the capital they stupidly lost in speculations and how they are rewarding themselves with stock options worth millions, how profitable companies are throwing their workers out of their jobs to please the stock market, how a single company (Total) "pocketed" $14 billion of profit last year and was allowed to get away with it, and how all this (and more, far, far more) is not only shamefully wicked and vicious, but also unnecessary, for France could be just and prosperous if only it

First published by Liberty Fund, Inc., at www.econlib.org on May 4, 2009. Reprinted by permission.

threw out "the system" of producing for the market and not for human needs and aspirations.

The class war that many had thought extinct is back. It is no longer just a war of words, but also of deeds. Sequestrating management when it announces job cuts is now regular practice and is approved by 45 percent of poll respondents, while 50 percent "understand" it. The police are looking the other way. Curiously for a war whose bangs, shrieks, and battle cries are deafening, only one side is fighting it. On that side, the shock troops are the public sector unions led by the railwaymen, high school and university students (often egged on by their teachers), and union officials from the private sector who have few members but are paid in complex ways for "helping to administer" social insurance schemes. They are cheered on by the media which are overtly or with sham impartiality breaking their lances as well as their professional ethics to keep up the fiction that the class war is fought at the behest of the whole people.

Indeed, in this war there is an enemy: "the system," which "the people" and the television networks are attacking, but as good as nobody is defending. There is no discernible conservative, let alone liberal, resistance or counterattack. A part of the political Right seems actually to show sympathy for the class warriors, as if it were preparing a partial surrender and appeasement.

This does seem strange, but a relatively simple explanation can be read from recent French economic and social history. Appeasement as the preferred tactic in the class war originated after May 1968, when the government dreaded an alliance between the student revolutionaries and the workers on general strike, led by the Communist union CGT. The latter mistrusted the students as crazed Trotskyists and Maoists. To forestall the alliance, the government offered an unheard-of deal on wages and "labor rights" to the unions, carrying along the employers who had little choice but to follow. Since that momentous accord that incidentally also set off a wage-price spiral and a quarter-century of inflation, the appeasement has proved to be habit-forming. It became frequent during the 1981–94 Socialist administration and an absolutely predictable kneejerk reflex under the 1995–2007 Chirac presidency. During this period, the French economy was being pulled backwards by two main handicaps: chronic unemployment due primarily to the labor code and the social insurance schemes, and the declining standards of public education, particularly of higher education. Year after year, timid attempts have been made to reform both the labor market and the public education colossus (in France, nine-tenths of all education is state-run). No matter how modest and marginal the proposed reform, the answer by the unions that held these systems under their implacable control was always an angry "boo," a stamping of feet in the street, and the threat of worse to come unless the proposed reform is unconditionally abandoned. Hearing the first "boo," or soon after it, the government always capitulated and there was armistice till the next attempt at reform.

Any child will learn before walking and talking that if his tantrums pay twice in a row, they will probably pay a third time. If tantrums work thrice, the fourth can fail only if the parents by some miracle suddenly acquire a steely backbone and the patience of elephants. The child will go on acting as if he had no such miracle to fear.

French labor and student unions and interest groups have thoroughly learned the lesson that tantrums always pay and that after each payoff, it is worthwhile to throw another tantrum for a bigger payoff. (It is significant that this "game" works only against the government and public enterprises and services. The private sector has not established quite the same reputation for weak knees and soft backbones, and if it is blackmailed, it is usually indirectly, by pressuring the government to put pressure on private business.)

How to break this vicious circle and how to gain at least a respite by ceasefire in this sterile class war in a country that some believe to have become ungovernable? More precisely, how to bring back sweetness and light without first traversing a painful period where tantrums are met by riot police—especially as today is about the worst moment for embarking on such a painful course?

> It is not from the benevolence of the butcher, the brewer, or the baker that we expect our dinner, but from their regard for their own interest. We address ourselves not to their humanity but to their self-love, and never talk to them of our own necessities but of their advantages. . . .

His words have been quoted umpteen thousand times, but we still tend to forget Adam Smith's teaching that it is not from the benevolence of the butcher, the brewer, and the baker (and, yes, the banker, too) that we must expect our daily dinner, but from their regard for their own. There is now a groundswell of mainly non-party clamor in France (probably more shrilly than elsewhere) for a New Economic Order, for mastering the "blind forces" of the market, for a Moral Capitalism. Nobody seems to be troubled by the utter meaninglessness of these phrases. Nobody notices that the only "moral" capitalism is one of doing the best you can by square dealing and taking calculated risks (also known as long-term profit maximization). Instead, the idea seems to be that business should be motivated by benevolence, solidarity, and fairness. Profit should be sought only to ensure future development and stability.

There is an inner circle in the Élysée Palace, very close to the president, that is launching trial balloons to prepare ground-breaking legislation for a Golden Rule for a sort of purified, moralized, benevolent, and above all New Capitalism to end all class wars. Its cornerstone would be the Rule of Three, meaning roughly that profit would not belong to the owner (e.g., the shareholders) of an enterprise, but would have to be divided into three equal parts, one for dividends, one for the wage-earners, and one for investment. The future profit yielded by this investment would again fall under the Rule of Three, and so on to eternity. This would serve a "more just distribution of wealth."

Economically, the scheme is incomprehensible (the Golden Rule is a Christmas wish list) and where comprehensible, as in the Rule of Three, it is harebrained. It is certain to undergo much reshaping before it can become a legislative proposal. If and when it does, this column hopes to offer some comment on it. Meanwhile, this country will go on muddling through.

The thirty years from the end of the war to the mid-1970s were the Glorious Thirties of Europe on the nicer side of the Iron Curtain. Spurred on by a sense of dire necessity, people went hard at work to clear up the rubble, repair the damage, and get over the grim phase of post-war reconstruction as fast as they could. In 1948, the Marshall Plan came in to fill up empty economies with working capital, and Western Germany amazed all by taking off into the *Wirtschaftswunder*. Robust economic growth, exceptional by historical standards, became a commonplace.

By about 1975, Europeans started to feel rich, or at least no longer under pressure to make good the catastrophe of the war. Inspired by the earlier British example, which started the post-war epoch with the Beveridge Report establishing an embryonic welfare state,[1] Europe "never had it so good" in 1966 and never ceased to invent fresh good ideas for making social progress by more public expenditure. In Britain, this was the era of building a universal free health service that could never stop growing, of destroying a world-class system of secondary education by flattening out its peaks and ironing "elitism" out of it, as well as of establishing social security systems against many of life's risks. Left behind while focusing on post-war reconstruction and taking off into new growth, other European countries hurried to catch

First published by Liberty Fund, Inc., at www.econlib.org on April 2, 2012. Reprinted by permission.

1. The Beveridge Report is the shorthand name of a report drawn up by a bipartisan committee of the British Parliament during WWII to examine how the provision of health and welfare might be reformed. Its full name was the "Report of the Inter-Departmental Committee on Social Insurance and Allied Services" and was called the Beveridge Report after the economist William Beveridge who chaired the committee. The report was published in December 1942 and became the cornerstone of the new welfare state which the Labour Party built in Britain after winning the 1945 election. One of its key provisions was the National Health Service Act, enacted in 1946.

up with the British example and were constructing welfare states of diverse forms but uniformly high cost, a process which was well advanced in the 1980s. Parallel with ever more elaborate social "entitlements," unemployment emerged and went on rising by fits and starts. It was always understood and explained away as accidental, transitional, and ready to be put right by the next round of full-employment policies. In fact, it proved to be a rock-hard part of the new European "socio-economic model." The Glorious Thirties of the immediate post-war period was imperceptibly replaced by the new Inglorious Thirties, which was a period of sluggish growth, a pressing political appetite for more and more elaborate social welfare, and menacing budget deficits, culminating in the deep recession of 2008–09.

During most of the Glorious Thirties, the overall economic performances of Europe and America were comparable. The European Common Market, as it then was, led in productivity per hour worked, and this lead was compensated by the u.s.a. in a longer work-year and in higher population growth thanks to the stream of Latino immigration. Large-scale Turkish and Arab immigration to Europe got going somewhat later. Steadily rising unemployment accentuated the slowdown of European growth after 1975. The United States was distinctly pulling ahead from that point.

While during the Glorious Thirties, Europe was rather proud of itself, of post-war reconstruction and the Common Market, and was counting the years before it caught up with America, in the Inglorious Thirties opinion split two ways. One half persuaded itself that Europe, despite its lagging economic performance, was still the stronger party and its superiority over the United States would become apparent as the construction of a federal Europe progressed. More important, America was ruthlessly hard on the poor and the helpless, who were being left by the wayside, while Europe made "social justice" prevail.

The other half of European opinion did not fool itself about America and its ways, but instead became frankly envious of American success. Deeply frustrated that Europe was stubbornly heading the other way and may be digging itself into an economic hole, this pro-Atlantic and (in the original sense of the word) liberal opinion had an image of the United States that was partly realistic, but also partly illusory. They regarded it as a rich place where markets were free, opportunities were wide, taxation moderate, political power decentralized, and government activism resisted. There was tremendous social mobility upward and downward; risk-taking was encouraged and admired. Far from being a little shameful, profit was to be proud of as a sign of usefulness and service to society. Thus the pro-Atlantic liberals asked themselves the obvious question: "Why, oh, why could Europe not be a bit more like this America?"

No, Europe could not, and would not try if it could. Instead, there are recent signs that it is the U.S.A. that may be tiptoeing to join the European way. The Bush administration could have given the opposite impression to the distant observer; it did cut taxes, it arguably made the fiscal system less progressive, and it kept cozy relations with a particular segment of corporate America. Greatly outweighing such concessions to political incorrectness, however, was the massive increase in federal expenditures, the mantra of transparency, and corporate governance. There was a proliferation of freshly defined rights of nearly everybody to nearly everything and in particular to protection against economic, social, and environmental risks. As a consequence, the already massive apparatus of federal regulatory agencies became even larger and more influential. Society as a whole, the regulated industries and their customers, all have their particular tradeoffs between the benefits of regulation, such as dealing with damaging externalities, and the cost of being regulated, including both actual operating complications and expenses and forgone business opportunities. An avalanche of paperwork as well as reduced employment for the unskilled and semi-skilled swell the cost of regulation suffered by the regulated. The trade-off indicates the optimum intensity of regulation, which may actually be zero or very limited. However, what is true for the regulated is not true for the regulator, for he suffers none of its costs, but could be severely sanctioned if "too little" regulation resulted in damage. Thus, his incentives never hold him back. For him, regulation is not too costly so long as it eliminates some risk, no matter how low the probability of the risk may be. Safety First is always the dominant rule to obey.

The primacy of Safety First, so alien to what the spirit of America was supposed to be, is a strong feature of the European mentality. Under the name of "principle of precaution," it is a clause of the French constitution. It sounds a tall story but it is the literal truth that when in 2007 the French president named a commission of experts to suggest measures to stimulate economic growth, and the commission recommended repeal of the precaution clause of the constitution among 300 other moves, the president agreed to pursue 299 of them but refused to touch the principle of precaution, which allowed innovations to be vetoed to protect society against the most far-fetched of risks.

The Obama administration is in many ways the watershed in the gradual Europeanization of the American economy and the whole social structure. It is the first presidency since that of Theodore Roosevelt that looks and feels antibusiness. Unwilling to stand up to the teachers' unions, it has let promising educational reforms be shoveled away. It has fought against state initiatives to pass right-to-work laws. It kept as close to the labor unions as did its predecessor to the Petroleum Club of Houston. Though it can share the guilt with a more than usually demagogic Congress, it helped to produce two of the most burdensome major laws that ever punished the American economy, Sarbanes-Oxley on corporate governance and Dodd-Frank on banking and finance. They promise to be inexhaustible sources of paperwork and lawyers' fees, and to outdo European management style in bureaucracy, rigidity, and timidity. Dodd-Frank, in addition, looks as if it tried to remodel American banking to make it act as Mom and Pop money shops were supposed to act on Main Street a century ago.

The biggest single step in the transformation of the American economy and the embedding of Safety First as its overriding priority is, of course, the 2010 health care legislation. Its core thesis is that no one has a right to expose himself and his dependents to risk of ill health (Safety First all over again), hence health insurance is compulsory, but if a person's employer does not provide it (as normally he must) and the person has insufficient means to pay for it himself, the state will buy it for him. There is a certain logic in this core reasoning. It is easier to accept if you close your mind to the incentive structure of the law, inducing as it does both health care providers and consumers to overspend. Whether the Supreme Court will judge it unconstitutional, the near future will tell. Either way, however, the bill raises questions about the American ethos and its affinity with Europe. The answers were obvious enough a generation ago but are far from obvious today.

8. COME AND GET CAUGHT IN MY TRAP

Enterprise and job creation now involve a new type of risk, that of being trapped by a "blocked exit."

France has twelve oil refineries with a total capacity of about one hundred million tons and an actual throughput of seventy-two million tons per year. The capacity is heavily skewed toward light distillates, while tax policy has biased consumption away from gasoline and toward diesel oil. The industry turned to exports, selling twenty-five to thirty million tons of gasoline per annum to the United States at declining margins. Consumption of motor fuel in both France and the U.S. has been shrinking at an average of 1 percent per annum in the last ten years, and refining in both countries is in a poor way. In France last year, the industry was losing money at an annual rate of 1,800 million euros, burning up about 1 percent of GDP.

France's flagship oil company Total owns and operates six refineries in the country. They made a loss of about nine hundred million euros last year. Total has signified its intention to close down the one at Dunkirk. The plant has 370 workers of various grades. Total has promised to find alternative employment for all of them in Dunkirk in new research and training facilities and an LNG terminal. The union refused the offer, insisting that the refinery be kept open, and to press home the demand, the 370 employees went on strike. Total's five other refineries immediately went on strike too, and the country's foreign-owned refineries also stopped for a short period by way of warning. Similar warnings were issued by the personnel of the country's oil product storage depots. The reader should bear in mind that for French governments and the media, picketing is an almost sacred institution, so that a handful of pickets are free to close down large plants for as long as it takes to be bought off at or close to the unions' terms. This, in fact, was the wholly predictable outcome of the refinery strike.

First published by Liberty Fund, Inc., at www.econlib.org on April 5, 2010. Reprinted by permission.

The president of Total was promptly summoned to see the president of the Republic, and a bargain was struck with the CGT, the ex-communist labor union that has taken the lead in running the strike. Total was allowed to shut down Dunkirk on condition that comparable jobs on the spot are offered to all employees. In return for this permission, Total had to undertake to keep its five other refineries running for a minimum of five years. Given the government's virtuous intentions about reducing greenhouse gas emissions, the capacity of the remaining five Total refineries might prove even more excessive than that of the original six up to now. Annual losses of one billion euros or more are not unlikely.

The strike at Dunkirk is continuing, though given the bargain with the CGT, it will no doubt peter out before the present text appears on readers' screens. The Dunkirk strikers claim that they have been betrayed. That is perhaps a pardonable reaction. What is less pardonable is the fury poured out by a large part of the public against Total. Here is a company—so the thundering rhetoric goes—that has made a profit (rather a shameful thing to do at the best of times) of eight billion euros in 2009 after making thirteen billion the year before. Their pockets bulging with billions, they have the cheek to shut down a plant that is perfectly capable of going on doing what it was designed to do. As they are making a profit, and an indecently large one at that, there is no justification for wanting to make even more by amputating the country's industry and jeopardizing the jobs of their workers. They simply must not be allowed to do it.

By refining its own crude instead of selling it on the world market, Total is destroying value instead of adding it. The value of Dunkirk's inputs exceeds the value of its output by about four hundred thousand euros per worker per annum. If the workers gracefully agreed to retire on any pension less than the princely four hundred thousand they now cost the country, they, Total, and the nation would all be better off. Before long, one or more of Total's remaining refineries will reach a similar position, or is perhaps already in such a position. Such considerations did not stop the government from obliging Total to keep the plants running for a minimum of five years, and much of the public feels that this was being too lenient with a company that is "obscenely profitable."

The case of the oil refining industry, which ought to shrink gradually in response to market trends or, better still, in intelligent anticipation of them if government and its electorate allowed it to do so, is but a straw in the wind. Every day brings news of a proposed plant closure or staff redundancy that sparks violent reactions including sequestration of the managers, the blocking of communications and transport, and lurid menaces of worse to come. Since the strike is hardly ever allowed to run its course, but is brought to a relatively successful end by intervention of the prefect, the labor court, or the industry minister, the unions and their wildcat rivals on the far left come to believe that they can walk on water and behave accordingly with utter confidence. The public, seeing this, also believes that the unions are almighty, while the government, sensing the public mood, has no hesitation to capitulate or persuade the management to capitulate.[1]

All this industrial skirmishing and its outcomes cultivate a very particular belief in public opinion about the nature of privately owned business enterprise. Entrepreneurs are cheered on to found new businesses and expand existing ones. Investors are urged to back them with capital, banks to lend them money generously. The job creation that results is welcomed. All this is as it should be. However, all this must be strictly one-way. The entry is free—indeed, it is held almost suspiciously wide open. The exit, on the other hand, is very hard to find; it is narrow, full of obstructions, and may be altogether blocked. If the business is not in danger of failing, it must carry on. The key watchword is, "They are making a profit," so they have no right to close down a subsidiary or shed part of an activity that is not earning its keep. Least of all must they be permitted to pack up key machinery and the client list and relocate to some other hospitable country. Those who do so are branded "cosmopolitan scum."

Above all, there is an unspoken but deep belief that if the entrepreneur owns his business, the worker owns his job. Once he is given it, it must not be taken away. Job protection is as much a duty of the gov-

1. The present writer once suggested to a neighbor, the chairman of the board of a bank by profession and a marquis by birth, that the government ought to break this vicious circle by standing absolutely firm and refusing to capitulate for a few times in a row until the lesson was learned. The gentleman replied, darkly: "Do you want blood to flow in the gutters?"

ernment as the protection of any other property. Indeed, it is more so, for the worker is more in need of it than the owner of land or capital.

It is very easy to grasp that such a doctrine, though vulnerable to reason when it is all spelled out, is so widely shared and cherished when it remains just an unspoken moral intuition. It is hard to think of a people that holds this intuition more fervently than the French.

It is the spoilsport's, the killjoy's deeply unpopular task to say that if jobs are owned by those who are given them, entrepreneurs will think twice before giving them, since they may have great trouble getting them back again. Hiring looks very risky if firing almost passes for a crime and is costly in money and trouble. The same is true, though less dramatically, of capital investment. Apart from the commonplace business risks, it is now deterred by a new risk as well: the risk of the blocked exit, the difficulty of disentangling capital, of winding down an activity that is no longer warranted by its prospects. Entering a business is now somewhat like stepping into a trap, a trap that society holds open with an inviting smile.

9. THE USE AND ABUSE OF
TAXES AND TAX HAVENS

Europe is fairly well equipped with tax havens. Swiss bank secrecy is not what it used to be, due mostly to the rashness of Swiss bankers establishing substantial operations in the U.S. which laid them open to arm-twisting by the Internal Revenue Service and banking regulators. The Channel Islands gave up part of their banking secrecy under pressure from the British government. But this still leaves tax havens in Austria, Belgium, Luxembourg, Liechtenstein, and Monaco (for non-French residents). Among them, Liechtenstein is perhaps the most exclusive and has long been regarded as the safest.

Early in 2006, contact was made in the most elaborate spy-novel manner between the BND, Germany's intelligence service, and a dismissed employee of LGT, Liechtenstein's top bank, which is fully owned by the princely family, chaired by the reigning prince's brother and managed by his second son. After what seem to have been difficult and very involved transactions, the BND paid 4.2 million euros to the employee for a list of about fourteen hundred clients of LGT holding accounts worth a total of between four and five billion euros. Some six hundred of the clients were Germans, the rest French, British, Italian, Spanish, and Swedish. The German authorities passed their names on to the respective countries' tax services and started audits into the affairs of the German residents, going public with the whole matter in February 2008. Prosecution was started against the first two hundred or so suspects; many confessed and threw themselves on the fisc's mercy in exchange for restitution of the funds that had escaped German tax. Some names were disclosed, the political repercussions were deafening, the Left marched triumphantly up the moral high ground, the Right was deeply embarrassed, and the German govern-

First published by Liberty Fund, Inc., at www.econlib.org on April 7, 2008. Reprinted by permission.

ment threatened Liechtenstein with the most severe though unspecified retaliation for its complicity with immoral German tax fraudsters. There was also a loud chorus of demands from many governments and the media for redoubled efforts to do away with tax havens by forcing the guilty countries to lift bank secrecy and provide data on foreign holders of accounts. The OECD and the European Union had for many years exerted maximum pressure to this effect and it is not clear what more they could do short of bombarding Luxembourg, Vaduz, and Vienna. But agitation is bound to continue. This is how matters stand, or rather this is how they swirl, at present.

It may be noted in passing that when bullied to show more "transparency," banks in tax havens say that it is not part of their duty to assist the work of foreign tax collectors. The OECD replies that "transparency" is required for fighting money laundering, a criminal offense. The banks retort that they accept new customers only after exhaustive cross-examination (which is certainly the case of the reputable banks) and that they are ready to provide information on clients' affairs if there is presumption of criminal activity. It is also the case that as pressure on European tax havens is kept up, fugitive accounts tend to move to banks in the Caribbean, certain Pacific islands, and (for really borderline customers) to the Ukraine and Russia. Nevertheless, as long as they exist, tax havens undoubtedly facilitate tax evasion, and this is where questions of morals arise. Some are simple, others are not.

Different societies pass different moral judgments on tax evasion. In Britain, it is still "not done," at least not by the "right sort" of people. On most of the Continent, it is widely done and freely admitted among close friends and relatives. In some circles, it counts as an exploit and in others an act of resistance against Leviathan. The main deterrent is, of course, the risk of being caught, although public education and the media try to inculcate the idea that paying one's taxes is a moral duty that springs from solidarity with others, and not paying them is free riding on those who do. Whether this is all that needs be said depends both on the uses the tax is put to and the demand for tax made upon the individual taxpayer. The tax may be financing the reasonable provision of public goods and services that are arguably to the benefit of all, even if the benefit to each cannot be interpersonally compared.

However, it may well happen that far too much public expenditure is skewed in favor of hare-brained schemes the individual taxpayer considers absurd (the Common Agricultural Policy or Galileo might rank high on the list of monstrosities he is furious to have to finance). It also may be that taxation is too blatantly redistributive, benefiting only one group or class while financed almost wholly by another. Finally, it may be that the "ability to pay" or the "we must take the money where we find it" principles of taxation are pushed too far for even the docile taxpayer to take them lying down.

We can have only subjective opinions on when taxation is just (or whether it ever is) and when it is abusive. Most people are ready to tell the well-to-do that he must play by the democratic rules and submit to the tax laws of his country. It is in their manifest interest to say so. But it is not shocking that the well-to-do is left unimpressed by the argument that it is a moral duty for the minority to pay for the good ideas of the majority.

If tax evasion were unfeasible or impossibly risky, the majority could go further to exploit the minority. In that sense, facilities for tax evasion are safety valves against taxation becoming more abusive than it is at present. Tax havens are one such facility. This is not to say that their operations are just. But they do fulfill a useful function in tempering the democratic juggernaut.

It has always been a function of the state to protect the property of its subjects against all comers except against itself. Confiscation was a prerogative of the early state, though it usually had to practice it selectively. Among modern states, dictatorships felt free to carry on the practice, restrained only by what they deemed inopportune. Democratic states have forsworn confiscation; they expropriate or, more prettily still, "nationalize" and provide "due" and "fair" compensation for the owners. Arguably, it is an oxymoron to call a price "fair" if it is paid in a forced exchange. Legislation, including what passes for "international law" regulating how sovereign states must compensate expropriated owners, including foreign ones, is largely shaped by the expropriators themselves. Its caricature image would be a conference of thieves adopting rules regulating how fair thieving is to be conducted.

Musing about this leads again to tax havens. Tax havens are not just instruments that facilitate tax evasion. They are also safe havens, or believed to be such. Anyone who knows what happened to all noble and bourgeois property except personal chattels in Russia in 1917–19 and to peasant property a decade or so later, to all Jewish property in Nazi Germany after 1934 and in the Nazi satellites before and during World War II, to nearly all property in the Soviet satellite states after 1947, or to most large industrial and financial firms in Labour Britain after 1945 and in two waves under Presidents de Gaulle and Mitterrand in France, might go to some lengths to shift at least his mobile assets to some Liechtenstein or other. States, taken as a class, are morally in no position to accuse the Liechtensteins of this world of immorality and of not playing the game. They have asked for it; they are not trustworthy and have only themselves to blame. There have been too many black sheep among them, and new ones may well be born any day.

10. RUSSIA'S SOCIALIST HERITAGE

Why is such a rich country so poor? Why should Russia lag so far behind other industrial countries? Why is it unable to make more of its obvious economic potential?

Admittedly, the country is penalized by a number of initial structural handicaps. Culturally, it is neither fish nor fowl, being neither wholly European nor wholly Oriental on personal characteristics and traditions, suspicious of and suspected by both worlds. It extends over too large an area compared to its population, saddling both the production and the distribution of its output with heavier transport costs than countries of denser population have to bear. Perhaps most important, it has an unfriendly climate. Some historians, tongue in cheek, explain the expansionary drive of Russia over the last three centuries by the longing of its people to escape from the climate of their homeland and settle under a sunnier, less humid, healthier sky, yet still remain in their own empire. As for cultivating the land, the saying goes that there are four natural catastrophes in Russia every year: spring, summer, autumn, and winter.

All in all, however, the endowments almost certainly outweigh the handicaps. Russia, even after the secession of the Ukraine, has enough high-quality farmland. It has inexhaustible resources of timber and vast deposits of every kind of ore from iron and bauxite to gold, much of it low cost. Using these resources, there is a reasonably educated work force of mixed quality, working nineteen hundred hours a year compared with about fifteen hundred in Western Europe. Russian workers are mostly obedient and bow to authority, they have weak unions, strikes are rare, and wages are settled on the level of the enterprise rather than of the nationwide industry, an advantage the Russian labor market has over the West and that keeps unemployment at just over 5 percent, close to the level of practically full employment. Skill

First published by Liberty Fund, Inc., at www.econlib.org on November 5, 2012. Reprinted by permission.

from shop floor to middle management level is adequate. Far more decisive than any of these more or less commonplace advantages is Russia's exceptional oil and gas wealth, of which more below. Taking a rough-and-ready account of both the obvious helps and hindrances, the visitor from Mars would expect Russians to be no less prosperous than Englishmen, Frenchmen, or Germans. His expectation would be legitimate, but very far out.

Accepting Russian statistics at face value, the per capita revenue of the population of 142 million is $17,000, though a different basis of calculation gives less than $15,000. This compares with the average in the main Western European countries of about $40,000. GDP has recently been growing at just over 4 percent per annum and is expected to maintain this rate in the near future, assuming that the price of oil remains above $100 a barrel. With the sharp rises in the price of oil since 1998, growth in Russia was relatively easy to achieve and should not be hard to maintain, though the shape of the economy would become ever more like that of an oil sheikdom, with the non-oil sector falling further and further behind and needing state protection to subsist. The Russian government has scores of good economic advisers and is quite aware of the dangers of such dependence on oil and gas, but cannot give up the great budgetary ease that oil provides. Nor can it conjure up industrial development by wishful thinking and exhortation.

Russia is inspiring confidence by running a current account balance of payments surplus of 3 or 4 percent of GDP. If oil and gas are excluded (and all other things remain equal, which of course they would not do), the surplus turns into a far less reassuring deficit of 10 percent of GDP, meaning that the Russian economy produces only 90 percent of what it absorbs—a ratio that cannot be sustained for any length of time.

The state levies a hefty export tax on oil, which is good for the budget and popular with consumers because it keeps the domestic price down. However, it also causes careless and uneconomic use of energy. Russia uses about twice as much energy to produce a unit of output of all goods and services as the best modern practice in the West. Waste of energy is the beginning of the explanation of Russia being so much poorer than it should be. Waste of everything else furnishes a bit more of the explanation.

Three generations of Russians now living have inherited some quite nasty things from socialism, one of which is a vacuum where in a non-socialist society certain incentives would direct people's behavior. Under socialism in Russia from 1917 to 1989, nearly everything belonged to the state, that is in practice to nobody, and very little belonged to anybody in particular. The result was the withering away of some of the habits that are formed by the incentives bred by ownership. Looking after one's own property, respecting that of others, and disapproving and discouraging senseless waste as well as theft in general (and not only the theft of one's own chattels) are some of these habits that go almost without saying in normal civilizations but that have been "bred out" of far too many modern Russians. Even after two decades of capitalist practice after 1989, the waste of time, the quantity of spoiled output, and the waste of material that goes uselessly into the typical Russian industrial product are staggering to see. Twice as much steel is used to manufacture a Russian tractor, a bicycle, or a tool as in the West simply because it does not occur to producers that economizing is a good thing even if they do not directly profit from it. Ceaseless sermons under socialism used to teach them that to be economical and avoid waste is good for the community, but the vacuum of incentives acted more strongly than the sermons. It is still acting fairly strongly, as a lost habit that will take time to restore even if government policy does not frustrate the process by counter-productive tinkering.

While socialism left a vacuum where there used to be an incentive, and thus has educated people not to bother about economizing anything that was not directly their own, it left another incentive to run wild. In normal civilizations, the incentive to appropriate anything valuable belonging to others is, to a greater or lesser extent (and in very honest countries like Finland and New Zealand, almost completely), neutralized by the threat of retaliation by the owners, by organized law enforcement, and by social ostracism. Where these checks are eroded, theft, robbery, usurpation, and the abuse of mandates' "agency" (e.g., power delegated to the police, the judges, and the officials entrusted with spending the public funds) can run rampant. In Russia, they do.

The checks, deterrents, and social sanctions have been weakened to the point of extinction under socialism.

The Berlin benevolent organization Transparency International prepares and keeps up to date a rank order of countries according to how corrupt they are. Among the forty OECD member countries, it ranks Russia in fortieth place, i.e., as the most corrupt. The type of corruption that Transparency International seeks to measure concerns government to business, business to business, and government to people relations. Some economists argue that much of this corruption is in fact useful, for it does the job of efficient allocation that competition would do if there was enough of it. The government official will award the bridge-building contract to the builder who offers him the biggest bribe, and this is as good as awarding it to the lowest bidder; the builder who can afford the highest bribe is the one who could tender the lowest price for building the bridge. Efficient allocation is ensured either way.

This reasoning does not quite hold water, but there is no place here to demonstrate why. Instead, it is instructive to look at another version of corruption where organized crime has police officials, prosecutors, and judges as sleeping partners and that is thriving in post-socialist Russia.

An enterprising Russian launches a business, runs it successfully for a while, and when it has taken root, two strangers visit him. They declare that henceforth the business belongs to them or to friends of them, and ask the owner kindly to give them all keys, passwords, and vital documents, sign a bill of sale, and say goodbye. Resistance is mortally dangerous and appeal to the police futile. Former President Medvedev used to announce campaigns to "strengthen" the rule of law and among other practices it was this type of unchecked robbery he must have had in mind. Nothing ever came of these pious campaigns. The tight network of mainly ex-KGB officers who exercise supreme executive power always shrugged off Medvedev initiatives with a pitying condescension.

However, the precarious tenure of business property, one of the heaviest items in Russia's socialist heritage, has turned out to be the source of a most interesting phenomenon. Russia's businessmen, from oligarchs down to proprietors of medium and even small firms, are beating a path to the West and some of their money is going along with them. Their favorite destinations are London and the French Riviera. House property coming up for sale in Knightsbridge, Belgravia, and Chelsea is likely to be snapped up by Russian buyers, as are villas from Nice to the Italian border. Agencies in London, run by young women who know everybody who is worth knowing, specialize in finding property and domestic servants for Russian newcomers as well as performing such miracles as securing admission to Eton or Harrow for little Volodya, and maybe for other little Russian boys yet to be born. Most of these Russian pilgrims do not permanently remain in London or Cannes, but want to have a hidy-hole to run to and shelter some of their fortune outside Russia if and when things there turn really nasty.

The numbers generated by this flight to safety look awesome. Russia's current balance of payments has an annual surplus of $60 to $70 billion thanks to oil and gas. In addition, foreign direct and portfolio investment in Russia was recently running at about $90 billion (though this figure is not very reliable). Capital outflow from Russia must be the mirror image of the total of the sum of the current surplus and the inflow, or, say, $150 billion a year (for the balancing item, official foreign currency holdings, is not large enough to make much difference).

It is difficult to believe, but also difficult to dismiss the statistics that point to it, that capital flight from Russia has the colossal order of magnitude of $150 billion per year. What a heritage socialism has left!

11. OIL, GAS, AND BLUSTER

FALSE FRONT

Economic man orders his affairs so as to maximize his satisfaction, but we cannot always tell what satisfies him. American Sovietologists have written millions of words explaining the 1991 collapse of the Soviet Union by its failure to satisfy the Russian consumer. The Russian people got supposedly fed up with queuing for hours on end to buy the drab and shoddy products of Soviet industry and, being fed up, smashed up the regime. Even within the Party, faith in the system was wavering and then the time was right for the great change. In this story, it remains a puzzle why the people who bore seven decades of hardship and absurdity suddenly decided that they were fed up and would not have it any more precisely at a time when things were getting better, food was no longer scarce, and basic needs were starting to be met even in the countryside. Nor is it clear how the Russian people were supposed to go about smashing the system; there were no street demonstrations, no strikes, and public order in the regime's last years was just as undisturbed as ten or twenty years earlier. Sovietologists should have remembered that the Russian people are famously patient under oppression and misery. In the two revolutions of its history, 1905 and 1917, it was not the people who broke the regime, but the regime that knocked itself out by losing a war.

The truth is that 1991 happened not because consumer demand was not satisfied, but because Gorbachev and the other modernizers in the Party and the army relaxed it to make it more innovative and competitive with the capitalist West, and in so doing, inadvertently undermined the authority of the apparatus that enforced obedience to the regime. The result was not revolution, but a shambles. "Red directors" stole the state factories and mines they had directed; KGB officers became their firms' "security" officers, contract killers, or both at the

First published by Liberty Fund, Inc., at www.econlib.org on October 6, 2008. Reprinted by permission.

same time; the armed forces were starved of resources; but at the same time, centralism declined and regional autonomy began, and the rudiments of a civil society surfaced.

Under Yeltsin's easygoing presidency, economic policy was relatively liberal. Anatoli Chubais, the privatization czar, made haste to get state property into private hands to drain the government of power and prevent any relapse into dictatorship, and did so even at the expense of tolerating monstrous corruption and the rise of an oligarchy. The outlines of a bourgeois order have nevertheless begun to show.

During these years, the price of crude oil fell from the mid-1950s to reach bottom at $15 a barrel in 1998. Russian oil output that peaked at twelve million barrels per day back in 1982, when oil used to fetch $66, declined to half that level by 1998. The joint effect of the two nosedives was, of course, devastating; Russia defaulted on its international obligations and stood ashamed and humiliated before the world. Looking weak and losing the respect, admiration, and if possible the awe of others was manifestly something that hurt the Russian people far more than had the "lack of consumer choice" in the drab treadmill of the Soviet years.

At this juncture, in August 1999, enters Vladimir Putin, a wholly undistinguished ex-KGB officer. He takes over from Yeltsin as acting president and is elected president by the dutiful people the following year. The oil price gains 40 percent in 1999 and continues to recover, as does production that gradually climbs to just under ten million barrels per day, a level which for the time being is the limit of its capacity. Price, not output, proves to be Putin's fabulous luck. By 2006, the average barrel fetches $65; by 2007 it reaches $100 and money is streaming into Russia.

During his first four-year term, Putin moves cautiously, allows economic policy to be influenced by sensible economists and is praised by ("classical") liberals in the West. The growth rate of GDP is 7 percent or better. Urban wages increase at double-digit rates, and more Rolls-Royces and Bentleys are sold in Moscow than in any other city in the world. Admittedly, property is not wholly secure, the borderline between business and gangster rule is fuzzy, and German Gref, the economics minister (who has since lost his post and has become a banker) declares that Russia "lacks one factor of production, the rule of law."

But during his second term, Putin, increasingly confident, uses the judiciary as his obedient tool to retake for the state the ownership of "strategic" enterprises and control over many more. Shell violates Russian environmental standards (!) and is evicted from its multi-billion-dollar investment on Sakhalin Island; BP is refused a pipeline linkup to the Gazprom network in the North, cannot produce the gas that it has no means to deliver, and loses its license and its investment; TNK BP does not respect the Russian labor code (!) and management control is wrested from it, and so on.

Putin explains his doctrine at length: ownership may be state or private, but the management must accept the state's close guidance so as to serve the national interest. (He also mentions, casually, that since Mahatma Gandhi is gone, he, Putin, is the only real democrat in the world.) The state's guidance is mainly carried out by a solid network of siloviki, ex-KGB or ex-army men, who often hold posts both as directors of enterprises and government officials at the same time.

Much of this looks bad, but most commentators accept it as something that works, for the growth record of the Putin years is unblemished. Or is it?

When Putin "took the reins" in 1999, GDP was $894 billion. It grew to $1,490 billion by 2007, a rise of $600 billion. During the same time span, the value of oil production at world market prices rose from $45 billion to about $350 billion, an increment of $305 billion. Natural gas was responsible for perhaps another $40 billion. The calculation is not quite fair to Russia, for not all oil and gas enters into GDP at world prices, but all in all, it looks as if up to a half of economic growth during Putin's first two terms was due to the hydrocarbon windfall. Allowing for some catch-up effect after the abysmal 1998–99 period, Russian performance is at the lower end of the group of "emerging" economies.

This finding fits perfectly into the Russian historical pattern. Like the false fronts of the rickety stores and hotels of the small towns of the American West, Russia has always presented a false front to the world. Potemkin put up stage-prop villages to embellish territory taken from the Turks, and wrote his name indelibly into history to stand for fraudulent make-believe. The practice of the false front took on gigantic proportions during the Soviet era, fooling the CIA into quite derisory overestimates of Russian economic and military strength. It also gave the Russian people something that satisfied them more than a more ample choice of consumer goods might have done: it gave them pride, a sense of righteousness and of being feared by the wicked America. The rising value of hydrocarbons is not a lie, but the claim of successful economic management is one. The flood of money that has inundated Russia serves as a false front, masking their intrinsic weakness. Except for the extraction of natural resources, industry is catching the "Dutch disease" of petroleum exporters. There are more fundamental weaknesses, too. Male life expectancy at birth is fifty-eight years, the population is falling by seven hundred thousand a year, public health is a disaster, underinvestment in electricity foreshadows a great power shortage, and bad reservoir maintenance hastens the coming decline of oil production. The morale of the army is poor and its equipment is getting obsolete. If the generals are to get new high-tech toys, the pile of accumulated oil money ($400 billion in currency reserves and $100 billion special reserve) may quickly melt away in a near future where oil production may be declining and the oil price may not come to the rescue. If there is no flood tide of oil and gas money, there will still be the old Russian standby of bluster which gives the people the delightful sensation of being feared. In February 1945, a battle-weary brace of Soviet soldiers told the present author that they were about to take Berlin, after which they would go on to take Paris and London. Nikita Khrushchev told the capitalists of the West that Soviet superiority will "bury them." In August 2008, General Borisov, commanding the Russian peacekeepers (!) on Georgian soil, told a French reporter, "Let the Americans come here, we will kill them all." Putin promised to give all aggressors a "bloody nose" and warned America "not to push us around." His docile assistant, President Medvedev, made it clear that Russia did not care a fig about what Europe said or did in response to Russian moves in Georgia. Such bluster involves no risk, flatters the people's vanity, and is the surest means of cementing popular support for the regime. It also upholds the traditional device of the tall false front hiding the modest building.

UNSPOKEN THREATS

At the time of the upheaval about Georgia and its separatist provinces Abkazia and South Ossetia, in August–September 2008, it was widely noticed that in trying to find a common tone of European protest to Russia, the U.K., Sweden, the Baltic states, and Poland advocated a very stern language but were pulled back by Germany and Italy. It so happens that Germany and Italy are markedly more dependent on Russian natural gas than the rest of Europe. It was also remarked that President Medvedev found it useful to remark that sanctions would do more harm to Europe than to Russia, though he refrained from elaborating what kind of harm he had in mind.

Nor do European energy administrators speak explicitly of dependence on Russian natural gas when they call for a more integrated gas transport grid and the diversification of sources of supply. But each knows what the other is thinking of.

Natural gas is more awkward to transport and more restricted in use than oil. As a result, it is worth only between a half to three-quarters of oil of equal thermal value. One thousand cubic meters of gas corresponds to six barrels (BOE: Barrel of Oil Equivalent) but may fetch only about $300 in North America. In Europe, the bulk of the gas is priced in long-term interstate contracts with complex formulae linking it to the free market price of oil with a lag. Prices actually paid vary widely. Russia has recently been charging the Ukraine $180/1,000 cubic meters and is talking of renewing the contract at $400/1,000 cubic meters, while it is understood to be buying natural gas from Turkmenistan at $13/1,000 cubic meters—a healthy spread indeed.

The economics of Russian natural gas is not easy to unravel. In 2006, the country produced 612 billion cubic meters (3.7 billion BOE) and consumed 430 billion of that. This seems inordinately high—five times the consumption of Germany whose GDP is twice that of Russia. The explanation is the obvious one: the domestic price is kept at a small fraction of the export price. The result is appalling waste, most conspicuously in heating, but presumably in industrial use as well. Gazprom has a monopoly of both export and all pipeline transport (which gives it the whip hand over non-state sellers). The pipeline network leaks from countless joints and closures (as does the oil pipe network of Transneft).

Gazprom has done relatively little to raise its output, which seems strange in the light of its strong ambition to raise exports to Europe and the sharply higher needs that are forecast for the Russian power utilities. One is led to suppose that Gazprom expects the government to allow it to raise the domestic price nearer to the export market level, thus reducing home consumption, and release several hundred billion cubic meters for export. Alternatively, Gazprom may have secret doubts about Europe's capacity or willingness to buy very much more Russian gas.

Currently, Europe's own production from Norway, the U.K. North Sea, and Holland is running at about 210 billion cubic feet, imports from Russia at 150 billion, from Algeria 33 billion, and from a variety of overseas countries in the form of liquefied natural gas (LNG) 49 billion. LNG is expensive to produce and transport but has greater potential to expand than piped gas, thanks to vast unexploited reserves in the Persian Gulf and other areas. If need be, LNG could greatly reduce European dependence on Russian gas, but it would take a decade of building LNG plants and ships for this to happen. It would happen if Gazprom tried to squeeze Europe by ratcheting up the price. LNG can be considered as the long-run countermove to Russian moves of this type. The threat of the moves and the countermove are unspoken but no doubt understood.

All of Gazprom's exports to Europe are delivered by pipelines that pass through the Baltic states, Belarus, Poland, or the Ukraine. These countries are getting Russian gas at "friendly" prices. If Gazprom tries to raise the price sharply and enforces its demand by cutting off supplies, the transit countries can still draw gas from the pipeline that was meant for Russia's paying customers in Germany, Austria, and Italy. The Ukraine has done this in recent years, giving Gazprom a bad name as an unreliable supplier.

In order to get off this hook, Russia is seeking to bypass the transit countries with two new pipeline projects. One, Northstream, would go from Russia under the Baltic sea directly to Germany; the other, Southstream, under the Black Sea to the Balkans and then to a hub in Austria and Hungary to Italy.

Southstream is also meant to trump Nabucco, a $7.8 billion European project that would draw gas from Kazakhstan and the Caspian Sea and carry it via Azerbeijan, Georgia, and Turkey to the Balkans, avoiding any Russian territory (assuming that Georgia remains an independent state). Nabucco would open in 2013 with a capacity of eight billion cubic meters per year, rising in due course to thirty billion per year. At first sight, Nabucco looks uneconomic, far from sure of getting enough supplies to fill it to capacity, and many doubt that it will in fact be built. Even if it were, it would make little difference to Europe's energy balance. However, to judge from Russian blustering and cajoling to persuade Hungary and Austria to throw all their support behind Southstream and let Nabucco drop, even the puny competition of the latter is perceived in Moscow as a threat or at least an insult.

PART 4

The Best of the Worst

1. THE BEST OF THE WORST:
WHAT PRICE DEMOCRACY?

For the last twenty years or so, the European economy looked tired, sluggish, beset by chronic unemployment while straining such muscle as it had to spread the "social" safety net ever wider, ever higher. At the same time, the American economy showed vigorous growth, resilience, and innate energy. Europe was by and large social democrat, America unrepentantly capitalist. Opinions were deeply divided about the merits of each, mostly because they sprang from the ineradicable gut feelings of each side. Lately, however, the clean cut between the two systems has become more and more blurred. America has acquired a hugely expensive public health care system, an interventionist monetary policy to make Keynes blush, an inexorably rising deficit that made the Director of the Budget throw down his job in despair, a solid complicity between the labor unions, the tort lawyers and the administration, and an economy that seems unable to respond to doping and is crawling along as sluggishly as the European one. Perhaps a little too soon, some observers are now saying that the u.s. has "Europeanized" itself; both continents have become democratic in the same sense.

VALUATION AND DESCRIPTION

Any language worth the name makes a clear enough separation between words that evaluate and words that simply describe. Consider pairs of words that perform the former job and pairs that do the latter. In the first set, you find such pairs of opposites as "good-bad," "handsome-ugly," "nice-nasty," "right-wrong," "true-false," and "just-unjust." In each pair, the first word is indisputably, self-evidently superior and preferable to the second. It simply makes no sense to say

First published by Liberty Fund, Inc., at www.econlib.org on November 1, 2010. Reprinted by permission.

that bad is better than good, that nasty is more agreeable than nice, nor that false is worthy of more respect than true. In the second set of words, you find such pairs as "like-unlike," "great-small," "many-few," "long-short," and "equal-unequal." The first word in each pair is no more valuable, desirable, or commendable than the second. They both describe; any ranking we give them comes from some particular context in which "long" is preferable to "short" or vice versa. "Equal-unequal" is such a pair of words, though you would not believe it from listening to everyday political rhetoric. So is "democratic-undemocratic."

THE MAXIMIN RULE

Winston Churchill is supposed to have said that democracy is the worst political system except for all the others.[1] This is a good enough aphorism, but it is rather poor decision theory. It is hardly an ideal of rationality to adopt it as a rule.

There is a great multitude of possible political systems from theocracy to technocracy, feudalism to plutocracy, hereditary monarchy to populist mob rule, dictatorship of the few to democracy. Each system is capable of producing a range of good and bad outcomes, with probabilities we can only guess. It is no use saying that we refuse to guess at such uncertain outcomes; for whether we have guessed or not, or guessed right or not, the outcomes arrive just the same, and it is better to at least try and anticipate them, even if we cannot be confident to guess right, than to give up hope and not try at all. Perhaps needless to say, the outcomes a given political system produces depend not only on the system itself, but on the kind of people and the kind of historical conjuncture to which it is applied.

By opting for a political system, we opt for what game theorists would call a "strategy" in a game we play "against" destiny. Each strategy is geared to produce one out of a range of outcomes from very good to

1. "Many forms of Government have been tried and will be tried in this world of sin and woe. No one pretends that democracy is perfect or all-wise. Indeed, it has been said that democracy is the worst form of government except all those other forms that have been tried from time to time." Speech in the House of Commons, *The Official Report, House of Commons* (5th Series), November 11, 1947, 444: 206–7.

very bad. Rationality, understood as being true to one's likes and dislikes, requires us to opt for the strategy that offers the best combination of outcomes weighted by their probabilities.

One famous strategy, maximin, deviates from this rule of rationality. It is not the one that offers the best combination of good or bad (where "best" combination is by definition better liked than any other), but the one whose worst possible outcome is better than the worst possible outcome of any other available strategy. Its name, maximin, means "maximizing the minimum," and that leads you to the strategy whose worst outcome is the best among the worst outcomes of all the others, and never mind any of the universe of outcomes that are better than that. Democracy locks us safely into maximin. It is truly the best of the worst.

FREEHOLD OR LEASEHOLD

"Democratic" is not a word of approval, nor is "undemocratic" a word of condemnation. Like "equal" and "unequal," such words are descriptive and anyone who uses them as evaluative ones is a victim of the linguistic trap laid by politicians, media people, and second-rate academics over the last half-century or so. It is an error, too, to conflate democracy with the rule of law. Prussia under Frederic the Great, France under Louis xv, and Austria-Hungary under Francis Joseph were undemocratic and adhered to the rule of law.

All tenure of political power except democracy is like freehold property that perdures until some exogenous factor terminates it. Tenure of power under democracy is like leasehold property; it has a built-in expiration date at which it is terminated and needs to be renewed. Getting a fresh leasehold is a matter of competition. The lease is awarded by majority vote to the competitor who offers the highest price to a potential coalition for its support. The price must then be paid by society as a whole, but principally by the potential minority. The result is a net redistribution from the better-off to the worse-off, for rich-to-poor transfer can always outbid the poor-to-rich one. The basic mechanics of political competition for a lease on power ensure that on balance democracy is intrinsically egalitarian. Egalitarian ideology is a consequence of this mechanism and not its cause.

On the road to equality of income and wealth, a terminus that is never reached and is not even seriously striven for, governments must outdo themselves at embellishing and nourishing a welfare state. Friedrich Hayek, of all people, positively commends the further expansion of the state to this end: "The only question which arises is whether the benefits are worth the cost."[2] A very good question indeed. "Government may render . . . many services which involve no coercion except for the raising of the means by taxation."[3] Government is induced by competitive pressure to pre-empt a growing share of the national product for its own expenditure, leaving a shrinking proportion for individual disposition. Short of revolt, individuals must submit to this, for majority rule ensures that collective choice trumps individual choice. The process of adopting new good ideas for "useful public goods and services" "whose benefit exceeds their cost" reaches a frenzy as the regular expiration date of the leasehold on power approaches. One has the impression that election fever begins ever earlier and election campaigns are becoming ever more massive and all-encompassing as democracy matures.

The maximin-type safety of the democratic system provided by the government having to face the expiration of its tenure at regular intervals is paid for with a heavy price. Capital accumulation and investment tend to be lower, structural adaptation meets more resistance, and budget deficits are more chronic in democracy than in some, though of course not all, non-democratic systems. One need not select such extreme examples as France or Spain compared to Korea, Singapore, or Indonesia to perceive the general tendency. Democracy has produced a "social model" in Europe, and is busily at work to produce one in the United States, whose attractions are visible enough, but whose costs are concealed or too easily imputed to causes other than democracy itself.

What all this suggests is not that we should somehow get rid of democracy and put in its place the miraculous "new order" stuffed with empty phrases and little else. Rather, what it suggests is that democ-

2. Friedrich A. Hayek, *The Constitution of Liberty* (Chicago: University of Chicago Press, 1960), 222.

3. Friedrich A. Hayek, *New Studies in Philosophy, Politics, Economics and the History of Ideas* (London: Routledge, 1978).

racy does not deserve the awestruck adulation and praise, due only to some ultimate good, that it is receiving. It deserves constant critical scrutiny and resistance to its encroaching creep at the margin; the very same treatment that should be meted out to any and every other kind of political system.

2. IS SOCIETY A GREAT BIG INSURANCE COMPANY?

Every epoch and every culture tends to have a magic form of words, an argument-stopper that trumps contrary thoughts, contrary wishes. Throughout the Christian era, "It is God's will" sufficed to settle an issue, and in the Moslem world, much the same words still suffice to do so. During the Enlightenment, the voice of an idealized Reason took over. "Progress" had its day, as did "The National Interest." "Democracy," "Equality," and "Social Justice" are currently running neck and neck. "It is Not Healthy" is a strong contender for filtering out what must not be done, but probably nothing is now more powerful than the knee-jerk rejection of anything that "Is Not Safe."

A great variety of reasons conspire to create a "safety first" culture. Many originate in one of the perverse features of modern society: that the risks, costs, and benefits of a given course of action accrue to different persons. Since September 11, 2001, hundreds of millions of airline passengers have suffered delay and inconvenience and the airlines and airports were made to incur billions of dollars of extra expense to maintain pre-boarding "security." The security checks may cause an infinitesimal reduction in the risk of a terrorist boarding the plane with explosives round his waist, and possibly an infinitesimal increase of the risk that he will place the bomb in the suitcase he consigns to the luggage compartment. Patting down millions of respectable matrons before letting them board their planes costs a great deal, causes irritation, and provides no perceptible improvement in security. It causes neither irritation nor cost to the regulators who impose these checks at the airports. However, if they relaxed the controls, all the benefits would go to the airline industry and its hundreds of millions of nameless passengers, and none to the regulators. The passengers would not

First published by Liberty Fund, Inc., at www.econlib.org on July 5, 2010. Reprinted by permission.

think of thanking them, nor would they have a face-to-face chance of doing so. However, should a suicide bomber blow up a plane after controls have been relaxed, the regulators would be lucky to escape being crucified by the media.

The same kind of mismatch between the interests of the risk-bearers and the regulators who "save" them from the risk prevails wherever and whenever collective choice exercised by some authority forcibly crowds out individual choices.

Often in recent history when a situation would inflict losses on some business interest if left to individual choices, collective choice steps in, indemnifies the losers, and spreads the loss over all taxpayers. To stay with the airline industry, such a case occurred when in April 2010 a volcano blew clouds of ash into the European airspace and the regulators stopped air traffic for six days on the grounds that not a single passenger's life must be exposed to avoidable risk. The airlines are estimated to have lost $1.12 billion and there is a strong likelihood that they will be indemnified from some European or national government purse.

A somewhat different but equally powerful mechanism operates in the notorious Common Agricultural Policy, where the community shoulders much of the losses that excessive production would otherwise inflict on dairy farmers, pig breeders, or winegrowers. What used to pass for an ordinary business risk that business was expected to bear is gradually transformed into a social responsibility. The progressive transfer of responsibility for losses from individual businesses to the state suppresses much of the penalty for losses and hence removes much of the incentive to get rid of the causes of the losses.

Quantitatively, the most important field where the "safety first at any cost" principle holds sway is health insurance, especially where the health insurer is directly or residually the government itself that is vulnerable to electoral threats. The service providers have a financial incentive to furnish more and costlier medical, hospital, and laboratory tests and seek to avoid the risk, however minute, of a mishap and a ruinous lawsuit in case they did less than the very maximum service. Patients have no interest to check this tendency, for in the majority of cases most or all of the cost is borne by the insurer and ultimately by society as a whole.

The very last word in the matter of "safety as the supreme guiding principle" is said by social contract theory that seeks to justify the individual's obedient subjection to collective authority. Except in revolutionary situations, individuals obey choices imposed upon them by the dictator, the constitutional monarch, an oligarchy, or a democratically formed majority. The principle that such choices are made according to some collective choice rule (that may but need not be a full-fledged constitution) is matched by the "principle of subjection" that obliges subjects to obey.

David Hume, usually wiser than any rival political philosopher, held that government is born not endogenously from social evolution, but exogenously from foreign conquest or "quarrels with other societies."[1] Once it is installed, individuals acquiesce in its exercise of power over them. In sharp contrast to the Humean view that sees passive acceptance of a tolerable modus vivendi, social contract theory sees people actually seeking a contractually defined command-obedience relation with authority and positive *consent* to collective choices made according to some implicit or explicit constitutional rule. They *consent* in full knowledge that collective choices will not be unanimous and some future ones may damage their own interests. On balance, however, they all expect to be winners. If they did not, they would not unanimously consent to the contract, which according to contractarian theory they are supposed to do.

Next to Rawls, the most thoroughgoing version of contractarianism is that put forward by Buchanan and Tullock in their *Calculus of Consent*[2] and in much of James Buchanan's subsequent work. The basic idea is that everybody, well-to-do and needy alike, will consent to a distribution of incomes which protects them from the risk of adverse changes in income: everyone will opt for a society that, like a great big

1. David Hume, "Essay V: Of the Origin of Government," in *Essays Moral, Political, Literary,* ed. Eugene F. Miller, rev. ed. (Indianapolis: Liberty Fund, 1985), 37–41. Also available at http://oll.libertyfund.org/?option=com_staticxt&staticfile=show .php%3Ftitle=704&chapter=137486&layout=html&Itemid=27.

2. James M. Buchanan and Gordon Tullock, *The Collected Works of James M. Buchanan,* vol. 3, *The Calculus of Consent: Logical Foundations of Constitutional Democracy* (Indianapolis: Liberty Fund, 1999). Also available at http://oll.libertyfund.org /title/1063.

insurance company, indemnifies losers from the "premiums" it collects from the gainers, the currently well-to-do. The well-to-do willingly accept this one-way redistribution from rich to poor because their preference for a safety-first society is stronger than their desire to remain well-to-do.

At first sight, this is an implausible conclusion drawn from extravagant or at least very strong assumptions. The chief one is that there is a "veil of uncertainty" that hides the future from the well-to-do (though, as some reflection must show, not from the needy). Untoward events may be lurking in the future that would reduce the income of the well-to-do to that of the needy. Suppose that the mean lifetime income is running at eighty, with that of the well-to-do averaging 100 and that of the needy seventy. There must be an untoward event that would cut the remaining lifetime income of the well-to-do to some low level, the event occurring with a certain probability at some future date which is also subject to a probability distribution. The probability of the adverse event, the reduction in income, and its probable date (imminent, medium-term, or distant) jointly give a result that would persuade the rational well-to-do to vote for a transfer of twenty of his present income to the needy. His remaining lifetime income would now be running at eighty, and so would be that of the formerly needy; there would be equality at the mean level. Should the untoward event in fact occur, the formerly well-to-do would stop transferring part of his income to the formerly needy, but he would presumably still draw an income equal to the mean eighty, benefiting as he would from the transfers of other well-to-do contractarians. As long as the mean income did not fall below eighty, everybody would be assured to get it one way or another. Society, functioning as an insurance company, would have vanquished risk.

This scheme has the charm of a bedside tale for wide-eyed children. It spoils this effect by the claim that it is describing the presumable behavior of the rational "risk-averse" utility maximizer. Two remarks undermine this claim. One is that the rational maximizer is not necessarily "risk-averse." He does buy insurance, but he also takes risks. His behavior suggests that he is risk-avoider for some ranges of his income and risk-taker for other ranges. The second and perhaps more important commonsense objection to the contractarian fairy tale is that the well-to-do have a better option than the one of willingly accepting redistributive taxation in order to benefit from it if some uncertain future event cuts down their income. Instead of deliberately reducing their income in favor of the needy, they can devote a corresponding part of it to accumulate capital. If the adverse event does occur, they can fall back on their savings. If it does not occur, or occurs only in the distant future, they can leave it to their heirs. Under credible probability distributions, they are better off this way than by deliberately contracting for a redistributive society.

Needless to say, we do have a redistributive society, essentially because he who wants to govern needs to buy popular consent to it. This is something that, with David Hume, we must probably acquiesce in. But I think we should protest against being told that what is happening happens because this is our preferred way of going for "safety first."

3. INCOMES: EQUALIZING OR CHURNING?

Preoccupation with the distribution of incomes has become more intense lately. Anger at the rich because the poor are poor fuels it, and so does the idea, inherited from "defunct economists" served in the public subconscious, that if total income is unequally distributed, some mythical entity they are pleased to call "total utility" will be smaller than it need be, and could be expanded by policies that equalized real incomes by acting on both the revenue and the expenditure side of the budget.

There is, to the great grief of the old-style interventionist economics, no such thing "out there" as total utility since the "utilities" of different persons do not add up to a homogenous quantity. The total of a cherry and a prune is a cherry and a prune and never two cherries or two prunes. At best, one can make the value judgment that it would be better to have two cherries and no prune. However, the phoney arithmetic of interpersonal aggregation combined with the misunderstanding about the "diminishing marginal utility of income" (which may or may not work for a person but does not work across persons) creates the belief that redistribution is not only a moral imperative, but also makes a society "objectively" richer.

In tirelessly battering "neo-liberalism" (but why "neo"?), such eminent economists as Joseph Stiglitz and their hordes of followers condemn "globalization" as a scheme for making the rich richer and leaving the poor by the wayside if not actually making them more miserable. On the part of the eminent economists, such claims show how passion and indignation can cloud logic and the perception of evidence. On the part of the horde of camp-followers, they show for the umpteenth time that a little economics is worse than none.

Two fallacies support the demand that incomes on a world scale ought to be made more equal. One is that just as wealth creation is

First published by Liberty Fund, Inc., at www.econlib.org on September 5, 2008. Reprinted by permission.

good per se, inequality is bad per se. Since "globalization" jointly produces wealth and inequality, a good and a bad, a balance must be
struck between them. Maybe "globalization" is bad on balance unless
its inequality-generating effect is "corrected."

The other fallacy is rooted on the recognition that since the age-old
process of "globalization" has gathered such momentum in the last
two decades or so, factor shares in developed countries have shifted in
favor of capital. Except for the highly skilled, labor incomes fell behind
economic growth. Seeing the relative share of capital increase, and the
"multinationals" piling up the billions, the cry went up that the rich are
getting richer. However, the day when capital was mainly owned wholly
or even mostly by the rich is long past. Today, the "multinationals" are
almost without exception majority-owned by middle- and low-income
people through pension funds and other intermediaries. The benefit
accruing to them does not show up in the statistics of personal incomes,
or does so only after a long time lag. Changes in the share of profits vs.
the share of wages no longer clearly signal a change in income distribution between rich and poor.

Where inequality has become glaringly greater and more obvious
is in the remuneration of top corporate executives who deploy other
people's assets in the markets for goods and services, and in that of
fund managers who deploy them in financial markets (though the latter
is probably no more than a passing aberration that should soon correct itself, while the former depends on whether shareholder activism
will gather much needed strength). These somewhat perverse results
of the principal-agent conflict are plainly offensive and in bad taste,
but in terms of total national or world income, not as big as the noise
they provoke.

As regards the large-scale problem of income equalization, the theo-
retical perspective could hardly be simpler. When the mean income exceeds the median, a majority of a self-interested electorate should vote
for rich-to-poor redistribution, and go on doing so until income distribution attains equality. (At this point, any further redistribution would
start creating inequalities, though that is no reason for expecting it to
stop.)

Any government that would falter in the progress toward complete
equality should be voted out and replaced by its rival that promised

to go further. Why, then, is there no trace of any strong trend toward income equality? To all appearances, governments and their oppositions fight their main battles over redistributive measures, and vast programs to that effect are constantly born or reshaped, yet the statistics do not show that inequality is being ironed out.

In abstract theory, the competition for capturing a majority of votes takes the form of groups of candidates for office making bids to pay voters with below-the-mean incomes sums of money taken from voters with above-the-mean ones, the highest bidder(s) forming the government. Redistribution is a neat rich-to-poor money transfer. In reality, however, the scope for such transfers is very limited, squeezed up as it is by three huge blocks of in-kind transfers governments make from rich and poor to rich and poor, with little net redistributive effect. They are old-age security (pensions), healthcare, and education. They are financed by general taxation and compulsory social insurance (payroll taxes). Both rich and poor contribute to them, income taxes weighing more heavily on the rich, value added or sales taxes and petrol taxes more heavily on the poor, with the incidence of payroll taxes being hard to assess but likely to hit the poor harder. (Corporation taxes should be regarded as part of personal income taxes paid by corporations on behalf of their ultimate owners.)

In advanced Western-style economies, pensions will absorb 15–18 percent of GDP, healthcare 7–12 percent, and education 5–9 percent, a total of 27–39 percent. Not all of this will be financed by taxes, compulsory social insurance premiums, and deficits (borrowing), but most of it will be. With public administration, defense, law and order, and the service charge of the national debt also to be financed, the scope for straightforward rich-to-poor transfers, as envisaged in pure theory, is obviously constricted. Willy-nilly, the state takes on in-kind, paternalistic commitments in old age and healthcare and education that bind its hands but that it cannot significantly lighten without hopelessly spoiling its image as the caring and civilizing guardian of the common good.

Redistribution of the sort that reduces the measure of income inequality and strongly favors the poor is popularly called "social justice." Naming it so is a clever and audacious stroke of one-upmanship, for the words, though strictly meaningless, pre-empt for it the moral high ground that rightly belongs to justice. However, the redistribution that goes on in modern economies is of a different sort. It leaves inequality mostly unaffected, though it absorbs up to (and in some cases more than) one half of people's incomes in order to hand it out again in various in-kind benefits to much the same people. It is, in plain language, "churning" the national income without there being much evidence that all its mixing, shaking, and heaving is leaving any identifiable class of society noticeably better off.

4. THE FAT CATS, THE UNDERDOGS, AND SOCIAL JUSTICE

Except the stars of showbiz and spectator sports for whom all is forgiven, fat cats do not have a good press. Even those who have done great things, built and run vast and vastly productive organizations employing thousands of men and women who are all at least a little better off as a result—even captains of industry are widely blamed for their income and wealth that is regarded as ranging from the provocative to the obscene. When, by a combination of gross collective misjudgment, ill luck, mass hysteria fostered by the perverse incentives governing the panic-mongering media, and equally perverse solvency and accounting rules, the fat cats of finance got themselves in deep trouble, the jubilant public all but cheered. Admittedly, as the music stopped, many bankers displayed singularly bad taste, but even perfect discretion would not have saved them from the detestation owed to fat cats.

At the other extremity of society, the underdog enjoys general sympathy. There is a presumption that he must be in the right and the top dog (or should it be overdog?) is in the wrong.

This is so not because of what either may have done, but because one is now beneath the other. The top dog may be blameless, but sympathy goes to the underdog and sympathy is easily mistaken for an imperative of justice.

All these sentiments and attitudes spring from deep-seated emotions that cloud cooler judgment. One such may be the shock and fear at the sight of gross inequalities of any kind that hurt what Isaiah Berlin called the "love of symmetry." Another may be the emotive appeal that playing Robin Hood holds for most of us (and hang the sheriff of Nottingham). Half emotion and half calculation inspire the gut feeling that rich-to-poor redistribution enhances the common good (the "ag-

First published by Liberty Fund, Inc., at www.econlib.org on March 2, 2009. Reprinted by permission.

gregate utility" of superannuated textbooks) while incidentally also raising the income of the person advocating it. Finally, pure emotion excites good old-fashioned envy; take down the fat cats, chop off the tall poppies, even if the person feeling that way expects to reap no profit from it.

Emotions are joined by expediency and both pull policy the same way. Under a democratic form of government (though probably in a less overt fashion than under any other form of government), competition among leaders and their supporters for the capture and tenure of government takes the shape of an auction ring. Rivals seek to outbid each other by offering to buy enough support to form a majority coalition. They can pay for it by redistribution through both the revenue (taxation and deficit financing) side and the spending (public goods and services) side. For obvious reasons, rich-to-poor redistribution can always beat a poor-to-rich one. The auction ends for the time being, and a winning coalition is formed when its marginal member cannot be bribed by a better offer to join a rival coalition. Normally, this will be the case when the winning coalition comprises half the voters plus one person, and its redistributive offer exhausts politically tolerated taxable capacity. Politics, of course, is less orderly than the tic-tac of this precision machinery, but they keep to the same beat.

Having got this far in setting out the emotional and the opportunistic springs of using political power to help the needy at the expense of the better-off, the scene is exposed in all its brazen moral nakedness. Emotion and expediency may fully account for what goes on, but is it ethically admissible, let alone mandatory? Is it in any rigorous sense *just*?

Redistribution has needed at least a fig leaf of respectability. In social justice, it has been handed a moral garb offering more ample cover of irreproachable virtue.

The name—or might we say the brand?—"social justice" alone is of tremendous effect, a superb specimen of the successful semantic fraud. For by thus calling itself, social justice is disguised as just one branch of justice, like commutative, civil, or criminal justice, each dealing with a different subject matter but enjoying the same legitimacy and respect. Honorably opposing social justice is just as impossible as being against justice in general. All its branches are protected by the same shining armor.

Social justice also calls itself distributive justice. The word "distributive" is supposed to point directly to its subject matter as "civil" or "criminal" point to theirs, while "social" points to everything and nothing and is just an almost meaningless decorative adjective. Perhaps because of that, social science writers prefer to use the word "distributive." However, that usage gives much of the game away. For any distribution of valuable things among individuals in a group is a result of property relations and contracts agreed on, and in the last analysis it is the result of the exercise of their freedoms. Protecting freedoms and barring unfreedoms is, in turn, the subject matter of all justice. Whether adjudicating property or liability claims, enforcing contracts, or handing down verdicts and sentences, justice always distributes. Talking of "distributive" justice is like talking of wet water. Pretending that it is a distinct branch of justice is another form of the verbal fraud the advocates of social justice, mostly unbeknown to themselves, are putting across. But it is a less invulnerable form.

For what social justice, also known as distributive justice, does is to condemn and override the distribution that results from the operation of the rules of justice itself. It is not a branch of justice fitting harmoniously into its whole and enjoying its legitimacy; it is instead its antagonist seeking to undo what justice has done. It is frank and matter-of-fact to speak of this as redistribution, but fraudulent or at best question-begging to claim that it is social or distributive justice. The latter implies a moral claim superior to the moral claims of justice in general.

Social justice does appear to imply one moral claim that is distinctly its own, namely the obligation of charity to relieve absolute poverty, and hence the legitimacy of coercive taxation to that end. This supposes that voluntary charity is inadequate, that compulsory charity is preferable to it because it gives a right to charity to the poor, and that there is general agreement on where absolute poverty ends and relative poverty begins. It is a pity but a fact that no such general agreement is in sight and hence the obligation of charity is open-ended. In any event, however, only a small part of the practices of social justice can be imputed to it, for much if not most redistribution has little to do with the relief of poverty and a great deal with compulsory insurance against life's contingencies and evening out inequalities of many kinds.

In fact, social justice is identified in the public mind with concern for equality, and though the relation is not so straightforward as that, the prima facie dependence of social justice on some egalitarian warrant invites a closer look.

It is albeit sloppily and superficially but confidently treated as self-evident that an equal distribution of good (and also of bad) things among a given set of individuals is morally better than an unequal one. However, there is nothing self-evident about this proposition. There is not even a presumption of equality based on some asymmetry between equality and inequality in the same way as there is a logically derivable presumption for liberty, for title to possessions, and for innocence. All the latter are based on claims to the contrary being verifiable but not falsifiable, hence on the burden of proof lying squarely with the accusation that can verify and not with the defense that cannot falsify the accusation.

No such asymmetry favors an equal distribution of goods, nor an unequal one. You can say that the distribution is to be equal unless sufficient reason is brought why it should be unequal. But you can no less sensibly say that it should be unequal unless sufficient reason is brought why it should be equal. The two statements are formally equivalent.

There is equivalence in form, which does not do much for social justice, but in substance the argument actually favors inequality. Real-world situations abound with reasons for inequality that explain why a given distribution is unequal. On a company payroll, some employees receive more pay because they worked longer hours, are more skilled, produce more, have served for more years, or bear more responsibility. Some of the variables responsible for different pay scales may themselves differ as between persons; e.g., one skill or one responsibility may be greater than another. The payroll will show much apparent inequality and many naturally occurring reasons for it. It would have to be shown that they are insufficient and that simple equality ought to prevail instead. On the other hand, there are few or no real-world distributions, apart perhaps from small army units or prison camps, where simple equality reigns and sufficient reason for it occurs as a matter of course. For the egalitarian cause, there should be an overriding sufficient reason for equal distributions that is stronger than all

the naturally occurring reasons for inequality and one that would justify political action to level them out.

Yet it is hard to see where such an overriding reason could come
from if not from high-flown rhetoric. Perhaps differences among men
and their endowments are "morally arbitrary" (as Rawls has it), but
what if they are? Perhaps "all men are created equal," but if they were,
why are they manifestly unequal? People have by and large grown out of
looking for the philosopher's stone. Why do they still keep looking for
the self-evident moral truth of equality and its satellite, social justice?

5. EQUAL POVERTY, UNEQUAL AFFLUENCE

It is not people being poor that causes social ills from school failure, teenage pregnancy, crime, and short life expectancy, but the fact that some people are poorer than others. It is not the level of income, but the differences between levels that really matter. It follows that fighting poverty is the wrong battle except if it reduces inequality. The right target is inequality and never mind if reducing it were to leave the poor as poor as before. They, and society as a whole, will still be healthier and happier.

This, stripped of rhetoric, is the latest twist in the convoluted chain of arguments for altering a more or less liberal order out of all recognition until justice proper is decisively subordinated to what some call "social" justice. Explicitly shifting the target from poverty to inequality, to the point where poverty becomes irrelevant as long as it is the same for all, is a radical novelty. It is interesting to look at why it has become fashionable.

From its beginnings, there has been a vigorous egalitarian streak in Christianity, much of it inherited from Judaism. Without being replaced, modern religious egalitarianism has been superseded by a lay doctrine, partly Benthamite and partly Kantian, that sought to make equal material well-being a requirement deduced from some self-evident moral axiom. Equal material well-being was a condition of the greatest social utility. Alternatively, it was a corollary of everybody having equal "rights" or equal moral entitlements to fair shares.

Such attempts to deduce egalitarianism from morality, though not really extinct, have not been very successful. They lay down that men have all been created equal, yet this is daily contradicted by their being strikingly unequal in vital respects. They claim that the talents and other endowments that enable some individuals to enjoy greater material riches than others are "morally arbitrary." Though most people

First published by Liberty Fund, Inc., at www.econlib.org on April 6, 2009. Reprinted by permission.

may subconsciously read this to mean "morally wrong," on further thought it turns out to be no more wrong than right, and supports an equal distribution no more than it does an unequal one.

Though the abstract moral argument was and remains weak, for a long time it was propped up by a widespread feeling that aiding the really needy was a duty intrinsic to human fellowship or citizenship. It was also accepted that the duty should be transformed into an enforceable obligation through the tax system. Welfare entitlements did mitigate poverty to a limited extent, though it has been argued that they not only relieved poverty but also aggravated it by inducing dependency and irresponsibility. However, what really brought about a massive decrease of abject poverty and misery all over the world in the last two or three decades was "globalization" that enabled hundreds of millions of mainly Asian but also Latin American and African poor to start earning wages. There is reason to expect this development to spread and intensify in the decades to come. If that would not abolish poverty, it would at least greatly ease it as a pressing problem used to justify redistributive taxation for its relief.

If poverty is destined to be an ever-weaker reason for reshaping society, there is still a last-resort case to be made by setting up inequality itself as a source of our major ills that could be cured by equality. Hence the shift of blame from levels to differences of material well-being, a shift that is now unfolding.

A variety of empirical studies has been targeted to show that equal distributions of privileges or affluence display fewer socially dysfunctional features than do unequal ones. Privileged baboons living in isolation from others do well, but when mixed with other baboons, some of whom may surpass them, they develop hormone and other troubles. British civil servants differ little from baboons, at least not in this respect. Those on the top rung are healthier and live longer than their subordinates, with health getting poorer and life expectancy shorter with each step down the ladder of hierarchy. Clearly, the cause is that those on the lower rungs are poorer than those above them. At least, this is what we are being invited to conclude. But how conclusive is the evidence?

Applied to entire societies, the new empirical egalitarianism boils down to this: if Country A and Country B have the same average real income, but in A it is distributed more equally than in B, then A will have better school results, less juvenile delinquency, less crime, better health, and greater life expectancy. This, we are meant to understand, is because compared to B, in A fewer people are more affluent than the rest, or fewer are poorer than the rest.

The two alternatives look symmetrical in form, but are not so in substance. If what makes a society sick is that when looking upward, people see many fellow countrymen who are more affluent than themselves, there is an explanation that is at least not counterintuitive: people are gnawed by envy or self-reproach for their own inadequacy or bad luck in the face of the success of others. A few years back, Lord Layard of the London School of Economics diagnosed this and proposed to punish success, a source of unhappiness for others, by a tax just like a tax on pollution or some other negative externality.[1] Readers will judge this proposal without being nudged either way by this essay.

The opposite case, where Country A is socially healthier because few people in it are poorer than the rest, is very different and more intriguing. Why should children do better at school if fewer of their classmates are poorer than they? The case is just conceivable, but stretches our good will a bit. Would the children in A do better still if the few poor ones were segregated into separate schools and the rest had no classmates who were poorer than themselves? Would the trick work equally if it were the few very affluent children who were segregated?

The logic of the neo-egalitarians, namely that it is not low levels but differences between levels that make society sick, tells us that if Country A were blessed with a new, even more equal income distribution where no one was affluent and no one was poorer than the rest, society would function ideally, even if in this new and equal distribution all were as poor as the poorest used to be in the old distribution. This looks nonsensical and as far as I am aware, the new egalitarians do not choose to push their logic this far.

All or most of the social dysfunctions they explain by the presence of income differences can be explained more simply by low levels of

---

1. Richard Layard, *Happiness: Has Social Science a Clue?*, Lionel Robbins Memorial Lectures (London: Centre for Economic Performance, 2003).

income, the old-fashioned poverty that egalitarians feel they can no longer rely on to serve as their battering ram against the ramparts of liberal order. They show empirical evidence that of two equally affluent countries, the egalitarian Country A is scoring better than the less egalitarian Country B. But the same evidence fully warrants a different interpretation. Country B has by definition more poor people as well as more rich. It is the prevalence of poverty that makes for the low scores, rather than the fact that not everybody is equally poor or equally affluent.

CONCLUSION

There are more potent ways of fighting poverty than soaking the rich. Inducing people to form and preserve two-parent families, if indeed they can be induced to do so, could be wonderfully effective. Another very potent means is to raise the demand for labor, the main or only thing the poor have to sell. One obvious cause of rising demand for labor is capital formation which, in turn, is fed by public, corporate, and personal saving. We can't predict what would happen to corporate saving, but we know that public saving is generally negative. Personal saving is typically a much greater proportion of high than of low incomes. Hence the same national income unequally distributed yields more saving than if it were equally distributed. By saving more, the very affluent are, so to speak, raising the price they will have to pay for labor tomorrow. In any event, unequal affluence holds out more hope for the poor than equal poverty.

6. TOPPING UP WELFARE

Throughout Western Europe, redistribution remains an electoral must. Right practices it no less than Left. However, the doctrinal climate in which it flourishes is undergoing a change. Capitalism is still condemned as selfish, inegalitarian, and chaotic, but it is no longer treated as the evil that must be uprooted, destroyed, and replaced by the purposeful, responsible, and just socialist order. It is only the half-crazed, wild-eyed intellectual flotsam that still clings to the old dreams of doing away with exploitation. More and more socialists quietly realize that since private industry is better at exploitation than state-owned enterprises, it is better at capital accumulation too, and will create more riches for governments to lay their hands on.

This new shrewdness was amusingly illustrated in the recent grand debates about the modernization of the derelict French Socialist party. Touchingly candid, its mainstream reformers declared that the party is not anti-capitalist, because it is for wealth creation; if no wealth were created, how could they redistribute it?

The question is well taken indeed. How could you slaughter a fat pig if it was not fattened first? One wonders whether capitalists are encouraged to create wealth if it is destined to be redistributed.

Economists of socialist inspiration have always brushed such questions aside. They persisted in treating national income as something that is produced first and distributed afterwards. Production can be left to the soiled but capable hands of capitalist entrepreneurs, with the resulting product being divided by the state along lines dictated by "social justice." The stage of distribution reacted back but little or not at all upon the stage of production. Statistical proof that taxation undermined incentives was difficult to find.

Lately, however, it has dawned even on left-leaning politicians and union leaders that there is a trade-off between redistribution and eco-

First published by Liberty Fund, Inc., at www.econlib.org on August 4, 2008. Reprinted by permission.

nomic growth. One cannot have an extensive system of welfare provision in kind, complex protective regulation, high taxes, and endemic budget deficits as well as low unemployment, technical progress, and vigorous growth. Scared a little by the perspective of stagnation or breakdown, since before the turn of the century Britain, Holland, Sweden, and Germany have tried to put a brake on the luxuriant spread of the welfare state. The share of GDP taken by government and the social welfare agencies seems to be leveling off. The European average is now hovering at just over 40 percent, with Germany at 44, Britain at 45, though France is still defiantly leading the pack with 54 percent.

Most governments now recognize that it is no longer clever politics to go on topping up the welfare state by throwing ever more money at the gaps that keep showing up in it. Clever politics now demands that the task be delegated to others. Business and Europe have started to be solicited.

"BUSINESS ETHICS"

The "Third Way" that Tony Blair learned about from his sociologist guru Anthony (now Lord) Giddens (and that Vaclav Klaus branded the fastest way to the Third World) included the idea that business enterprises did not belong to their owners alone. Along with its shareholders, a corporation had other "stakeholders" to whom it owed some responsibility and who ought to have a say in its conduct. Employees, suppliers, and customers were the obvious ones, but the townspeople, cultural and educational institutions, the environment, and for that matter the whole nation had a "stake" in each business, and it was management's clear duty to respect these stakes.

The spread of this doctrine is paralleled by the rise of "business ethics" as an academic subject. Believing that such a subject really exists is tantamount to treating business as an individual, a person who can have ethical codes and duties to follow them. But business is not a person. Its conduct is directly chosen by managers, who are persons and have ethical duties. The overriding one is their fiduciary duty to the owners who employ them. Whatever the managers do in their private life, in running a business their duty is to maximize the present value of all future net profits, all of which belong to their employers, the shareholders. It is clear that if they are worth their salt, they will always deal squarely, for in business "honesty is the best policy"; i.e., it is the profit-maximizing one. There is only one maximizing policy; the distinction between short and long run is spurious and must be replaced by "present value" in which both short and long run profits are discounted to their present worth.

Maintaining employment when there is not enough work in prospect for all earns kudos for the "socially responsible" management. In fact, the managers are not only spoiling the chances of more efficient resource allocation that can only come about if labor is mobile. They are also stealing money that belongs to their owners and was entrusted to them. The same goes for all expenditure, or forgone revenue, favoring the interest of a "stakeholder" that will not yield sufficient future profit through the effect it may have on goodwill for the corporation rather than for the social standing of its managers.

For well-known reasons, managers can get away with vast generosity to "stakeholders" without owners curbing them. "Business ethics" courses teach them that on the whole this is how they ought to behave, albeit "with due consideration" for the "legitimate interests" of shareholders. The media and the economically illiterate political class go one further. They brand it as scandalous that a corporation makes a net income running into billions; why can't it be content with hundreds or tens of millions, which would still be a thousand times an ordinary workman's annual wage? And why can't such profitable corporations contribute more to protecting the environment, financing community projects, and providing housing and social services?

Thus, public opinion and the media are hectoring managements to be "ethical" and spend for the benefit of the "stakeholders" the money entrusted to them by the shareholders. Corporations are sternly asked to be "good citizens," though only individuals can do that. Managements do yield to this moral pressure; doing so passes for "best practice" in most business ethics courses. The net effect is that state provision for welfare and good works, running at a level that stretches government finances to critical limits, is topped up by the private sector without taxation and budget deficits being further increased.

A TRULY "SOCIAL" EUROPE

Governments, cheered on by public opinion, now delegate downwards, to the corporate sector, some of the "topping up" that the welfare state always requires. They also try to delegate some of it upwards, to the European Union that they, egged on by their electorates, stridently demand to become really, truly "social."

It is a fair guess that the proposed European constitution was rejected in 2005 by the Dutch and particularly the French referendum because it was not "social" enough. This may have been a misjudgment on the part of the French, for the most innovative part of the draft constitution, the Charter of Fundamental Rights, bore within it the seeds of a vast and irresistible expansion of "workers' rights" and social protection, with member states forced to comply by the European Court of Justice.

This abortive effort was repeated in 2007 by the "simplified" Lisbon Treaty in which the Charter of Fundamental Rights has reappeared in all its cack-handed absurdity. All twenty-seven member states should have ratified it; but the Irish in a referendum have rejected it. They will be asked to vote again, the right way this time, and perhaps go on voting until finally they vote as Europe's federalists tell them. However, if this eminently democratic procedure does not work itself out as now expected, the most "European" member governments are determined to push for the nearest approximation to a socialist ideal that they can possibly get.

Europe, the program of the current six-month French presidency of the Union declares, must above all be a protective entity, sheltering its citizens from the risks of globalization, unregulated capitalism, and imported food that endangers health and undermines the capacity of European agriculture to feed the people; it must harmonize upwards corporation taxes, and do many other things that member states would rather delegate to Brussels, lest they be accused of being irresponsibly populist.

Trying to get Brussels to do the topping up may or may not produce much of a result. But it is yet another testimony to the wishful thinking that blithely supposes that if someone else can be made to carry out our task, we do not end up paying for it one way or another.

7. IS SOCIETY A GREAT BIG CREDIT CARD?
PART 1

Most of us have credit cards made of plastic. All of us have a credit card made of laws and the apparatus that enforces them. It is called the state.

Next to the contraceptive pill, the mightiest agent of social change in our age has been the credit card. Urged on by such friendly invitations as "fly now, pay later," with a self-assured swipe of our magic card we get instant gratification of our wishes for whatever money can buy, at least within a reasonable order of magnitude. For wishes of a higher order, we can use the mortgage on our house as a credit card, topping it up if it had been paid down or if the value of the house has gone up. The "pay later" part of the formula is not just trickery meant to reassure you, though it does mean to do that, too.

If "buy now, pay later" is so often chosen instead of "buy when you can pay," it is because of time preference. Future goods are worth less than present ones; they are devalued by a time discount. Despite its commonsense appeal, many economists and philosophers have condemned time preference as irrational or non-existent. In the burgeoning environmentalist literature, the damage a given amount of global warming would do to future world product is either not discounted, or discounted at only 1 or 1.5 percent. This justifies a much higher expenditure to prevent future damage than if future world product were discounted at, say, 3 or 4 percent.

Time preference cannot rationally be less than the expected marginal productivity of capital. If it were less, a rational person would contradict his own preference if he consumed his marginal dollar instead of saving it and thus augment his future product. A rational person with a low or zero time preference would, in other words, starve

First published by Liberty Fund, Inc., at www.econlib.org on May 3, 2010. Reprinted by permission.

himself to death. He could only escape this sad fate decreed for him by his zero time preference if the marginal productivity of capital fell to zero or was expected to do so. It is, of course, problematical whether the market interest rate is a good proxy for the expected marginal productivity of capital, and if it is, which is the relevant interest rate that balances the marginal dollar saved against the marginal dollar consumed? The real medium-term rate may be a reasonable candidate, and thus 3 to 4 percent could be the minimum annual rate by which "fly later" might be worth less than "fly now." While it can hardly be much lower than this, it can very well be higher.

Credit card interest rates are, of course, much higher than 3 or 4 percent. One reason on the supply side is that credit card debt is of poor average quality. A flight, a good restaurant dinner cannot be repossessed if the debtor defaults; recovery by other means costs too much, so that the average debtor must pay both for himself and for the defaulter. On the demand side, the time preference of certain types of card-users may be almost astronomical. Weakness of will, or simply a failure to realize what they are doing, might plausibly explain the behavior of habitual heavy credit card borrowers.

Time preference incites to overspend, i.e., to dissave. It is usual to cite the precautionary motives as the main incentive to save. We save to cushion us against unemployment, illness, and old age. Some primitive peoples used to take care of the infirm and the old by gently taking them by the hand, leading them to the deepest forest, and leaving them there. Mostly, however, care was incumbent on grown-up children, and families with many children and many relatives fitted well into that system. Modern China's one-child rule is its opposite pole. A corollary is that Chinese household saving is now extraordinarily high. Another corollary is that in order to stimulate consumption, the Chinese government is advised to introduce state provision of health care and pensions. Gradually but inevitably, this will be done.

There are, of course, alternatives. In continental Europe, where state paternalism is deeply rooted, both healthcare and pensions are provided by compulsory social insurance, but not generously. Household saving, typically between 10 and 20 percent of GDP, supplements them. In the U.K., healthcare provision by the state is supposed to be as comprehensive as it can get, but the state pension is rudimentary, and is supplemented by corporate pension schemes. Household saving has been shrinking, approaching zero but moving back to about 5 percent under the shock of the 2008–09 recession. In the U.S., healthcare is mainly employer-financed; basic pensions are a federal responsibility and are largely supplemented, as in the U.K., by private pension schemes, some of which are corporate, others individual.

What members of a society do not do for themselves in these domains, either by saving up for it or by having their credit cards do it, is done for them by the state. Having the state do it is like using a great big collective credit card which allows them to have public goods, social services, subventions, and tax breaks simply by voting for them. Getting the state to furnish these good things is the equivalent of "fly now." The "pay later" is understood to come at some point — maybe.

For it is only "maybe." One is not really sure. Though the national accounts balance in the aggregate, the accounts of particular individuals need not; some end up as suckers, others as free riders. Well over a century before "public choice" or "rent-seeking" became passwords among the initiated, Frédéric Bastiat described the state as the instrument by which everybody is trying to live at everybody else's expense.[1] All cannot succeed to ride free, but many will. Political economy and political science analyze these subsurface goings-on as the product of rational opportunism, the calculating exploitation of voting strength, the sale of souls to the highest bidder, and so forth. All that is valid enough but tells only half the story. The other half, perhaps the more important one, is about the uncalculating, unconscious, and unwary manner in which the majority of people regard and handle the collective credit card. It is as if they sincerely believed, without consciously believing it, that the state is sitting by a vast reservoir of good things and useful deeds, rivulets and avalanches of which are regularly re-

---

1. Frédéric Bastiat, in his pamphlet *The State* (1848), defined the state as follows: "L'État, c'est la grande fiction à travers laquelle Tout Le Monde s'efforce de vivre aux dépens de Tout Le Monde." [*The state is the great fiction by which* everyone *endeavors to live at the expense of everyone else.*]. See Frédéric Bastiat, *Selected Essays on Political Economy*, trans. Seymour Cain, ed. George B. de Huszar (Irvington-on-Hudson, N.Y.: Foundation for Economic Education, 1975), 140–51. Quote is on p. 144 in a slightly different translation.

leased. The stock has perhaps all been paid for beforehand, or need never be paid for—the question does not arise. If the state is on the side of the people, it lowers the floodgate, releasing more milk and honey; if it is Scrooge-like and ungenerous, it restricts the flow. The people are not divided by divergent interests, trying to live at each other's expense. Rather, they are united in the purpose of bending the state towards more liberality and generosity. It is "fly now," and there is no "pay later" at all. Any attempt to "cancel a flight" is fought tooth and nail by all as arbitrary and unfair, even if it is in the real interest of some that some expenditures should be restricted.

If the public can have a split personality, this is one of them. The other is conscious, calculating, and even crafty. Each of its subgroups benefits disproportionally from some good or service, some subsidy or other privilege that the collective credit card can procure and that will be collectively paid for at future dates. Clearly, each of these subgroups can be a successful parasite only if it steals a march on the others. If half of the subgroups—say, the railwaymen, the teachers, and the fruit growers—successfully claim favors and the others do not, it is the former who will be parasitic on the latter. Hence it is a matter of elementary self-defense for the latter—say, the dairy farmers, the policemen, and the pensioners—also to agitate and make strong claims of their own. In fact, pre-emptive attack may be the only effective defense they have.

None of this rational but sterile and self-defeating roundabout would be really feasible (or at least it would have little scope) if there were no "social credit card." It is because a government can borrow from the future that it has little hope of resisting popular pressure for expenditure today. Through most of history, royal treasuries were emptied when ambitious kings made foolish wars, and got filled up in periods of peace. Modern democracies function differently: big budget deficits in rough times alternate with smaller ones in better days. Big or small, the deficit is endemic, a surplus quite exceptional. When society works with a great collective credit card and can yield to its own time preference, it would be hard to expect a different result.

8. IS SOCIETY A GREAT BIG CREDIT CARD?
PART 2

"We can/cannot live above our means." Tick the right response!

It is the literal truth that "pay later" need never become "pay now" as long as old credit card debt can be repaid from new credit card debt. No musical chairs, no Ponzi scheme, no fraud is involved. As long as such parameters as interest rates, income-to-debt ratios, and income growth remain within the right range, we can go on and on, spending more than we earn.

But can this be really true? Output must equal input, expenditure must equal revenue; how can consumption permanently exceed production? Plainly, for a single economic agent alone in an inhospitable environment, it cannot. But if he interacts with a fertile Nature, or with other persons, interesting and instructive possibilities open up. They have obvious relevance to a burning problem of our day, the catastrophic or at least catastrophic-looking budget deficits that dominate the economic landscape. Some alternative cases may be worth a brief review.

Case 1. Economic agents know what they are doing.

Case 1a. A fisherman lives off a stock of 100 fish that reproduces itself and grows by 3 percent each year. The fisherman eats 103 fish in the year. He is aware that he consumes the growth potential. He can raise his consumption to 104, knowing that it will have to start declining in the distant future.

Case 1b. Walter and Li each have capital yielding 100. Walter consumes 103, borrowing 3 from Li who consumes 97. With each maintaining his consumption, Walter will have mortgaged all his capital to Li in 33 years. With compound interest, this will of course happen sooner. Walter will have nothing left to live on. The parties will have

First published by Liberty Fund, Inc., at www.econlib.org on June 7, 2010. Reprinted by permission.

to "restructure" the debt. At some point, they will both be aware that something of the sort will probably have to happen.

Case 2. Economic agents are largely unaware of the effects of their actions. Since Keynes, economists have become fond of pointing out that what is true of the individual economic agent need not be true of an entire society; thrift, for instance, may be a virtue for the individual but a vice for society.

Case 2a. GDP is 100, of which 75 is consumed. Households save 7 and corporations 18. Of the total saving of 25, investment in fixed capital and stocks absorbs 20, net exports 2, and the budget deficit (i.e., government dissaving) 3. The national debt is 100. The year's deficit is added to it, raising the debt to 103. However, since GDP is also rising at 3 percent per annum, the ratio of debt to GDP remains a constant 100 percent. Of the annual growth of 3 percent, 1.5 percent is real and 1.5 percent is due to inflation. With inflation no higher than this, the debt can probably be financed with the 10-year rate of interest at 4.5 to 4 percent. These numbers are probably close to the situation of most major Western economies as of 2011–12, and suggest that, as the saying goes, the worst is not inevitable. Though governments would still be living above their means, the course of these economies could be self-sustaining.

Case 2b. Like the flutter of a butterfly's wings in chaos theory, a relatively minor event in 2007 is magnified by self-fulfilling prophecies into a collapse of confidence in the financial system in 2008, and GDP falls from 100 to 95. Consumption sinks to 70, household saving is 10, corporate saving 15, and net exports zero. Gross capital formation falls to 13 and the remainder of 12 is the budget deficit. The "output gap" between potential and actual GDP, 5 in the present example, would be higher if the deficit were lower, and vice versa, though the relation between the two is, of course, not one of simple addition or subtraction. At all events, it must be recognized that the budget deficit is to some extent (and some would say, completely) redeemed by the "output gap" being smaller than it would otherwise be. It is equally clear, though, that a double-digit deficit is not sustainable for more than a very few years, and must be followed by years of corrective action that everyone approves in principle but will ferociously oppose in practice.

Case 2c. For an average Western European economy, a national debt of 100 percent or more of GDP is a zone of acute danger. Japan's national debt will probably cross the 200 percent mark this year or next. One must conclude, perhaps unjustly, that the Japanese must be unaware of what they are doing.

The national debt of a country is owed either to its own residents or to foreigners, and is denominated either in the home or in foreign currency. These variables permit four possible combinations. Three are currently topical. Greece owes most of its debts to nonresidents (including very rich shipping magnates with their accounts in London or Cyprus), and the debt is mostly denominated in euros which the Greek state cannot print. The next-worse situation is that of the United States of America. It owes far too much of its debt to nonresidents—perhaps 2 trillion dollars to East Asians—but all of it in dollars, which it can always reimburse by printing new dollars, new Treasury bills and Treasury bonds to replace the old. The best combination is that of Japan, all of whose debt is in yen and all of it is owed to Japanese residents. If the worst comes to the worst, the Japanese government can always repay its creditors by levying on them whatever taxes it takes to do so. Meanwhile, there is no pressure to repay. The Japanese state these days raises medium-term loans at 1.5 percent per annum (The extraordinarily low rate is the market's way of saying that it expects deflation to be resumed.) At such conditions, even a national debt of 200 percent of GDP is sustainable.

9. CLASS WAR BY JUDO

Marxists and most Frenchmen hold that since all value is produced by labor, all of it should be paid out in wages except the part taken by the state, a body which by rights ought to belong to the workers anyway. All private profit is stolen from the working class. It is incumbent on the state to claw it back from the capitalists.

Class warfare is the mode of clawing back the profit, though complete success requires actual revolution. For the hard Left, this is the true aim of class warfare. For the soft Left, well-drilled labor unions in closed shops squeezing profits by tough collective bargaining are fighting the good fight. A more formidable arm of class war as practiced by the soft Left is the collective mandate an electoral majority hands to the state to "slice the national cake" by transfer payments and public goods, so that its distribution will be more favorable to the working class than the original distribution intended by those who had arranged the baking of the cake in the first place.

THE LOGIC OF DISTRIBUTIVE SHARES

Class war scenarios drawn from Marxist metaphysics can neither be verified nor falsified, and arguing about them is not the best of fun. Disciplined common sense, on the other hand, has conclusions to offer about the shares of labor and capital in the "cake" that help us understand the world even if we disagree with them.

It is a truism that if a firm wishes to maximize the present value of its profits over time, it must so deploy its resources that the marginal unit of capital it hires and puts to work has the same productivity as the marginal unit of labor. If it made a mistake and one of the factors it employed had a higher productivity than the other, it could improve its position by redeploying its resources and employing more of the

First published by Liberty Fund, Inc., at www.econlib.org on May 7, 2012. Reprinted by permission.

more productive factor while releasing some of the less productive. All firms that survive in a market with reasonably free entry must at least roughly approximate this balancing act. The result is a reasonably efficient economic system.

However, auxiliary assumptions are needed to make the system work properly. Factor productivities must be decreasing in the sense that if more labor is employed, all other things being equal, its marginal product would decline, and so would the return on capital if more of it was invested. However, the "all other things remaining equal" clause is never satisfied, so that the decreasing-returns-to-scale proviso serves only the criterion of logical completeness. Far more important in practice is the assumption of price flexibility. If an influx of foreign capital depresses the marginal return yielded by it, but the rate of interest remains rigid and does not decline, there would be excess supply of capital and some of its stock would be left idle. Similar disequilibrium would result in the labor market if the supply of labor increased or the demand for it fell, but wages remained at a rigid level fixed by the legislator or collective contract.

The deus ex machina in this system is the progress of technology, which may increase the productivity of capital (e.g., data processing, computerized design), labor (school teaching aides, ambulatory surgery), or both in much the same proportion. The labor-saving or capital-saving bias of technological innovation obviously impacts the distributive shares, but is not necessarily impacted by them. Taking a very long-term historical perspective, we might suppose that since the stock of capital tends to grow faster than the working population, innovation preventing the return on capital from declining would be good for stability and hence might be favored by the innovators, but this idea is perhaps too clever by half and it is wiser to treat technology as an exogenous variable.

WHEN WORKERS OF THE WORLD UNITE

The neo-classical theory of factor shares sketched above makes plain good sense intellectually, and it offers a fairly reassuring world view. Failing major rigidities, such as fixed wages or regulatory obstacles to capital market movements, the incentives in the system would seem to keep it in a balance that undergoes no brutal swings and is efficient at keeping the available factors at work in the most efficient manner. Neither capital nor labor has some obvious built-in handicap exposing it to exploitation by the other.

This suggests that we should expect the distribution of incomes to be fairly stable, with only moderate ups and downs over time in the measure of income inequality. Capital would go on accumulating, raising corporate profits and personal incomes from ownership and enterprise, but the accumulation would increase the demand for labor, hence raising incomes from wages.

However, for the last three decades or so, this has stubbornly failed to happen. The return on capital tended to rise, profits grew with little interruption, and inequality of personal incomes expanded spectacularly. Unskilled and semi-skilled wages in the developed economies stagnated.

Opinion that was formerly reconciled to the "Washington consensus" has now become bitterly hostile to it, deciding that capitalism was intrinsically unfair. There is probably no intellectually respectable way to give a clear meaning to the notion of fairness, for unlike justice, it has no clear rules which define it. Nevertheless, people of good will and good sense will have notions of rough justice, rough equalities, and a rough sort of "Buggins's turn"[1] in life's ups and downs when they mean that an outcome is fair. By that standard, the sharp divergence of wages and profits in the recent past is at worst not unfair. At best, it should be welcomed as a giant advance against world misery, hunger, and hopelessness.

Over this very inegalitarian period, half a billion breadwinners in China, Vietnam, Thailand, Indonesia, and the Indian subcontinent have migrated from rural underemployment and near-hunger to urban employment and a somewhat more hopeful future. They got their well-deserved Buggins's turn. As long as the pool of Asian rural underemployed was not at least partly drained, the wages of the European and American semi-skilled could not rise in response to capital

1. This is a British expression which means that the next person in line for the task is the person who has been waiting the longest. It is thus a way of allocating resources based on seniority rather than merit.

accumulation all over the world. Globalization made sure of that. For
the last few years, the pool of the Asian labor reserve being now partly
drained, wages in that region have taken off, rising about 10 percent
per annum over the inflation rate. It must now soon be Buggins's turn
for the European and American semi-skilled.

It is as if the workers of the world had united to achieve equality
among them, with the poorest uplifted and the better off pausing to
wait for the poorest to catch up with them. Meanwhile, the lucky rich
served to bring about the capital accumulation which made the whole
process possible. Their easy rise is now probably also drawing to a less
auspicious close.

HOW JUDO LETS THE WEAK DEFEAT THE STRONG

In the customary mode of class war, organized labor wrestles with capitalist employers by collective bargaining aided by the odd strike or
work-to-rule as well as by using its electoral weight to bend policy so
that it should redistribute income from profits and the rich towards
wages and the poor. Such wrestling is the daily fare of both business
and politics in the developed world, and it is normally successful to
some extent. Diverting income from corporations and the well-to-do
who save much to wage-earners and the needy who save little reduces
the rate at which the capital stock is increasing, and hence also the
rate at which the demand for labor increases, wages rise, and jobs are
created. For a small though immediate victory, labor and the soft Left
trade away the far greater long-run winning trend that would carry
them along to great heights if they gave up the old-fashioned wrestling
for crumbs, yielded in judo fashion to the force of the adversary, and
allowed unfettered capital accumulation to curb the return on capital
and lift the income of the labor it seeks to use.

The unconsciously judo-like tactics of the South Koreans, and of
course the Japanese who started the practice by working merrily on
while they were officially on strike, achieved in two generations a level
well above the highest ambitions of the average European wage earner.

Standard economic history teaches that labor during the Industrial Revolution rose from abject misery and subjection by organizing
and resisting exploitation. It is more plausible to conclude that labor

rose from misery thanks to being too weak to be able to depress high profitability and hence the rapid accumulation of capital. The judo fighter yields to his stronger opponent by calculating design. Labor in nineteenth century Europe and twenty-first century Asia yielded to capital, not by design, but by its intrinsic weakness. Yet the result is much the same. One wonders whether the clamor for social justice can be powerful enough to undo such a slow but benign outcome of the class war.

PART 5

Risks' Return

1. SOLVENCY AND LIQUIDITY: SOME FINANCIAL "CRISES" ARE MORE CRITICAL THAN OTHERS

The eminent American economist Joseph Stiglitz speaks with the authority that a series of glittering appointments, including the Drummond chair at Oxford and the title of chief economist of the World Bank, lend him. His Nobel Prize places him out of range of the everyday technical snipings that economists like to aim at each other. It is a pity that time and again his visceral left-wing convictions get the better of his professional competence. At such junctures, he is fair game. His book[1] on globalization was a case in point.

Recently, Professor Stiglitz accused the financial powers-that-be of hypocrisy[2] for prescribing bitter medicine to the poor when a financial crisis hits them, but treating the rich with the greatest mansuetude when they get into similar trouble. He recalled the draconian measures the IMF imposed upon poor developing countries during the 1997 Asian financial crisis and indignantly compared them with the generous flood of money with which the world's major central banks inundated the banking systems of the rich Western world in 2007. One justice for the rich, another for the poor.

It is an elementary but still useful exercise to sort out the two fundamental variables, solvency and liquidity, that underlie any financial upset, albeit in different proportions.

Solvency is an attribute of a person, firm, or state that in its perfect form signifies the ability to discharge any of its obligations on the date it falls due. It means that the debtor has sufficient assets in cash or in such other forms that can with virtual certainty be converted into

First published by Liberty Fund, Inc., at www.econlib.org on January 7, 2008. Reprinted by permission.

1. Joseph Stiglitz, *Making Globalization Work* (New York: W. W. Norton, 2006).

2. Joseph Stiglitz, *Financial Hypocrisy*, November 13, 2007. Project Syndicate [online] available from http://www.project-syndicate.org/commentary/financial-hypocrisy.

cash by the due date. When sufficient assets are available, but in such forms that converting them into cash on reasonable terms takes longer than required, we may speak of imperfect solvency or temporal insolvency. Temporal insolvency has a probability distribution of the dates on which the asset will be converted into cash; for instance, there may be some probability that it will be sold and the settlement take place within a month after it is put on the market, with the remaining probability being that this will happen within three months. At all events, these contingencies are different from absolute insolvency, when the debtor simply lacks sufficient assets in any form, or when the probability of converting them into cash is very small or very remote in time.

Liquidity is an attribute of assets (though one does say that a firm is very liquid when much of its assets are in cash or quasi-cash). It signifies that the asset has a market with several active or potential participants, and can be instantaneously converted into cash at or just under the market price, or can be bought for cash at or just above the market price. The price at which a buyer will come forth is the Bid and the price to bring forth a seller is the Ask. The measure of liquidity is the inverse of the spread between Bid and Ask. A $100 bill can be sold for $100 and also bought for $100; the Bid-Ask spread is zero and the bill's liquidity is perfect. A widely held share may have a Bid-Ask spread of one-sixteenth of a dollar, a less active one a quarter. Exotic securities may trade at spreads of five percent or more, used cars or secondhand machine tools at thirty or fifty, or indeed at almost any spread into which a clever buyer can talk a hapless seller. They are "liquid" in a strict sense, though it is not reasonable to regard them as liquid. (This is one of the numberless cases where it is reasonable to use the vague word "reasonable," for nothing more precise will suit the case.) Information about the asset will heavily impact on its Bid-Ask spread. The used car, like the pig in a poke, may be very illiquid because too little is known about it. Liquidity, like solvency, also has a temporal dimension: the Bid-Ask spread will normally be highest when sale and settlement must be instantaneous, and will narrow down if the asset can be left in the market for short, medium, or longish periods. Here is one area where solvency and liquidity shade into one another at their margins.

Now we may briefly consider some of Professor Stiglitz's charges. By the time the 1997 crisis set in, certain Asian countries got themselves heavily into short term debt, some of it "hot" money ready to move in or out at electronic speed. Typically, local banks borrowed from Western ones at interbank rates and re-lent the funds to local business which put them into inventories and equipment. The accompanying balance of payment deficit and other signs of overheating then reached a critical point at which all the Western lenders tried to get their money out again. There was at least temporal insolvency, for assets located in Asian countries could not be converted into foreign currency unless long-term foreign capital was streaming into the country. Manifestly, the contrary was the case. An Indonesian timber logging concession did not attract a single foreign bidder at two year's purchase. The IMF had to step in and bail out the Asian countries. The alternative was default and shambles on the 1998 Russian model. It is worth remarking that the Asian countries had positively asked for the IMF to bail them out, and knew the conditions—fiscal austerity, monetary squeeze— they had to accept to get it. Perhaps they should have chosen to default, like Argentina, but that is an entirely different question.

Professor Stiglitz points out that two countries, China and India, remained untouched by the crisis and these were the two countries who had resisted the liberal doctrine and kept controls over capital movements. Now it is true that capital controls should be used when necessary; the word "necessary" tautologically means that this is so. The trouble is that when they become "necessary," it is too late to slap them on, while if they are kept on permanently, they occasion very high permanent costs. They frighten off the inflow of foreign investment. They also cause a trickle of capital outflows by using a variety of devices that nobody has yet found the means to stop. On the whole, liberalization of capital movements seems the better bet. Professor Stiglitz may also be reminded that China and India had truly miserable economies as long as, true to the spirit of Mao in China and the Nehru dynasty in India, they clung to socialist controls and regulations, and did not "take off" until they had begun to scrap them. It is hard to believe that capital controls are the one exception that must not be scrapped.

While the Asian, Russian, and Argentine crises were crises of solvency, the Western financial crisis of 2007–08 is a crisis of liquidity. It is different in kind, and also less critical. It sprang from two sources. One was a bout of perfectly commonplace overlending in the American residential mortgage market. Too many mortgages were written for nearly the full value of houses owned by residents with too low and precarious incomes. Once house prices peaked and started mildly to decline, many of these mortgages were no longer serviced and foreclosure involving heavy loss, or patient waiting for better days, were the lenders' only options. However, all this was, so to speak, in a day's work.

The second source of the crisis that, combined with the first, made an unstable mixture was feverish financial innovation. Two devices proved particularly fragile. One was the creation of "collateralized debt obligations," or CDOs. They gathered essentially illiquid assets, such as residential mortgages, into packages serving as collateral for securities of various yields, maturity dates, and risk profiles. Thus a vast potential market was opened for relatively illiquid assets rendered liquid by presenting them as securities suitable for financial investors seeking particular yields, maturities, and risks. This was undoubtedly a sensible innovation doing good for mortgagors, mortgagees, and third-party investors alike. However, when some mortgages within the collateral package started to turn sour, the CDO would turn to poison, for nobody wanted to hold paper whose quality suddenly proved to be quite uncertain. Lack of adequate information bred suspicion and turned hitherto liquid securities into illiquid ones, unwanted and hard to trade.

All this was exacerbated by another innovative device, the "structured investment vehicle," or SIV, which borrows in the money market and invests the money in higher-yielding securities, including about 55–60 percent in CDOs. When CDOs are suspect, SIVs become suspect and so do the banks which sponsored them or granted them borrowing facilities as a second line of defense.

At the core of this crisis, there is a relatively small dose of insolvency originating in the mortgage market. The layered structure of a highly developed financial system magnifies the effect of a small rotten core by what looks like a double-digit factor. Most of the damage is in the eye of the beholder. If, under such circumstances, losses had to be cut by selling assets that have fallen under suspicion, much damage that is now merely virtual would become real, thus exposing the banking system to needless shock and causing an arbitrary redistribution of wealth in favor of "vultures" of all kinds.

It is, then, neither "hypocrisy" nor partiality for the rich Western countries that makes central banks try and keep interest rates low and pump unprecedented volumes of money into the banking system, but good sense. The crisis needs to be digested, suspicions allayed, adequate information provided and when that is all done, liquidity will be found to have been restored.

2. A TRILLION-DOLLAR "CATASTROPHE"?

The French socialist and corporate lawyer Dominique Strauss-Kahn, as director-general of the International Monetary Fund, has joined the chorus of financial leaders calling for "something" to be done to solve the current banking crisis brought on by the American subprime lending "crisis" which came to a head in August 2007. He has used his position as the head of one of the world's leading financial institutions to utter shrill statements about the "crisis" being grave, very grave indeed, with the worst yet to come. At the IMF, World Bank, and G7 meeting in April 2008, the British Chancellor of the Exchequer went one better, claiming that we were witnessing the greatest economic shock of the last seventy years. The 1973–74 oil shock, the double-digit inflation of the 80s ending in the sharp 1991–92 recession, and the massive destruction of human and material capital in World War II must have slipped from his mind.

One might also distinguish between previous financial problems, such as Argentina's bankruptcy in 1998 and Turkey's overheating in the first years of this century, which are the sort of balance-of-payments problems that might both require and merit lending to them by the International Monetary Fund, and other "crises" which are the result of the loss of confidence in the market. The current "crisis," as every opinion-maker persists in calling it, is primarily the latter kind, one of loss of confidence. Financial markets are inherently skittish. However, all markets, even skittish ones, have self-healing capacities and the more highly developed they are, the more reliably these capacities restore a market to equilibrium. Cool and masterful action by central banks can be an additional help. What does not help is voluble and excited talk by authorities who should know better than to stir up panic among banks and institutions under their tutelage who are frightened enough without being told that Judgment Day is nigh.

First published by Liberty Fund, Inc., at www.econlib.org on May 5, 2008. Reprinted by permission.

Nor is it helpful for the self-healing process that greater and lesser authorities, and indeed all self-appointed experts who manage to get quoted in the media, keep calling for "coordinated global action," though there is no chance whatever of such a thing even if it meant anything specific. Trying to stave off the havoc they imagine to loom on the horizon, they sow the panic that might make it into a real danger. Draconian FASB accounting standards force financial institutions to mark down certain types of assets in ways that undermine such market prices they might otherwise reasonably command, and thus create a need for further cumulative markdowns. Under public pressure to "show it all," banks are deprived of the discretion that commonsense "prudent man" conduct would leave them. Looking weaker than they really are, and anticipating tighter regulation, they feel vulnerable to loss of confidence of their depositors and of the interbank market, and so they restrict lending. All in all, busybody babble, officious interference, and the urge to impose order on passing turbulence are helping to bring about the very effect they profess to dread. After the 1929 crash, much the same administrative ineptitude and busybodiness, plus a suicidal attack of trade protectionism, helped to deepen and prolong the Great Depression. That chapter of history is quite unlikely to repeat itself, but some high officials and august institutions seem to be having a good try at making it do so.

The IMF now estimates the losses from the subprime mortgage mistakes at $565 billion and from its secondary effects at another $380 billion, or a total of $945 billion. As they are presumably still counting, one might safely round the total to one trillion dollars. The sum does sound catastrophic, and the media chatter does present it as such. It is not. If it were really a loss to the world economy, it would be a bit of a shock, but not a catastrophic one. However, most if not all of the trillion dollars is only a loss to one side in a zero-sum game; it is a gain to the other side. If the mortgagee lends too much on a house to the mortgagor, the latter gains what the former loses; the house itself suffers no material damage. If the mortgagee escapes the loss by having the mortgage "packaged" with many others in a "collateralized debt obligation" that is passed on to some institutional or private buyer, it is the buyer who takes the loss if some of the mortgages in the CDO turn out to be worth less than their face value. There may be a whole chain of buyers sharing in the loss. Some in the chain may even gain. The whole process of securitizing a mortgage serves to transform it into marketable form, so that various cocktails of mortgages end up in hands that are willing to carry a given default risk for the lowest payment and are also willing and able to assess the risk. It is on the latter score that much error and negligence occurred because the old adage of caveat emptor was taken too lightly. If there is a remedy against that, it is not more severe regulation of financial transactions, but the painful lesson taught by burnt fingers.

Needless to say, even a zero-sum game can have substantial economic effects if the gains and losses, though cancelling themselves out, are big enough. The resulting redistribution of the stock of wealth, however, is partly a matter of luck and its effects must be a matter of guesswork. What is fairly predictable, though, is the impact of the event itself that triggers off the "trillion-dollar catastrophe" in the first place. In the subprime context, the event was the downturn in business and residential property prices in the U.S., the U.K., Spain, and Ireland. Besides hitting those who bought or lent on property and benefiting those who sold or mortgaged theirs just before the downturn, property owners as a whole suffered a paper loss on their holdings, as did owners of equity securities in the ensuing stock market decline in late 2007 and the first part of 2008. This "wealth effect" on spending is no doubt negative, but it is hardly catastrophic and given the puny personal savings ratios in the U.S. and the U.K., somewhat slower consumer spending may not be an unmixed evil.

However, the jump from predicting mundane and ultimately quite moderate economic changes to apocalyptic visions is a long one. Mr. George Soros is certainly one of the most successful speculators of recent decades; his long and spectacular run of winning bets must owe more to talent than to blind luck. His repeated attempts at earning intellectual fame with books explaining financial markets in near-mystic terms are on the whole less successful. He likes to conclude that capital is too mobile for its and the economy's own good, that financial movements are self-reinforcing and self-destructive rather than self-equilibrating, and that more and better regulation is imperative. In his latest book, *The New Paradigm of Financial Markets: The Credit Crisis of*

2008, he lays great stress on the danger of a swelling volume of credit derivatives. He puts the outstanding volume of credit default swaps at $45 trillion; since he wrote his book, they have risen to $62 trillion (yes, $62,000 billion). But despite the implied suggestion of an exploding economic universe, the astronomical number need not frighten us. These swaps are in essence bets on loans and bonds being or not being duly repaid. Every bet made on some outcome is necessarily matched by a bet taken on it. A given outcome has no effect on net wealth, though it does redistribute it. Banks should normally be net winners of the process just as bookmakers are net winners at the races, except when they act as punters. Some banks apparently did so act recently, and their bets did not pay off. However, none crashed and no depositors lost their deposits.

The redistribution of wealth engineered by credit and equity derivatives is voluntary, for it is the result of every player freely taking the risk he runs to earn some expected reward. Public opinion, the media, and the authorities condemn this voluntary redistribution with horrified indignation. Involuntary redistribution by taxation, on the other hand, earns overt or at least tacit approval.

Meanwhile, after the trillion-dollar horse has bolted, preparations are in full swing to lock the stable door. Banks have just about adjusted to Basel II regulators, and will apparently soon be confronted with proposals for a new set of more stringent constraints. One characteristically paternalistic object would be to make sure that there will never again be a trillion-dollar loss to the system, and never mind the trillion-dollar gain. It is to be feared that such new regulations would induce disintermediation and hence hinder efficient outcomes. This adverse effect, however, might last only as long as it took all interested parties to learn to get round the regulations. Even the cleverest regulation is no real substitute for the more flexible and discretionary common sense of the "prudent man" rules that financial institutions must observe in order to build and preserve the reputations upon which their future livelihood essentially depends. It is not more regulation but less that would spur confidence-dependent financial institutions to follow the "prudent man" rules, each in its own fashion, flashy or staid, to suit client preferences and needs.

3. BANK DEBT, SOVEREIGN DEBT, AND
THE DOGS THAT DID NOT BARK

Hybrid economies and hybrid banking systems, halfway between free market and command-and-control, have gotten us into trouble in 2008. Pundit opinion is near-unanimous that it is markets that are at fault and we must move towards more command-and-control, if not do away with capitalism altogether. Should we not think about going the other way instead?

Maurice Allais, one of only two French Nobel prize winners in economics, is a champion mathematician but has rather less time for plain horse sense. He considers, for example, that banks should be obliged to match the maturities of their assets to their liabilities. If they make a one-year loan, they must set it off by a deposit fixed for one year. Thus banks will always be safe havens.

The truth of the matter, of course, is that a bank is a bank if it borrows short and lends long. If this were prohibited in the sacred name of security, the clever innovations of Italian Renaissance goldsmiths and seventeenth century English wool merchants would have been for nothing. To be able to borrow short a lot and do so at little cost, they must be above all suspicion like Caesar's wife. Ordinary profit-maximization ("greed," as we are now asked to call it) would induce them to look prudent and opulent and selective in the risks they take. (Compulsory deposit insurance is the first link in a chain of regulatory measures that reduce the need to look prudent and selective.) Despite the confidence a bank may manage to inspire at some cost to itself, it still needs some ready reserve in hand to meet large cash withdrawals. The reserve may be minute, because if one bank is running short of money, others must be running long by roughly the same amount, and the first bank can borrow it back on the interbank market. This remains

First published by Liberty Fund, Inc., at www.econlib.org on October 4, 2010. Reprinted by permission.

true, and liquidity is not a problem of availability and willing help by the lender of last resort, but only of cost as long as unreasoning general panic does not overcome all confidence. Depositors nowadays do not take home billions in plastic grocery bags.

General panic hits solvency rather than liquidity (though the two shade into one another and cannot really be separated). When professional pundits are influential and the media are loud and both live by chilling our blood, general panics may become more frequent. Such a panic was set off in August 2007 by inordinately blowing up the dangers to the world financial system inherent in a mere $400 to $600 billion of securities backed by U.S. subprime mortgages. On these mortgages, the lending banks might have recognized some losses depending on the likely recovery value of the ones that failed. Transformed into marketable securities, they might have fallen under the FASB regulations, "marked to market," and as the market was both inexperienced and spooked, the carnage among banks holding, or even suspected of holding, CDOs (collateralized debt obligations) was gory—as we remember.[1] Paper losses were estimated in astronomical numbers and denials were disbelieved; prophecies of doom were, in the nature of the case, self-fulfilling. Banks were said to be casinos, bankers bashed as greedy thieves. Many were in fact a bit foolish and dim, relying on the rating agencies[2] and the regulations that would protect them from anything really bad. Many or most were solvent in reality while the accounting rules and the house-of-cards character of artificial safeguards struck them down as insolvent.

This inglorious tale began with a moderate house price bubble blown up by cheap money, continued with government encouragement of mortgage lending to credit-unworthy debtors, and finished by governments saving the banking system from insolvency with cash in-

1. The Financial Accounting Standards Board (FASB) is a private organization selected by the Security and Exchange Commission to develop accounting standards for U.S. corporations. "Mark to market" is an accounting practice used to value assets and liabilities by using the current market price of these assets and liabilities. "Collateralized debt obligations" are securities based upon a portfolio of fixed income-producing assets, such as home mortgages.

2. Such as Moody's or Standard and Poor's.

jections that totaled vastly more than the likely loss of value of the part of the housing stock that was "in hock" to the banking system. All this was volubly explained as the result of insufficient regulation of an inherently unstable free market system. Blaming the result on excessive regulation and interference sounds no less likely and no more capable of proof.

The received wisdom now is that the banks did not have enough capital. The new Basel III regulations will oblige them progressively to raise their solvency ratio from an average of 4 percent of total liabilities to 7 percent.[3] If their own capital remained unchanged, they would have to cut their lending and other asset holdings practically by half to get from 4 to 7 percent of own capital—an absurd result. Instead, they will have to raise new capital by siphoning it away from the non-bank sector of the economy—a result that governments must dread only a little less than a savage reduction of bank credit to the economy. The irony is that if another "bubble" rose up and then burst, banks with 7 percent of their own capital could become technically insolvent almost as easily as with 4 percent, and would in any event find themselves in breach of regulations as their solvency ratio started to shrink from 7 percent towards zero.

One way out of these dilemmas could be to forget about Basel III and the rest of the rigmarole of controls and leave it to the banks' discretion to adapt their posture to the conditions of survival dictated by the market. There would be casualties, but the net outcome might be much better.

After the banks, the forthcoming chapter is on sovereign debt. The yield on German ten-year government bonds is now 2.2 percent, on French ones about 2.6 percent, and on U.S. treasuries about the same, all absurdly low even if the world were heading toward the mother of all depressions. In the 1930–34 Great Depression, the ten-year rate moved in a range between 3 percent and 4.5 percent. Currently, Irish and Portuguese government bonds yield nearly 6 percent and so do in-

---

3. The Basel III accords were established in September 2010 by the Basel Committee on Banking Supervision. The committee organizes meetings which are attended by the finance ministers of the G20 group of industrialized and developing nations and by the governors of their central banks.

vestment quality European corporate bonds. European common stocks sell at twelve times current earnings, which translates into an earnings yield of 8.5. These yields, taken together, tell a strange story. Something looks very wrong. Government debt is unlike bank debt, and indeed any other private debt, in that the debtor is sovereign and cannot be hauled into any bankruptcy court. It is backed by no assets except the government's ability, often severely limited, to tax its subjects. It can always service the debt it owes in its own currency by printing more money, but foreign currency debt owing to non-residents is more problematic, particularly if its balance of payments is also uncomfortable. Much the same is true of euro debt owed by Eurozone countries that have no way of printing more of it for their own use. If the debtor government services such debt, it is because it wishes to. The consequences of defaulting on the debt are unpleasant and boil down mainly to trade finance and future government borrowing becoming difficult and extremely expensive. Russia in 1998 and Argentina in 2001 nevertheless defaulted and in later years made mostly good on their obligations without lasting damage to themselves.

Greece in 2009 might well have defaulted, abandoning the euro and adopting the old drachma again at a deeply depreciated rate. There were some fairly good reasons for taking this course. It was pre-empted by the richer European countries bailing out Greece in the last minute with loans costing only a charitable 5.5 percent and no doubt destined to be rolled over in some fashion as they fall due. The ostensible reason for bailing out Greece was to forestall domino effects, with Portugal, Ireland, Spain, and (rather unlikely) even Italy defaulting, abandoning the euro and engaging in competitive devaluations. The real reason probably was and remains officialdom's fear of the unknown, of what might happen if market forces are "let loose."

Like the banking "crisis," the sovereign debt "crisis" can be ascribed to many complicated reasons that still leave certain aspects unanswered. One of these is the question: Now that things have gone this far, why were no countervailing forces set off to slow them down and at least mitigate the "crisis"? Why did things reach crisis level before anybody noticed how bad they were?

A story will furnish, not the full answer, but an inkling of it. A man had a dog. The dog, having in his genes the job of guarding the house, broke into furious barking each time someone passed outside along the fence. The excited barking drove the master mad; he was losing his sleep and the neighbors were also complaining. He undertook to teach the dog better manners, punishing him if he barked before some stranger actually started to fiddle with the front door. The training worked well enough and the master was never disturbed by barking before the break-in was definitely in progress.

The dog had been treated and trained as European (particularly German) culture and official practice treat the speculator. Selling "short," i.e., without prior ownership, is severely frowned upon and, for government and certain financial securities, periodically prohibited. Using derivatives except for bona fide insurance is regarded as devilry itself. In fact, any purchase and any sale in anticipation of an up or down price movement is loudly condemned as immoral and threatened with sanctions ranging from punitive taxation to ostracism by peers and denunciation by the press. Mr. Volcker is telling the banks that they must choose between banking and speculating.

There is little excuse for failing to understand that since the speculator must sell high and buy low, if he is successful he must willy-nilly attenuate price movements that would take place if he were not speculating. In other words, if he survives, he must have an albeit involuntary stabilizing effect. Moreover, as he adopts the "long" or "short" position that will in due course yield him a profit when it is undone, he acts as an early warning siren that, like the barking of the dog, signals that something may be amiss and needs attention. It is a pity that like the dog that is bred to bark but punished when he does, the speculator is so unanimously condemned for doing what the market calls upon him to do. But then we do not trust markets, do we?

Is Standard & Poor's, the venerable debt-rating agency, a weapon of mass destruction reminiscent of the pre–Iraq War of George W. Bush and, like that phantom WMD, perhaps a merely imagined one? The answer is not easy to call, and has some relevance to how we should evaluate the strident demands for more and more regulation to correct alleged market failures.

After some early warnings in the new year of 2012, Standard & Poor's, in a massive artillery barrage, downgraded the debt rating of nine of the seventeen member states of the Eurozone, some of them by as many as two notches. It did so on a Friday evening, and the majority of the media promised a bloodbath in the bond and stock markets for the following Monday. There was no bloodbath. If anything, markets were firmer. Manifestly, a downgrade by one of the two dominant rating agencies is either a nonevent—which sounds very unlikely—or the nasty, wicked "speculators" have fully anticipated the downgrade and priced it into the markets well before it has actually taken place.

The spectacular mass reduction in the estimated creditworthiness of the majority of Eurozone countries has set off a storm of furious indignation and cranky proposals. Some of these were laughable, some dangerous. It was said that private debt could well be rated by private agencies, but public debt must be assessed by a public body—needless to say, a democratic one. An earlier proposal by the Brussels bureaucracy that the EU should establish its own rating agency to "break the monopoly" of the private ones was also revived. Many voices from the continent of Europe trotted out the truly lunatic conspiracy theory that the rating agencies, being undeniably "Anglo-Saxon," are promoting the interests of the U.S.A. and Britain who want to break the euro which, if it survives, would threaten the "ultraliberal" domination of the dollar.

First published by Liberty Fund, Inc., at www.econlib.org on February 6, 2012. Reprinted by permission.

Defenders of the agencies say that blaming them for the bad news they spread is to blame the thermometer for showing the patient's fever. This, however, is to draw a false analogy; for what the agencies announce is not a fact, such as the temperature, but their estimate of the probability that the patient will die prematurely, i.e., that the debtor state will default on interest or principal at or before the due date. Seen in this light, downgrading is not malevolent or outrageous, but logically correct. Only four countries in the Eurozone—Germany, Finland, Luxembourg, and the Netherlands—are judged by s&p to merit the top AAA grade, and even that may be a shade too generous, for the probability of default is, strictly speaking, never zero. AA is about as good as any long-term state obligation may possibly deserve. Where s&p is clearly blameworthy is the timing of the mass downgrade. In year after year of ominous overspending, the notes of most of the euro states were left peaceably unaltered, only to be brutally cut just when all these states seem to be more or less convincingly scrambling to change their ways and reduce their unsustainable budget deficits. Why downgrade them now when it was not appropriate to do so while they were still spending as if there were no tomorrow, and piling up the debt was only for petty, mean-spirited accountants to worry about?

A classic fairness rule holds that you must never kick a man when he is down. An eminent historian of ideas, John Plamenatz, once said in my hearing that this rule was typical of the silly English, for the man being down was obviously the most convenient time for kicking him. s&p must implicitly believe that this is so.

One downgrade that really looks shockingly timed is the lowering of Italy by two notches to BBB. Italy, in the last years of the shaming monkey-circus that was the Berlusconi era, was (as the unforgettable Lena Horne used to sing) "lying face down in the gutter" and seemed not even to mind it too much. During these inglorious years, its rating remained intact. When late in 2011 it became obvious that Italy's national debt was too much for her national income to carry, the incorrigible Berlusconi was forced to resign and was replaced by severely serious Mario Monti who, with admirable courage that only a non-elected statesman can afford, produced an admirable program of structural reforms. They fully deserve the hate-word "ultraliberal," though the author and the habitual readers of this column would be more comfortable with calling it simply "liberal" in the original freedom-of-contract sense of the word. If Mario Monti can defeat organized labor and the vested interests of business and the professions, Italy should have a brilliant future over the next few decades. It seems monstrous, then, that s&p is kicking Italy, not when she is still lying face down in the gutter, but when she is bravely scrambling to get back on her feet.

Does such infamy help to make the case for the bizarre Brussels proposal to regulate the rating agencies to have some public control over what they may or may not say about the creditworthiness of sovereign states? Such regulation would be a good way for ensuring that nobody paid any attention anymore to what they did say.

If a rating downgrade lastingly depresses the price of sovereign debt, *then* it is a self-fulfilling prophecy, for it makes the refinancing of its maturing chunks of the debt more expensive, hence the budget deficit larger than it would have been if the rating agency had kept quiet. It is, therefore, a WMD. However, since rating agencies will almost necessarily be created in a free market, and their self-fulfilling prophecy spoils the natural scheme of things and makes for market failure, such agencies ought to be outlawed or severely regulated. This, in a nutshell, is the view of much of the Brussels bureaucracy and of semi-educated European commentators. It is becoming parrot talk.

Remember, however, that the rating is not fact-finding, but a forecast. It is a judgment inspired by facts, like any other forecast. There are literally hundreds of such forecasts flooding the public forum every month, poured out by the OECD, the IMF, the ECB, the Brussels Commission, government agencies, universities, non-profit research organizations, and private consultants. Many of them employ more economic brainpower than s&p or Moody's. The institutional investors who make the bond markets routinely take some notice of the forthcoming forecasts. The cleverest among them may even anticipate the rating agencies, selling bonds prior to a downgrade and buying them back after it. But no market participant has good cause to believe that the agencies are any more prescient than the other forecasters. Why, then, do we assume that they are more powerful than the average of the others?

Much of the answer lies in one word: they have an *ally*. It is a non-market one, not a spontaneous growth but a political and institutional artifact: a legal rule, or self-regulation adopted to forestall it. Governments, believing that they are doing good, forbid certain types of investors, notably pension funds and insurance companies, to buy and hold debt securities that the agencies do not rate highly enough. Even nonregulated funds will conform to such rules because the fund manager may be more interested in looking prudent and blameless in case of accidents than in maximizing the return to the fund's owners. Such principal-agent conflicts may be the secondary effects of government regulation.

Once a country's sovereign debt comes to be graded below the critical level set by regulation, or even threatens to be set below it, the regulated funds must liquidate their holdings as an automatic knee-jerk reaction. The market, in other words, is artificially programmed as a safety-first mechanism and not, as a flawless market is supposed to act, a mechanism for balancing risk against reward, as risk and reward are perceived from day to day by the marginal buyers and sellers who are trying to do the best they can and are under no constraint to jump when the rating agencies say "jump." The ones who jump mostly do so, not because they fear the agencies as weapons of mass destruction, but because the regulators say so and public opinion discourages contrarian judgment.

5. NED LUDD, HANDLOOM WEAVING, AND FRANCO-GERMAN MORAL BANKING

When the steam-driven loom was replacing handicrafts in Britain and the handloom weavers were losing their livelihood, they were led by Ned Ludd into desperate acts of machine-wrecking. Their rebellion would today be called "industrial action" in English and "social movement" in French. Political correctness being unknown at the time, the Luddites were brutally repressed by the British Army in 1812. The choice was between appeasement and drastic suppression. Appeasement would have violated the liberty of manufacturers to employ any method of production they saw fit on any terms they could agree with the workers they needed—a principle that looks harsh but which is the one sure way of radical long-term improvement in real wages and the condition of the working class. Moreover, appeasement and the consequent setback to the rise of British industrial power was unthinkable at a time when, just prior to the Battle of Leipzig, Napoleon still looked like he was winning and Britain was straining every nerve to bring the Second Hundred Years' War against France to its successful conclusion in 1815.

Today's banker-bashing and the clamor for "taming" the financial services industry bears some, but only some, resemblance to the Luddite movement of two centuries ago. The main difference is that while the early Luddites faced a single-minded government, today's banker-bashers and would-be system reformers have the political authorities mostly on their side. Except for a tiny minority, French educated opinion has never understood how an economy worked, and if it did not, why it did not. French governments have long been notorious for administering heavy doses of policy medicines that were worse than the disease. This was the main visible reason why France, superbly endowed

First published by Liberty Fund, Inc., at www.econlib.org on January 4, 2010. Reprinted by permission.

with all that it takes to make a country rich and its economy to grow vigorously, has been a laggard since about 1975. The French government is now deeply convinced that the 2008–09 economic upset was due to the moral depravity, the devilish complication, and the unregulated excesses of the modern financial services. They conform to what Paris calls the "Anglo-Saxon model." Systemic salvation lies in its replacement by a strictly regulated "European model" in which banking serves the "real economy," by which Paris understands physical production with tangible capital and honest labor, rather than the shuffling of fancy paper. It fails to grasp that fancy paper is shuffled because it represents title to real things, and it is more efficient to shuffle it than to physically move tangible goods from one owner or one debtor to another.

Though it has started to emancipate itself in many ways, in the matter of financial services Berlin has fallen back into the bad habits, first acquired under Konrad Adenauer, of following the lead of Paris. French aversion to Anglo-American ways sits well with German ideals of seriousness, middle-class virtues, and middle-of-the-road solutions. When Germany and France are allied, they invariably get their way in common European policy-making (though Europe being what it is, it usually does not make much difference that they do). Germany and France both wanted a far-reaching re-regulation of the banking, insurance, and securities industry. Now they have got their way to some limited and as yet uncertain extent, aided by the singular ineptitude of London, the natural opponent of Luddite propensities.

The Lisbon Treaty has created two make-believe posts, namely a president of the council of ministers and a minister of foreign affairs, to head the equally make-believe government of Europe. Neither post has any real power. The British government has campaigned for Tony Blair to be the president and when that attempt fell through, it used the consolation prize offered to it on a platter to take the foreign minister's post for a harmless and low-profile Englishwoman. Henceforth it is she who will inaugurate all-European flower shows and countless summit meetings. The British choice left the road open for a French nominee to get one of the three or four posts of commissioners with real power, the commissioner for the internal market who is responsible for the regulation of financial services.

Two strident reactions followed. One was by French president Sarkozy, whose words often run ahead of his thoughts and who declared that this is a triumph of the European over the Anglo-Saxon model of capitalism. The other reaction came from the City of London and the press, where the French move was seen as a plot to cripple the competitive abilities of the British banking and securities industry and to help realize the old French dream, first articulated by Valery Giscard-d'Estaing, of making Paris the top financial center of Europe. Naturally, nothing the internal market commissioner can do could possibly bring this dream any nearer to reality. What it could do, though, is to wreak havoc with the whole European banking and securities industry just as the Luddites tried to wreck the modern machinery to weave cloth.

If the Franco-German conceptions of a more "moral," safer, and more bureaucratic banking really prevailed, London would suffer more than the rest, part of its people and their business emigrating to New York, Geneva, Hong Kong, and Singapore. Oddly enough, some of the British authorities seem almost to want this result, finding that the city is "too big" and of doubtful "social usefulness" (to quote the governor of the Bank of England). The primary targets of pruning would be investment banking and fund management.

These are the parts of the industry that have done most to provoke the indignation and fury of public and official opinion by their wholly outlandish system of astronomic salaries and bonuses which they are now defending by tooth and claw. Admittedly, football players and pop stars earn as much or more, but they entertain the public, while investment bankers and fund managers do not. Their remunerations defy the laws of supply and demand and are incomprehensible to outsiders (including the writer of this column), but interfering with them is unlikely to work, easy to evade, and may do more harm than good. Like many other absurdities, banking bonuses may eventually fall victim to normal economic forces. Until they do, however, banking will remain the industry everybody loves to hate, and will be poorly placed to defend itself against counter-productive attempts to overregulate it.

Other than "pruning" investment banking, Franco-German inspired regulation is likely to focus on solvency and on the whole modern generation of innovative financial products. Banks are already under pressure to increase their solvency ratios, and it would not be surprising if the present standards of about 8 percent of a bank's "risk-weighted" liabilities being their own capital were gradually raised to 10 or even 12 percent. Skeptics would remark that in case there is a "meltdown" in the market for one major asset class, such as mortgages, a few percent more or less of their own capital will not make the difference between solvency and insolvency, while a more massive increase in solvency ratios would suck the rest of the economy dry of capital, for far too much would be needed to fill up bank balance sheets. The only way out for the banks is to de-leverage, shrink their balance sheets to make their existing capital amount to a higher percentage of it. This result, which some authorities seem to want, is achieved by restricting credit—the "credit crunch" the authorities untiringly condemn.

The other main target area of regulation is bound to be all the recent innovative financial products. They include the transformation of non-marketable into marketable assets by securitization, as well as such derivatives as credit default swaps, put and call options, currency and commodity futures, and interest rate swaps. Their common function is to help distribute risk by creating instruments for insuring against it and for underwriting the insurance. They also serve as more efficient vehicles for the speculation that everybody bitterly hates and wants to eradicate, failing to understand that its function is to smooth out price fluctuations by buying low and selling high, thus pulling the price up in the trough and pushing it down at the peak. If it does the opposite, it bankrupts itself.

It is a sad commentary on our economic intelligence that we expect the regulators to order it to heel for being "destabilizing" as well as for being an offshoot of "immoral capitalism."

In his classic essay "What Is Seen and What Is Not Seen" (written in 1848 and published in July 1850), the shamefully underrated and neglected French economist Frédéric Bastiat (1801–50)[1] declares that what distinguishes a bad economist from a good one is that the bad one can see only what is to be seen, while the good one also discerns the as yet unseen consequences that are bound to follow the visible effect of an action. Present benefits must be painfully paid for in future costs, while present sacrifices tend to be generously rewarded in the future. The good economist must, of course, weigh up the merits of a law, a policy, or an institution by taking account both of the effects he (and others) can see and the future consequences he foresees (and others do not).

Stated this way, there is a built-in test that makes it very easy to tell the good economist from the bad one: we only have to watch the consequences as they emerge with the passage of time. Events will show up what the bad economist has overlooked and what the good one has correctly foretold.

Bastiat, in his summary introduction, states the problem in terms of a choice (to change something or to keep it the way it is) and the future, as yet unseen consequences of that choice. However, the choice also involves another, different implication that is unseen but, unlike the one that will emerge in the future, is condemned to remain unseen. For the choice of a law, a policy, or an institution has one effect that is not seen but will be, and another—namely, the future state of affairs—that *would have* prevailed had that choice not been made. This is the state of affairs that we forgo, that might have come about but did not, "what we do not see" and never will. It is what in modern economics is called

First published by Liberty Fund, Inc., at www.econlib.org on February 1, 2010. Reprinted by permission.

1. Bastiat's essay, "What Is Seen and What Is Not Seen," is available at the Library of Economics and Liberty: http://www.econlib.org/library/Bastiat/basEss1.html.

opportunity cost that the bad economist tends to ignore and the good one can only approximate by educated guesses, intelligent conjectures. Though Bastiat does not explicitly mention it in his summary of "what is seen and what is not seen," most of his examples also deal with "what might have been." It is probably fair to credit Bastiat with the discovery of the concept of opportunity cost.

When by mid-2008 near-hysterical panic-mongering got the better of a banking system that was admittedly overextended, but that by its very nature cannot resist a collapse of confidence even if it is ever so well capitalized to start with, governments guaranteed countless billions of bank assets and injected countless millions of equity and loan capital into key banks. Much of this money has since been repaid with ample interest. Some of it remains tied up in rather messy situations, but the operation as a whole, despite strident cries about the taxpayer having to rescue the fat cat bankers, will probably at least break even. The banking system, though a bit shaken, was saved. The opportunity cost—between five and ten major European banks being temporarily unable to repay deposits (especially the large and volatile wholesale deposits of institutions) on demand—might have been higher than the cost of government intervention. The rescue thus looks well worth it, though some diehard critics think letting big banks fail would have had salutary long-run effects.

The parallel operation of propping up the economy by raising public spending is, contrary to average opinion, less evidently justified. The major European states will have run deficits of 8 to 12 percent of GDP between 2008 and 2011 if not beyond. The effects on the national debt and the budgetary strain of servicing it looks too frightening to contemplate. That problem, however, is outside the scope of this essay.

The court of popular opinion has irrevocably judged that all the havoc, disorder, and misery is the fault of the banks and the greedy bankers running them. Though it should know better, educated opinion has rallied to this judgment and is busily engaged in explaining how the financial system has caused the "crisis" and how radical "systemic change" is needed to prevent another one before we know where we are.

Most of these reformers seem to want a tame, playing-by-the-book banking system that turns its back on innovation, wizardry, own-account trading, derivatives, securitization, and the financing of buy-outs and corporate wheeling-dealing. Instead, it should limit itself to the routine financing of the production of "real," tangible goods and earn only moderate, "morally acceptable" profits. It would be a nice research project to try and estimate the opportunity cost of this reform program. If it is carried out, which the baying of the revenge-hungry renders very probable, two functions of the system will be impaired: the smooth and audacious reallocation of capital in response to changing profit prospects, and the reallocation of risk from where it arises to where it is most readily borne. The opportunity cost of the reform is the enhanced efficiency that these functions would ensure if they were left unimpaired—an efficiency that "is not seen."

The most ominous of the reformers, however, seek reform of the financial system not by stricter regulation and moral suasion, though they are in no wise against these things. What they propose is a radical shortcut: they want simply to weed out the part of the financial system that is *not socially useful.*

It is the gut feeling of many that the proper function of the economy is to supply the population with wholesome homegrown food, no-nonsense long-life garments, and decent housing. The rest, the services sector, is debatable. Public services, mainly law and order, health care, and what goes by the courtesy title of "education," are more or less all right. Beyond these, however, what is left is what Harold Wilson, an inglorious British Labour leader and prime minister of the 1970s, called the "candyfloss economy." As the name tells us, it is not "socially useful." Hence it must be a candidate for weeding out.

No lesser authority than the governor of the Bank of England has publicly suggested that the British financial services sector is *too big* and it would be a good thing to cut it back to size. Liberal economists and philosophers must be shaking their heads in troubled disbelief. In what sense, in what perspective is an industry "too big" if, taking good years with bad, it is vastly profitable and is getting bigger?

A service is profitable if Everyman, the businessman and the final consumer, buys it. Buying it is the one indisputable way he has to show that he *wants* it. But Superman is unimpressed by what Everyman wants. He wishes Everyman to get what he *needs.* For only what he needs is "socially useful."

Superman, looking on from his lofty perspective, has a shrewd idea of what is socially useful. A true humanist, he would gladly give Everyman the chance to help define it, but the latter can only speak by spending his euros and dollars. That, as we have seen, merely expresses wants, not needs, and in any case some have more of it and hence speak louder than others—on both these counts, it just won't do. It remains for Superman to speak all by himself for Everyman.

Superman, of course, is not only the governor of the Bank of England, but all those who have the supreme arrogance to assume the role, as well as the chance or the sharp elbow to occupy the pulpit. The last time such men and women could actually decide what was socially useful, what was to be weeded out, and what was to be fostered and expanded, was when they were members of the Central Committee of the Communist Party of the Soviet Union. The reader will perhaps join me in trusting that history is not getting ready, in some less odious disguise, to repeat itself.

PART 6

Cheap Talk as a Weapon
of Mass Destruction

1. CHEAP TALK, A WEAPON OF MASS DESTRUCTION: ASSET VALUES, EXPECTATIONS, AND THE APOCALYPSE

Complex questions of biochemistry are usually discussed by biochemists and those in civil engineering by civil engineers. For discussing the economy, the news media offer their columns and screens to anybody, or nearly so. The main qualifications are an acquaintance with the current buzzwords, a glib tongue, and a store of explanations of what has happened and threatens to happen that can rouse enough readers and viewers to indignation and dread of the future. Media men need not know much, but they know that good news is no news.

Cheap talk about the economy these days revolves around two topics. One is the "abject failure of neo-liberalism, capitalist free-for-all, and Thatcherism." Since World War II, but even more painfully since the demise of the Soviet Union, all on the Left were forced silently to suffer derisive comments about socialism that does not work and capitalism that does. Their halfhearted mutterings about social justice and inequality were swept aside with the reminder that it was capitalism that has lifted over a billion Third World people out of poverty. Now, however, the tables were at last turned. Subprime mortgages were worthless, asset-based securities were "toxic," banks were falling like ninepins, and stock markets had no bottom. Deregulation proved to be irresponsible and gave free rein to bankers' greed. Governments had to step in at every turn to shore up the rickety edifice.

The other central topic of cheap talk is the dreadfulness of the recession that is now enveloping the world (for has the IMF not reduced its 2009 world growth forecast from 5 to 3 percent?). Parallels between the present and the Great Depression that broke out in 1929 are made. The U.S. economy may still be growing, much as a dead man's nails

First published by Liberty Fund, Inc., at www.econlib.org on October 21, 2008. Reprinted by permission.

keep growing for a little while, but the U.K., Germany, and France are already in recession and worse is to be expected. Most disturbingly, China is slowing down; the government expects only 9 percent growth for 2009.

(It is interesting to reflect on the ways the same statistics can be put before the public. French GDP was reported down 0.3 percent for the second quarter of 2008 and was forecast to fall by 0.1 percent in the third and fourth quarters. This has set off shrieks of horror and despair by the commentators. The general public took its cue from them. One wonders what would have been the reaction if the report had stated that output in the second quarter was 99.7 percent of that of a year ago and was expected to rise to 99.9 percent in the next two quarters. Likewise, unemployment in 2009 is likely to rise by 2 percentage points—something deeply to be regretted. But would it sound just as ominous to be told that the payroll of the representative firm will decrease from 100 to 98?)

Needless to say, the round-the-clock barrage of half-literate panic-mongering can hardly fail to have some self-fulfilling effect. Told again and again that it may be 1929 all over again, though it is more likely to be just a very nasty recession, any businessman may feel duty bound to defer his expansion plans, for even a small probability of a 1929-type collapse will drastically reduce the (probability-weighted) expected value of his project. It must be added that while central banks all over the world have been busily cutting their discount rates and helping to push up bond prices, the near-collapse of stock prices is acting in the opposite direction and on a vaster scale. It is ironic to note that while government, through the central banks, is pushing both short and, indirectly, long bond prices upward, the most fervent advocates of government action are pushing stock prices downward by their rumor-mongering about the fragility of financial institutions (a perfectly self-fulfilling prophecy and cheap to spread, too) and by the talk of "the worst is yet to come."

Warren Buffett, the most successful investor alive, calls financial derivatives "weapons of mass destruction." Much could be said about their effects. However, their destructive power, massive as it can be, is as nothing to that of cheap talk.

From January 1 to October 10, 2008, the stock market valuation of all listed European companies was roughly halved — an apocalyptic result. How can European business be worth half of what it was less than a year ago?

By rational calculus, a company's equity is valued by the marginal holder as the sum of all future net profits discounted to the present at his private discount rate. The latter, in turn, is the riskless pure interest rate (e.g., the yield of long Treasury bonds) plus a subjective risk premium he needs to compensate him for the possibility that future profit may not be as good as he expects. This premium is a bit too much like "double jeopardy," or two hits for one fault, for his sum of expected future profits must be a composite of alternative likelihoods, the certainty equivalent of good, bad, and middling profit figures, which allows for bad outcomes. However, let that pass. It may be noted that the present value of the stock will be greater if seven fat years are expected to be followed by seven lean ones than if the lean years come first and the fat ones later. In any case it is barely thinkable, to put it mildly, that either the discount rate, or the sum of probability-weighted future profits, or their time pattern between fat and lean years, or all three together, should change sufficiently in less than a year to cut the value of all European companies by half. Can we all be out of our minds?

The answer is, maybe we are. Economics offers a sort of possible explanation by using the concept of "elasticity of expectations." Suppose that an asset is priced at 100 today and we expect it to be priced the same 100 in the near future. If the actual price falls to 90 and our elasticity of expectations is 0, we still expect it to be priced at 100, providing us with some incentive to buy today. If our elasticity is 1, our expected price goes to 90 and we might as well stay put. An elasticity of, say, 2 makes us expect the future price to fall to 80 and our best bet becomes to sell before it does go to 80. Elasticities of less than 1 (including the somewhat eccentric "contrarian" case of negative elasticity) are consistent with market stability; elasticities above 1 are inconsistent with it. In fact, they are consistent with the notion of a "bottomless market" when triggered off by a downward move and with a "bubble" when set off by an upward one. (The dot-com bubble of 1999–2000 was the most recent example of people being driven out of their minds by cheap talk of a brave new world.)

Why, or when, is the elasticity of expectations of a wide enough swathe of marginal economic agents, businessmen, future pensioners, and institutional asset managers likely to be greater than 1? Economics is not psychology, and strictly speaking it has no answer. (Psychology probably has none, either.) Nonprofessional common sense suggests, though, that cheap talk—the ever wider avalanche of frightening scenarios, self-feeding dire forecasts, and the round-the-clock battering of our senses by data that can be read and commented on in more than one way—does unsettle the mind. A febrile atmosphere is created by the great firepower of modern media with the bias toward bad news (for good news is no news), and the instinctive wish of the majority of commentators and politicians is to consign the capitalist order of things to hell and replace it with "something better." As a result, our sense of proportion is gradually worn down.

It is as this atmosphere thickens that the elasticity of expectations may overshoot the mark of 1 and all kinds of self-feeding processes may gather speed. There was no good reason why the European and American economies should lose their cruising speed, kept up with some variations since 1992. However, some potholes in the housing markets, messy consequences in financial markets that were poisoned by the undermining of confidence beyond all measure, and perverse effects of regulations (such as "marking to market" and solvency ratios) that made things much worse than they needed to be, were blown to epic proportions by cheap talk. Once expectations became very elastic in the climate of nervousness, every adverse move generated a greater one. Thus were reasons contrived for a recession that was on "objective" grounds quite unnecessary.

2. WE ALL PREFER GROWTH TO AUSTERITY

Galactic Happiness Consultants L.P. have just released the results of a survey of ten thousand adults in twenty-seven European countries who were asked to rank chocolate cake and thin gruel in order of preference; 72.6 percent chose chocolate cake, 4.3 thin gruel, and 23.1 thought the question was daft. The Scientific Advisory Board recommended that the latter be considered as preferring chocolate cake.

These startling findings provoke a train of further thought. The common people all over Europe complain bitterly about having to get by on the thin gruel of austerity. Their governments point to the debt mountain that must at least be stopped from growing faster than incomes, and if possible stopped altogether from growing, in order to remain bearable at all. Professor Stiglitz, the most popular oracle these days, tells Europeans that they are about to commit suicide, for austerity will only increase their debt load; only economic growth of some vigor can stop it from rising. At present, Europe's economies, bar one or two, are stagnating. Quarterly changes in output of plus or minus 0.3 percent are well within the margin of error of official statistics. How to get growth going? Knee-jerk economics would spend more, increasing consumer demand and initiating infrastructure projects. However, this is precisely the policy of the last twenty years, and look where it has got us: to a debt mountain that is still growing and to output that is not. Growth, it seems, must be stiumlated without relaxing austerity, one foot pushing the accelerator, the other forcing down the brake to the floor. Unsurprisingly, nothing much happens. Governments in their awkward posture must face an electorate reluctant to be deprived of chocolate cake.

First published by Liberty Fund, Inc., at www.econlib.org on June 4, 2012. Reprinted by permission.

REACHING THE END BY ACTING ON THE MEANS

John Stuart Mill believed that the pursuit of happiness was a mistaken notion, for happiness was not reached by pursuing it.[1] There is a commonsense test: ask passersby on the street where they are heading. One is going to the football match, the other to meet his wife, a third to a job interview and the fourth to get a cup of coffee. In fact, they are pursuing happiness and using for that the means that seems best to each at the moment. In fact, there is simply no real activity called "pursuing happiness."

Much the same is true of another famous abstraction that is a cornerstone of economic theory, namely maximization. A rational agent may be said to seek the highest indifference curve he can reach, or the outcome offering the greatest mathematical expectation of "utility," or aim at the maximum present value of all future profits. But none of these activities exist as such; each is the purpose of activities intended to reach it. The rational agent does his shopping, takes a risk or declines it, and runs his business the way he thinks best. The best way may be the most likely to maximize his profit, but we cannot say that he is maximizing his profit. All we can observe is his use of the means that may produce such an end.

John Kay is a British management expert and a popular newspaper columnist. He knows that if you correctly define some hitherto ill-understood phenomenon, people will at best nod and then forget you, but if you give the phenomenon a name, people will remember you

1. In "Utilitarianism" (1861), J. S. Mill states, "If by happiness be meant a continuity of highly pleasurable excitement, it is evident enough that this is impossible. A state of exalted pleasure lasts only moments, or in some cases, and with some intermissions, hours or days, and is the occasional brilliant flash of enjoyment, not its permanent and steady flame. Of this the philosophers who have taught that happiness is the end of life were as fully aware as those who taunt them. The happiness which they meant was not a life of rapture; but moments of such, in an existence made up of few and transitory pains, many and various pleasures, with a decided predominance of the active over the passive, and having as the foundation of the whole, not to expect more from life than it is capable of bestowing." In *The Collected Works of John Stuart Mill*, ed. John M. Robson, vol. 10, *Essays on Ethics, Religion, and Society* (Toronto: University of Toronto Press, 1985), chap. 2.

as the inventor. Perhaps with this as his motive, he explains that firms attempting directly to maximize their profit tend to fail, for the way to maximization is not the direct, but the "oblique." What he must be saying is that there is no direct way to attain such an aim, for, like the pursuit of happiness, profit maximization is an abstraction. He cites the example of Imperial Chemical Industries that had set out to build up a world-class pharmaceutical research capability and by so doing, have maximized their profits. There was nothing "oblique" about this. If you think some merchandise will sell well, there is nothing "oblique" about organizing facilities to produce and market it. It is the direct way to profit maximization. There may be alternatives: buy a stock of the stuff for resale, become a wholesale distributor, develop a brand name that earns your stuff a premium price; but none of these means to the end is "oblique" if the word means anything we can recognize.

A board of directors would look silly as can be if it devoted its meeting to "profit maximization." (This is not to deny, though, that boards sometimes have agendas that are as silly as can be.) A serious meeting must devote itself to serious matters that have a serious chance of enhancing profits or reducing losses.

The same must apply to the Ecofin[2] and heads-of-government "summit" meetings that are about to be devoted to the objective of re-starting growth. The Maastricht Treaty that snapped shut the trap of the euro and laid down rules of good budgetary behavior that Germany and France predictably proceeded to break before their signatures had the time to dry was initially called the Treaty of Stability. It was then re-membered that everybody wants growth, and the treaty was renamed Stability and Growth—the stability prescribed in the treaty hopefully serving as the means to the desired growth.

MAKING IT OR LETTING IT GROW?

Europe's economy, subjected to the good ideas of overriding govern-ments armed with the power of collective choice, fits well enough the

2. ECOFIN, or the Economic and Financial Affairs Council, is made up of the Economics and Finance Ministers of the twenty-seven member states of the Euro-pean Union.

metaphor of a human body under perfusion subjected to the good ideas of a well-meaning but hapless quack. The body is covered by a thicket of red and blue plastic tubes, the red ones siphoning off its vital juices, the blue ones drip-feeding them back in. The man under such perfusion is not doing too well, and the quack, desperate to improve matters and bring about recovery, keeps adding more red and blue tubes to the bewildering tangle.

The plastic tubes are symbols of good ideas in matters of fiscal and monetary policy and the perfection of welfare entitlements. Each is meant to correct the perverse effects of the previously installed jungle of tubes. Each is destined to help, or at least not to hinder, the resumption of economic growth. As a rule, each is largely ineffective, for the thicker the tangle of tubes, the less responsive is the body to further tubes meant to stimulate it.

For the last quarter of a century, the Japanese economy was ceaselessly stimulated by profusion of public works until there was hardly any space left for more new bridges that nobody needed and new roads that led nowhere, yet growth has never taken off.

There is an obvious alternative to the self-contradictory policy of austerity combined with spending to stimulate growth. It is not to make growth, but to let it happen by resolutely taking off the tubes. The recipe is to apply that almost forgotten arch-simple medicine, rhetorically called liberty.

The labor laws of most European countries run to several thousand pages and in at least three major ones, France, Italy, and Spain, they provide job protection of such severity that in terms of severance pay and judicial process, dismissing an employee is almost prohibitively expensive and complex. As risky as filling a vacant job is made by job protection, employing the unemployed demands reckless courage. For every hundred jobs benefiting from job protection, ten or more new jobs may fail to be created due to the risk built into hiring labor. Yet the greater the resulting joblessness—now having passed the 10 percent mark in the Eurozone—the more electorally suicidal it seems for a government to relax job protection. Similar though less strong reasons perpetuate government regulation of the minimum wage, the "legal" work week, and the "legal" retirement age, all of which violate elementary freedom of contract and obstruct growth.

Some people are no doubt flabby and let themselves be carried by the flow, but most try to better themselves as they know how. For this very fundamental reason, an economy where the rule of law and the freedom of contract are not wholly absent has a natural bias to grow. There is a presumption that if a largely free economy existed, it would grow briskly and be resilient to shocks. There is, alas, also a presumption that although we all prefer growth to stagnation and chocolate cake to thin gruel, we are stubbornly inclined to use political power to try and make growth by multiplying the plastic tubes of policy instead of letting it happen by not standing in its way.

3. MICRO, MACRO, AND FANTASY ECONOMICS

There are two branches of genuine economics, the micro and the macro, and a third and phoney one, the fantasy economics that feeds on wishful thinking-demagogy and the rantings of pretentious charlatans. As micro and macro are tangled up in one of their periodic conflicts of mutual misunderstanding, the stage is clear for the fantasy economics of "new order," "need, not greed," "equitable distribution," "stability," and so forth. None of this rhetoric is harmless, and the seductive apple-pie-and-motherhood language it uses makes it difficult to combat. Microeconomics finds support in common sense, the lessons of everyday life, and perhaps also in inherited instincts that favored genetic survival in evolutionary selection. Microeconomics teaches that no sane man will try to increase his income by borrowing more heavily on his credit card so that his increased consumption should stimulate consumption, fill factory order books, and permit him to earn more by doing overtime. Yet macroeconomics suggests that something of the sort is a quite plausible sequence of events. Plausible, however, is sometimes mistaken for necessarily true. "It all depends"; macroeconomic plausibility may or may not point to correct conclusions.

When in 2000 France's socialist government reduced the "legal" work week to thirty-five hours, the main plea was that this will spread the available work among more people (i.e., reduce unemployment) which of course it did not. It increased costs and caused much disruption. On the other hand, when in 2008–09 a large proportion of German employers reduced both the work week and wages, the result was that German unemployment rose significantly less than that in neighboring countries. Could this be a negation of the French experience? It was nothing of the sort; it was simply that other things were not equal: in one experience labor costs increased, in the other they did not. Micro and macro are fairly unanimous that you do not increase

First published by Liberty Fund, Inc., at www.econlib.org on December 6, 2010. Reprinted by permission.

the demand for labor by making it more expensive. Higher unemployment pay has no direct incidence on wage cost, because it is paid out of general tax revenue and leaves unemployment insurance rates (a kind of payroll tax) unchanged. However, wherever the incidence of a higher cost first hits the economy, the indirect incidence will inevitably work through to labor cost, too.

The contemporary quarrel between micro and macro rages around the sustainability of growing government debt, the potential of the fiscal stimulus to induce growth and create jobs, and the risks of unorthodox central banking. In all these areas, the instinctive, micro-oriented "know-nothings" confront the educated Keynesians. The latter keep desperately trying to hammer into the thick skulls of the former the basic blueprint of John Maynard Keynes's system. More government spending (i.e., dissaving) generates income that is greater than the spending itself, with part of the income being consumed and part saved to generate the saving that matches the government dissaving. In Keynesian parlance there is the multiplier effect and it is greater than 1. As long as there is spare capacity (unemployment) in the economy, the government ought to go on spending more, working through the multiplier, because the extra private saving takes care of the government dissaving and the extra consumption is, so to speak, a welcome windfall gain. Timidly refusing to generate it is criminal waste.

Despite truculent voices to the contrary, the Keynesian logic is faultless in that the conclusions do follow from the assumptions. Why it does not really work, and why it singularly failed to work in 2009–10 and maybe beyond, is that other things do not remain equal. Part of the extra spending stimulus fails to stimulate domestic income because as much as 0.3 of the multiplier might leak out through extra imports. Much of the rest may be offset by industry taking fright of the rising budget deficit and reducing investment, and by consumers striving to reduce their indebtedness, producing some saving to balance the government's dissaving. The total effect of higher imports and lower investment might be a multiplier barely higher, or maybe even lower, than 1 and the stimulus stimulating nothing except the national debt. This is not the fault of Keynes but of those whose macroeconomics exist in Fantasyland.

This is instinctively understood by the know-nothings, but rather harder to accept by the kind of public instructed in the rudiments of economics. Sex education these days begins at age eight and economics is taught as early as fifteen. These may be necessary, or necessary evils, but seem premature all the same. Economic education much before economic experience may well act as the little knowledge that is worse than none. It is this public that is a sucker for the fantasy economics peddled in profusion today, which borrows the language of economics but has no roots in either micro or macro logic.

One of the charms of fantasy economics is that it fits so well into metaphors. Industry and commerce are benign activities, but when they go across frontiers, they become warfare where our side loses because the other side is not fighting fair. There are many remedies against this unfairness. Outright protection is no longer politically correct and must be dressed up as something else to be respectable. International cooperation, however, is always a good thing; there is never too much of it. It also provides occasions for pointless summit meetings where jetlagged politicians and their long tails of assistants can listen to each other's prepared statements. Currently, one proposal for international cooperation is that Germany ought to restrain its exports and increase its consumption to let its neighbors have a chance. In a similar vein, Beijing ought to cooperate by somehow persuading American consumers to buy fewer Chinese T-shirts and tennis racquets. More broadly, no country should allow its current account balance to exceed 4 percent of its national product. In Fantasyland, governments can achieve these things if only they will agree to cooperate.

In Fantasyland, it seems obvious that China has injured America by cunningly fixing the official exchange rate of their currency, the yuan, so low as to make their T-shirts irresistibly cheap, and hoarding the u.s. dollars they received for them. The upshot was that China accumulated $2.5 trillion of "reserves," an amount that still keeps growing with every month's u.s. trade deficit. The effect is tantamount to China making America a free gift of $2.5 trillion worth of merchandise, for what else can they do with these astronomical "reserves" than keep them on the books of their central bank forever?

Fantasy economics as a study of warfare or at best a bitterly fought football game helps to understand the self-inflicted pain most of Europe is currently suffering in the "crisis" of the euro—a "crisis" that is increasingly looking like a quasi-permanent state of affairs. The euro replaced national currencies in 1999 partly because it was promised to raise economic growth rates in the region by 5 percent or more, and partly because it would enable Europe "to look the dollar in the face," or better still, to become its equal as a global reserve currency. Milton Friedman was convinced that, failing fiscal unification, the euro experiment would collapse in a matter of months. Instead, it is still subsisting, though it has signally failed to fulfill the promises of growth and especially of prestige that had been made for it. It is being maintained by the Herculean efforts of the more solvent of the member states who seem determined to throw good money after bad to save their nearly insolvent fellow members without admitting that at least some of this money can be regarded as already gone down the drain. The mystery is that doing this is unanimously acclaimed as wise, constructive, and necessary because it preserves the integrity of the Eurozone. There is ominous talk of "fragilization" and "contamination" from Greece to Ireland, Ireland to Portugal, Portugal to Spain and so on, ending in some unspecified but catastrophic collapse. Nobody feels the need to ask why such language is the right one to use, and why the "integrity" of the zone and its common currency is so precious as to warrant the most painful economic and political contortions. Heavily loaded metaphors suffice to convince us that Greece, Portugal, Spain, or Italy reverting to their own separate currencies would be a bad thing for anyone, let alone (as is being asserted) for everyone.

Let us briefly conclude by glancing at the Christmas wish list that forms the core agenda of the G20 powers for the coming year. A new world monetary order is to be designed, the volatility of commodity prices and the instability of markets remedied, bank regulation further intensified, and "financial" (i.e., naughty) transactions Tobin-taxed. It is a safe enough bet that this agenda will bring about nothing worse than mind-numbing chatter in expensive meetings. What is saddening is that it is not solid understanding of micro and macro theory, the depressing history of exchange controls, fixed rates and commodity price stabilization schemes, nor the vacuity of fantasy economics that will preserve us from these hoary panaceas, but rather the sheer unlikelihood of reaching unanimous agreement among sovereign states on anything substantive, however foolish it may be.

4. NEGATIVE PRODUCTIVITY

As of January 1, 2011, the French "legal" minimum wage or *smic* was raised by 1.6 percent to nine euros ($12) an hour or 1,365 euros per month. About 10 percent of wage-earners, condescendingly called *smicards,* are paid the minimum wage. Their take-home pay is amputated by what is called "their" contribution to "social" insurance. Of course the remaining and greater part of "social" insurance premiums is just as much "their" contribution, but for cosmetic reasons is called the employer's contribution. The division into employer and employee contributions is stark economic nonsense. Both parts come out of the pay the worker would get if there were no compulsory insurance or if he paid the premium directly rather than through the employer paying it on his behalf. However, many or most workers fall for the cosmetic and live with the illusion that the benevolent, "socially" just government orders the employers to give them something on top of the wage.

With retail prices lifted by a value-added tax of 19.6 percent, the purchasing power of the *smic* is hardly above the bare subsistence level in an urban environment. People who have a heart must find it shamefully low. Yet people with a head regretfully find it too high; for within the great mass of unemployed, the proportion of the unskilled who would be candidates for the *smic* is much higher than the average, i.e., the skilled and the unskilled taken together. Average unemployment is at 9.5 percent, but among the unskilled it can locally be 25 percent or more. Is then the minimum wage too low or too high?

The answer is that it is both, due largely to the caring, "socially" just hand of the government. Paying 1,365 euros a month to a *smicard* costs his or her employer anything between 2,200 and 2,500 euros due to the highly complex social insurance schemes whose premiums the employer pays on his employees' behalf. The result is that it is cheaper to go capital-intensive—install automatic checkout counters in supermar-

First published by Liberty Fund, Inc., at www.econlib.org on January 13, 2011. Reprinted by permission.

kets, automatic ticket controllers at subway stations, and giant street-cleaning machines to sweep the streets—rather than employ *smicards* to do these lowly tasks.

Suppose for a near-delirious moment that freedom of contract is suddenly and miraculously recognized as a firm rule. Among many other things, "social" insurance against illness, old age, and unemployment ceases to be compulsory. The wage, with or without deductions for insurance, would become freely negotiable. Would a *smicard* give up all his entitlements under the various "social" schemes in exchange for a rise in his take-home pay? Some would not at almost any price, but some, probably many, would rather take a raise from 1,365 to 2,000 euros in cash than persist with the old system. The effect on employment of the unskilled might be very substantial indeed.

The author of this column was recently the tacit witness of a debate among a group of economists on low-wage employment. The majority thought that the unskilled were getting a rather miserable cash wage but a whole array of in-kind benefits (of which the three major "social" insurances of health, old age, and unemployment represent the greatest part) as well as housing, family, and other allowances, and that it would be a good idea if all or some of these fringe benefits were abolished and their cost returned to the workers in the form of higher cash wages. For liberals (in the original, not the American, sense of "liberal") this would be an obvious improvement, for cash that can buy the in-kind benefit but also anything else is necessarily preferable to the in-kind benefit alone. There are of course well-rehearsed weakness-of-will and other paternalistic arguments against the liberal thesis, but they become weaker as society learns to live with more personal responsibility and less collective care.

A different economist, however, had an interesting objection. Society, she explained, has over the past half-century erected an elaborate system of pipes that conducts vital fluids to parts of the body politic and economic where they are most needed. Dismantling what she called "the pipe work" would upset the political equilibrium and, more tangibly, throw the hundreds of thousands who "operate the pipe work" on the heap of the unemployed. Last year in this column, in pale imitation of Frédéric Bastiat's genial idea of the "negative railway," I spoke of the "negative marginal productivity of government." Treating government as a factor of production like labor or capital, the idea was that when it only enforces the rule of law, its productivity is very high. As it expands its scope to what Friedrich Hayek, with touching good faith, called "useful public goods and services," its marginal productivity becomes increasingly dubious. What is grievous about this large zone of government activity is that unlike the case of labor that is sacked and capital that is lost or withdrawn when its productivity is less than its cost, there is no market test to decide about the productivity, or lack of it, of governments. "Operating the pipe work" where the fluids of the welfare state circulate may or may not be positively productive. However, whether it is or not cannot easily be decided by what would pass for pure, non-subjective economics. It is a matter for political polemic and ethical convictions about what some people are entitled to impose upon the rest of us.

However, there are some extreme configurations of state and society where the negative productivity of government action is so blatantly perceptible as to make discussion almost redundant. It is hardly possible to think of the near-desperate condition of many African countries without attributing the blame, the frustration, and the repeated economic backsliding to their truly awful governments. Development economists who get consulting contracts from African governments or international organizations subconsciously repay patronage by not blaming governments, but discoursing instead about the better targeting of development aid, strategic investment in education and health, technology transfers, and so forth, but the wasteful stupidity, corruption, and cynicism of kleptocratic governments over the post-colonial half-century has been destroying all the good that good will attempted to do in these fields. Lack of democracy is cited as a reason; but the big and the little tigers of Asia and South America were not, and still are not, noticeably democratic, yet economically they have raced ahead while Africa has mostly stayed in the same place while its governments have been tormenting its hapless subjects.

At the other end of the spectrum of civilization, there are countries that abound in intelligence, capital (and are exporting it), and have first-class technology, a vast health-care and educational apparatus, and a reasonably clean-handed judicial and administrative class, yet are steadily falling behind in terms of material wealth. France is the out-standing example. It has been running a budget deficit without inter-ruption for the last thirty years and is now running one at 8 percent of GDP; 55 percent of GDP is spent by collective decision, leaving less than half for individuals to dispose of. By a colossal effort of political rivalry and administrative tenacity, 55 percent of economic lifeblood is siphoned out, to be re-injected by a staggeringly complicated tangle of perfusion tubes on places chosen and ceaselessly changed by the gov-ernment. The arteries and veins of the natural body make do with what is left. We cannot be absolutely sure of the operative reasons for the re-sulting underperformance. But ascribing it to negative productivity of the factor "government" offsetting the positive productivity of capital and labor is at least logically a sufficient explanation.

5. FINANCE IN PARROT TALK, PART 1

George Stigler, the 1982 Nobel Laureate, was almost as great a humorist as he was an economist. His deadpan irony was devastating. In his *The Economist as Preacher and Other Essays* he speaks of "that most irresistible of all the weapons of scholarship, infinite repetition."[1]

I call "parrot talk" the loud and relentless repetition of some plausible fallacy that is first launched as an original and debatable notion by some minor authority or small group, often with an axe to grind, and then, by a mysterious process of perverse selection, is taken up and hammered home by public intellectuals and the media, triumphantly becoming a firmly established truth. When used as prophecy or forecast it is liable to be self-fulfilling. When used as explanation and diagnosis, it dictates the remedy. In either case, it is capable of causing deep and lasting damage in political thought and the public policy the thought tends to shape.

In the present column and the one next month I will be dealing with a few particularly insidious and dangerous subjects of parrot talk. I will first recall a few that I had identified in earlier writings. Then I will present some more recent untruths, such as the idea of "financial capitalism," the supposedly vital need to stock up the banks with extra capital, monetization of the debt, and the alleged vices of modern capitalism, such as speculations and short-termism.

FUNDAMENTAL FALLACIES

Among my *Collected Papers* there is an essay entitled "Parrot Talk."[2] It treats a number of fallacies in political philosophy that, looking plau-

First published by Liberty Fund, Inc., at www.econlib.org on November 7, 2011. Reprinted by permission.

1. George J. Stigler, *The Economist as Preacher and Other Essays* (Chicago: Chicago University Press, 1982), 122.

2. See Anthony de Jasay, *Political Philosophy, Clearly: Essays on Freedom and Fairness, Property and Equalities,* ed. Hartmut Kliemt, part of The Collected Papers of Anthony de Jasay (Indianapolis: Liberty Fund, 2010).

sible and pleasing to most people's ears, are being repeated on every possible occasion with an air of assured conviction. Each time they are declared, more academic parrots take them up and relay them in ever wider circles until they become ineradicable common knowledge that feeds prevailing political thought.

One of these fallacies, pilloried in "Parrot Talk," is the separateness of production and distribution. The gross national cake is first baked according to the laws of economics, and then sliced and distributed according to the collective decisions of society. It remains unsaid that the very reason why a cake of a certain size is baked at all (rather than a sweeter, bigger, or smaller one, or indeed none) is that its distribution will be of a certain kind and not a different one. Income is not grabbed and redistributed with impunity without reacting back on production.

Another fallacy, often repeated to reassure the voter called "liberal" in *English* English that he has little to fear from the candidate called "liberal" in *American* English, is that it is possible to bring about equality of opportunity without enforcing equality of outcomes. It takes a minute of extra thought to realize that once preceding outcomes are allowed to be unequal, current opportunities cannot possibly remain equal.[3] But this extra minute of thought is suppressed by the rising noise of parrot talk. Finally, the essay notes that the most widely accepted modern theory of justice lays down as its first principle that everybody must have a right to the greatest possible liberty compatible with the same liberty for everybody else. One may ask why having a right to liberty is better, or different, than having liberty itself. Adding the "right to" should raise suspicious second thoughts, or perhaps it is just empty verbiage—but having a right always sounds nice, and passes well in parrot talk.

MUST SAFETY-FIRST ECONOMICS PREVAIL?

What the earlier "Parrot Talk" essay sought to do in political thought, the present one aims to do in the current language parrots use about

---

3. This point was made by Robert Nozick in his discussion of the earnings of Wilt Chamberlain in *Anarchy, State, and Utopia* (New York: Basic Books, 1974), "How Liberty Upsets Patterns," 160ff.

finance. It is written by taking as read certain well-established theses of neo-classical economics that are basic to what in *English* English is called "liberalism."

Thanks to incessant repetition in the last few years, public opinion is now convinced that risk is a bad thing and ought to be purged from the economy as far as possible. Economics, on the contrary, teaches that some risk is inevitable because the future is not predictable, and is necessary for efficiency. The size and severity of risk and its price should and under a regime of free contract would adjust to each other. The wish to avoid risk by paying the market to bear it (e.g., by hedging, forward dealing, or insurance) would, in equilibrium, be equal to the willingness of the market to assume that risk. This situation is an optimum, because neither the marginal risk-avoider nor the marginal risk-bearer can expect to do better by moving away from it. The spectacular stock and bond market losses of 2008–09 showed that the expectations of large operators, such as the insurer AIG, may occasionally be spectacularly wrong (especially if biased by existing regulations and Fannie Mae activities, as was the case in the U.S. residential mortgage market), but they did not invalidate the theorem. The losses were the outcomes of zero-sum games and as far as one can tell, they involved no destruction of tangible value. As Milton Friedman would say, for every loser, there was a gainer. Damage did occur due to massive mismanagement of the shock waves, but not because risk was allocated by price in the first place. After all the ensuing parrot talk, the received truth now is that risk is bad and almost reprehensible and should be purged from the system. Poor system! Risklessly, it would be heading for an unpromising future.

The condemnation of risk and particularly of its assumption by professional risk-bearers has become a rock-solid dogma. It is not the only one that is firmly believed because everybody else seems to believe it and is saying so. The overarching untruth that assiduous parrot talk is converting into a new truth is that the freedom of contract, the basic enabling condition for allocative efficiency in the economy, is "all right in theory but does not work in practice" and needs to be limited and regulated in an ever larger variety of sensitive contexts, many of them in finance. Losses made by any lame duck industry must be doctored because they are obviously bad things. Finance attracts the curiosity of the busybody because its techniques are ill understood and it is shrouded in an air of mystique and power.

"FINANZKAPITALISMUS"

German parrot talk has achieved the feat of uniting in a single word two of the most hated ideas that in other current languages would take two or more to express.

There must be some people, though not very many, who would be happier as cavemen or nomadic herdsmen battling periodic famine and the cruelty of elements than denizens of our urban civilization. For the rest of us, however, the populist dreams of abolishing the "dominance of money and the dictatorship of the market," as well as seeking "production for real needs, not for profit," should and can be dismissed as irrational ranting. It would be rational if we harbored a strong streak of masochism that could best be satisfied by self-inflicted economic and social pain.

At a more sophisticated level than masochistic oratory, a few standard accusations are obstinately leveled against finance, capitalism, or both. Often no distinction is drawn between the two, which can be excused on the ground that finance and capitalism have flourished together and though each can be imagined without the other, the result looks painfully contrived. Quantitative economic planning by input-output matrices, on the one hand, and market socialism on the other, are examples of such contrived monstrosities. You can perhaps run an economy without prices set in a single money of account, but it looks hardly promising. You can perhaps run a money economy while suppressing the profit motive, but it looks unpromising, too.

The steady stream of parrot-talk charges come under two headings. One is morality. Capitalism is immoral because it promotes immoral or at best amoral conduct in pursuit of a morally worthless objective, profit. It also generates inequality of material conditions among men, and relations of subordination. It is not realized that all economic systems, except perhaps subsistence farming, do these things and have done so throughout history. Where capitalism is superior to its real or putative alternatives is in its relation to morality. It is the only system where the optimal rule to follow in order to achieve success is "honesty is the best policy," (though following a rule is not the only or necessarily a better road to success than not following one). Capitalism, as has been recognized by the more intelligent among its defenders, systematically economizes morality: it needs less of it than other systems in order to function properly. It achieves more with morally fallible human agents than other systems could hope to do by relying on the scarce supply of clean-handed, selfless, public-spirited people they could find. Capitalism shrinks the opportunities for corruption, precapitalist and socialist systems open them widely.

Under the less high-minded heading of stability and efficiency, parrot wisdom, particularly since the mayhem of 2008, has it that an excessive financial superstructure renders the economy top-heavy, crisis-prone, and badly in need of reregulation after the decades of doctrinaire free-marketism of the latter part of the twentieth century. This charge, for all its plausibility with bank rescues and stubborn unemployment weighing on our minds, is nevertheless an arbitrary one. The capitalist economies, in particular their financial service sectors prior to 2008, were too lightly regulated in the view of some, too heavily in that of others. They were in either view hybrids. There is no earthly way of telling, from the performance of a hybrid system, what the performance of a pure system would have been. Maybe putting the banks in straitjackets would have averted 2008, maybe setting them really free to swim or sink would have done it. Maybe neither would have made much difference. But pretending to know that more regulation was needed, as Mr. Volcker, Mr. Mervyn King, Dodd-Frank legislators, and the Basel committee do, and as incessant parrot talk to the same effect raises to the rank of a self-evident truth, should not be allowed to serve as an argument-stopper.

Probably the best French current affairs commentator exclaimed the other day that every day hundreds of billions of money transactions flow through the exchanges without the least attempt by governments at regulating them, and this was truly terrifying and inadmissible. She might as well have added that every day hundreds of billions of hectoliters of water slosh about in the oceans without the least attempt by governments to regulate them, and this was truly inadmissible and terrifying.

6. FINANCE IN PARROT TALK, PART 2

In a breathtaking "Note on the Reform of the International Financial and Monetary System in the Context of Global Public Authority" issued by the Pontifical Council for Justice and Peace on October 24, 2011, this institution of the Holy See took it upon itself to urge the imposition of a tax on financial transactions (the notorious Tobin tax, advocated mainly by Germany and France, dismissed by Great Britain, and mostly ignored by the United States of America), the separation of retail and investment banking, and the strengthening of the equity capital ("recapitalization") of the banking system. If the International Chamber of Commerce issued a statement calling for brotherly love and charity and the regular practice of the sacraments, we should find it incongruous and out of place. However, the Holy See has since Leo XIII's encyclical of 1891 accustomed us to Church advocacy of large departures from a laissez-faire free contract economy. (The Catholic "Club Med" countries of Southern Europe are paying a heavy price for following this advocacy.)

STRENGTHENING THE BANKING SYSTEM?

A bank is solvent if it can pay off its liabilities to third parties, some on demand, others on their due dates, by liquidating its assets. As long as the bank is believed to be solvent, the necessity to liquidate all its assets to pay off all its liabilities does not arise. In the perhaps laudable attempt to provide a tangible foundation for the belief in solvency, an all-European panel of central bankers and officials sitting in Basel is empowered to require banks to maintain certain fixed proportions between various classes of their assets and their liabilities. These requirements have been progressively tightened from the initial set known as Basel I to the present Basel III. Greatly simplified, the requirements

First published by Liberty Fund, Inc., at www.econlib.org on December 5, 2011. Reprinted by permission.

amount to a solvency ratio by which, under Basel III, a bank is allowed to have 93 of third-party liabilities for every 100 worth of assets. This means that its own equity capital must be no less than 7 for every 100 worth of assets. Since the starting figure for the system as a whole was only 5, the average bank had to increase its solvency ratio by 2 to reach 7 before the deadline in 2017. Most banks were expected comfortably to surpass this level out of a few years' retained earnings. So far, so good.

However, behind this safe-looking outcome there lurks a fundamental doubt. External liabilities are fixed in nominal value; 93 is unambiguously 93 in the currency, e.g., euros, in which it was denominated. However, whether an asset is valued at 100 in the balance sheet to match the 93 on the liability side and leave an equity of 7 is a matter full of ambiguity. An immensely complicated set of guidelines laid down by the International Accounting Standards Board (IASB) tells the auditors what method of valuation by the bank of its assets they may accept, but there is room for different interpretations of the guidelines. By and large, an asset must be "marked to market"; if it was bought for 100 and its market price declines to 80, it must be inscribed at 80 on the balance sheet. It may then serve to support only 74.4 of liabilities. Since the latter still figure at 93, something has to give.

Not all marketable bank assets must be "marked to market," and not all bank assets are marketable. Most, in fact, are not quoted and are exchanged only sporadically or not at all. Mortgages may not have been packaged into tradeable mortgage-backed securities, and industrial and commercial loans may be valued by the lending bank at par as long as they are "performing," i.e., as long as current interest due is being paid. However, while these asset classes may escape the letter of the "marked to market" rule, should they escape its spirit? When recession threatens, is it not reasonable to say that if these asset types were traded on a market, their price would decline by 10 percent or more in a matter of months? Should the bank's balance sheet not reflect this? If half of the bank's assets are written down by 10 percent, the bank's own equity capital shrinks from 7 to 2 percent. Since Basel III says that for safety it should be 7 percent, should depositors, especially the big wholesale ones, panic and start a run? Worse still, if the spirit of the "mark down to market" is not respected and assets are not written down but the large depositors, indoctrinated by parrot talk, think that they ought to have been, the balance sheet will no longer be trusted and the eventual panic could be much worse.

The irony of it all is that if it had not been hammered home to the public that a solvency ratio of 7 percent is needed for safety, even the harsh "mark to market" rule could be endured without much damage — for the bank is solvent as long as it can pay off its liabilities, and technically it can do this with a solvency ratio of 0.

If the bank's solvency ratio were 7 but must not be breached, the effect is the same as having a 0 ratio.

Clumsy interference in misguided attempts to improve on matters knows no bounds, for even improvements can be further improved. No sooner did European banks get used to the idea that they must have at least 7 percent equity that Mme. Lagarde, the new director general of the IMF, in apparent haste declared that it was "urgent" to recapitalize them by raising their solvency ratio to 9 and the biggest banks to 10 percent by July 2012, a mere nine months. This was the classic case of bellowing "Fire!" in a crowded cinema. Some banks rushed to the stock market, raiding it for extra capital, leaving that much less for industry and commerce. All others began aggressively to reduce their assets, partly by dumping large chunks of their holdings of Italian, Spanish, and other sovereign debt, and partly by denying credit to their less important small and medium business customers. Absurd situations arose. Airbus, up to its neck in aircraft orders, cannot step up production because its subcontractors cannot get the credit they need to raise more working capital.

While a recession of sorts is being artificially engineered, the public is convinced that it must be a good and prudent thing to recapitalize the banking system, for more financial strength is doubtless needed in this time of "crisis." May we remark that if the authorities in their zeal to manage the recession and parrot cries shriek "Crisis!," a 9 percent solvency ratio would not give better support to the banking system than 7 percent. What might help instead are fewer cries of "Fire!"

7. FINANCE IN PARROT TALK, PART 3

The most recent occasion for the parrot choir to hit fortissimo was the October 8–9 "last-chance" Brussels summit to end all summits and save the euro, at least until the imperative need for another last-chance summit emerges in a few months' time. Britain went into this summit moderately concerned about the future of the euro, the money of its largest trading partner, but also anxious about the regulatory zeal of Monsieur Barnier, the commissioner for the internal market, and his distinctly non-liberal brain trust with its instinctive dislike of the city of London. Confronted at dawn with a complicated and in part puzzling draft agreement more or less accepted by twenty-six of the twenty-seven drowsy government delegations, the British asked for exemption from certain regulatory aspects, a demand angrily refused by the French president. By the unanimity rule, the twenty-six willing governments are thus prevented from amending the Union's basic treaty as desired by Germany (an amendment that may have taken several years to ratify and survive referendums in several countries), and must be content with intergovernmental agreements. The former would hardly be stronger than the latter, but perfidious Albion is loudly blamed for vetoing it.

France is behaving like the jilted bride who becomes embittered, and Britain like a clumsy lout. Each side blames the other and claims that the other has dealt itself a losing hand. The bad blood may last a couple of years but not more, for France needs British friendship to counteract the overwhelming weight of Germany.

Meanwhile, the regulatory steamroller is advancing, flattening the international financial landscape at a cost that lies between the stratospheric and the astronomical. According to HSBC and Barclays, two of Europe's half-dozen giga-banks, "ring-fencing" their retail operations to insulate them from the hazards of the investment banking

First published by Liberty Fund, Inc., at www.econlib.org on January 2, 2012. Reprinted by permission.

side will cost them up to two billion euros per bank in extra information systems and lost synergies. The added safety is problematical. The
Financial Times of December 9, 2011, reports that worldwide financial
service companies are hit with an average of sixty regulatory changes
every working day, a 16 percent rise over last year and no let-up in
sight. Regulators announced 14,215 changes in the twelve months to
November 2011. Compliance departments have to cope with an annual
increase of up to 20 percent per annum until at least 2013. The Dodd-
Frank bank reform act in the United States and the Basel III rules in
Europe are chiefly responsible. In addition to burgeoning compliance
costs, Basel III's jerking up the required solvency ratio of the banks
from 7 to 9 percent in a matter of months is, despite protestations to
the contrary, putting on a "credit crunch" in Europe that is turning
the danger of a 2012 recession into a reality at a cost in needlessly lost
output of the order of one hundred fifty to two hundred billion in one
year.

It is fair to say that if and when 7 percent of own capital turned out
to be insufficient for banking safety, 9 percent would be no more sufficient. Fractional reserve banking depends on confidence first and last.
No realistic solvency ratio can suffice if confidence is ceaselessly shaken
by cries of alarm by the powers-that-be who are competing for media
attention, and by their echo of shrill parrot talk. Regulatory houses of
cards built by eager busybodies cost dear and instead of restoring confidence, make for shyness.

"NAUGHTY, NAUGHTY CHILD!"

The December 2011 agreement "to save the euro" is alleged to provide
for a voluntary limitation of structural budget deficits to 0.5 percent
of GDP. This is to be the golden rule of every state. The key word, of
course, is *structural,* meaning roughly taking the good years with the
bad. If the actual deficit is, say, 4 percent, a state can always argue that
it would be 0.5 if this were not a bad year. In a good year, the same
policies would yield a surplus—and so on with jam, jam tomorrow, but
never have a balanced budget today.

The really interesting part of the golden rule, however, is that it is supposed to incorporate automatic sanctions against the offender. Each state will have the golden rule in its constitution. If it offends against the golden rule, the European Court of Justice will nudge the country's constitutional court to act. It, or the Court of Justice (it is unclear which), will "sanction" the state. But what the sanction may be is a puzzle. The constitutional court will not unseat the government, and its verdict may be just shrugged off. The Court of Justice has no armored column to send to occupy the capital. A fine looks a more feasible punishment. But for the fine to persuade a government to change its fiscal policy, its amount would have to be huge, probably no less than 1 percent of GDP. For a government desperate to survive the next election, even that sum would not be a deterrent—the less so as it may just drag its feet and not pay it, or be unable to pay it for the very reason that forces it to run a budget deficit in the first place. In other words, for all the talk about automatic sanctions, the new golden rule looks just as unenforceable as the 1991 Maastricht treaty rule that both Germany and France had simply shrugged off.

The sole realistic alternative is to punish the offending state by the Court of Justice and the other European institutions shaking an index finger at the offending state and saying, "Naughty, naughty child!" For the time being, no parrot-master is admitting this and the parrots are happily repeating that there will be no deficits because there will be "automatic sanctions." The painful awakening could then serve as the subject of the third or fourth next "last-chance" summit meeting to save the euro.

FUNNY BONDS, EUROBONDS

There is now a wide consensus that a major weakness of the Eurozone is to have seventeen different states issuing seventeen different sovereign bonds of different creditworthiness. "Speculators" (the common European word denoting financial institutions, pension funds, and widows-and-orphans who try to put their assets in instruments they expect to fall least, or rise most, in value instead of passively awaiting whatever their destiny will bring them) then "attack" (i.e., refrain from buying, or sell, or even short-sell) the weakest-looking bonds, so that the weakest state will be unable to service its debt and will have to be "saved" by stronger Eurozone states, while the "speculators" turn their attention to the next-weakest victim that requires the next bail-out—and so on. The remedy, all agree except the German public, is to have Eurobonds not identified with any one state but guaranteed jointly by all. Obviously, weak states are not very convincing guarantors for other weak ones. The handful of strong ones, principally Germany, are not sure that they wish to be the guarantors for all the rest of the seventeen.

However, like funny money that has neither hard assets nor a government's taxing power to back it, bonds are funny ones if issued by a body that has no revenues with which to pay interest and to help re-finance the principal when it falls due. In order for Eurobonds not to be funny, the body that issues them would have to have the power to tax Europe's citizens in some very substantial form—a power that no sovereign European state looks ready to concede. In the last analysis, asking for Eurobonds as the sole means of keeping the Eurozone in being is to ask for a federal Eurozone government with monopoly power to tax, but returning agreed parts of the revenue to member states to let them have some degree of autonomy. At present, governments and their electorates would angrily reject such a solution. It is more comfortable to ask for Eurobonds without thinking through the grim reality they would have to bring with them. This, in any case, is the standard way in which European public opinion likes to imagine the options it wants to believe in.

8. ECONOMICS TEXTBOOKS:
TEACHING TO DESPISE

After sporadic complaints that have been voiced for years, fresh concern is being expressed by German and French business circles and some intellectuals about the economics courses in secondary schools and to a lesser extent in the universities. Textbooks used in secondary schools are accused of being tendentious, calculated to persuade the young that the capitalist economy is an engine of instability, disorder, gross inequality, and injustice.

Textbook publishers say, in their defense, that they publish what the teaching profession demands. Teachers have wide freedom to choose the course books that pupils are more or less obliged to buy. Teachers almost naturally lean left, though there is always a minority of stalwarts to hold out against the spirit of the profession. The leftist bias is "natural" in the sense that teachers as a class are probably more brainy and certainly more educated than the vast bulk of people in other occupations who earn comparable or even higher incomes. Teachers, then, feel underpaid and badly done by in what they regard as the capitalist system. Such a system is despicable and in order to help replace it by a better one, teachers want the young to despise it too.

It is, of course, far from nonsense to argue that teachers are underpaid. However, it is a mistake to ignore that at present pay levels in Europe, there are no more unemployed teachers than unfilled vacancies. Apart from imbalances in certain locations and subjects, overall supply and demand are equal. Generally higher pay would therefore almost inevitably mean teacher unemployment, for more people would opt for the profession than there was place for. Remedying that would involve building more schools, having smaller classes, and raising the compulsory school-leaving age—one more dose of tax-and-spend (or

First published by Liberty Fund, Inc., at www.econlib.org on March 3, 2008. Reprinted by permission.

rather spend-and-borrow) medicine that is obstinately administered to cure society's varied ills.

Back to the textbooks, then, that seem destined to remain tendentious as long as teachers feel wronged by the existing order of things. I have argued here before that people in the northern half of Europe have an innate understanding of the most basic economic verities, including how wealth is created and what the state can and cannot do, while in the southern, Latin, and Catholic half there is a gut feeling against enterprise and profit and a thick fog of confusion about how an economy works. Most present-day teaching upsets the natural understanding and makes the confusion worse.

Teaching economics at secondary school level is relatively recent. It is meant to make education more "real"; finding out how "untrammeled" free trade leads to job losses is more "relevant" than learning to speak their own language without massacring its grammar, let alone studying Livy or Ovid to practice close reasoning. Economics at secondary school level is liable to be descriptive if not downright anecdotal. It is likely to produce just that little bit of knowledge that is worse than none.

The teaching profession defends itself by invoking impartiality. They teach that there are dark Satanic mills where women and children toil for starvation wages, that the caprices of the market can create waste and that in modern-day monetary disorder, currencies go up and down at the pleasure of cosmopolitan speculators. It is necessary, and only fair, to show pupils that capitalism, and its "wildest" version in "mondialization," has its dark side. It might be pertinent to add that if women and children did not work for starvation wages, they would presumably starve, and that the value of capitalism lies not in what it is, but in the difference it makes.

"Impartial" economics taught to adolescents relies heavily, though not always explicitly, on a number of very basic propositions that look so plausible that they pass for self-evident. Three of them seem to me particularly insidious. I will call them the distribution-independence, the worker-defense, and the property "rights" thesis.

High school textbooks teach that capitalism, leaving as it does the distribution of income to the free play (or, as some will say, the caprice) of the market, generates inequality. It goes without saying that inequality is bad both because it is "socially" unjust and because it reduces the aggregate "utility" derived from aggregate income. Therefore society must reduce inequality by "appropriate" policies.

For modern theory, nearly all of the above is undiluted bilge. Few university-level economists will still invoke aggregate utility. Perhaps the worst part of the thesis, though, is the implicit idea that if you change the distribution of income, its total rests unchanged. The national income is not an irrigation network where you can reduce the flow of water into one ditch and increase it in the other. The tacit supposition that income is independent of its distribution is absurd, yet it is just as plausible to the untutored mind as the idea that the earth is flat is plausible to all who trust their eyes and have never been told the contrary.

An equally plausible notion taught in schools is that employers, naturally strong, would abuse workers, naturally weak, if "workers' rights" were not defined, extended, and bolstered by legislation. Minimum wages, a "legal" work week, "legal" limits on overtime, strike "rights," and the legal immunity of unions are but a few high trunks in the dense thicket of labor legislation whose total volume may reach several thousand pages (as it does in France). Employers feel lost in the thicket, but what matters is that without it, employees would be lost in the capitalist jungle.

The dominant effect, albeit only one of several, of the defense of "workers' rights" is to create excess supply in the labor market by making employers shun the increased risk of hiring. Labor's bargaining power is drained off as a result. Even some trade unions (e.g., in Spain) have started to recognize the effect of labor legislation in causing unemployment and depressing wages. But for most of semi-educated public opinion, it is self-evident that defending workers' rights must be good for the workers. The young learn in school that it is by affirming workers' rights that we tame capitalism and "ultraliberal" pipedreams.

A third one of these prize specimens of self-evidence is that property is a "social construction." Owners hold what they do by the grace of society that has created property "rights" in the first place. The government, society's agent, is protecting them against all comers (except, obviously, against itself). In what is admittedly a somewhat involved chain of tacit reasoning, those who speak of "property rights" when they mean property show a symptom of having assimilated the "self-evident" truth that what owners have are "rights" conferred upon them by "society" and enforced by its power.

In reality, property "rights" do exist. They are generated by contracts and matched by the corresponding contractual obligations. Lending and borrowing, mortgages, leases, partnerships, insurance policies, options, and other derivatives represent property "rights." They are derivatives of property, and are offset by the corresponding obligations of counterparties as assets are offset by liabilities. Underneath it all is the residual net equity, the pure property. Confusing it with property "rights" gently guides teenage reason towards the legal system of which these "rights" are a part and which is created and upheld by society's agent, the state.

However, straightforward chronology tells us otherwise. Property originated with the caveman and, more pertinently, the cavewoman who have evolved the notions and rules of mine, thine, ours, and theirs. Customs of gift-giving and legacy and conventions like queuing, first-come-first-served, and "finders, keepers" strengthened the functions of property, and the development of voluntary exchanges has laid the foundations of society. All this has manifestly preceded anything re-sembling a state and a legal system upheld by it. Capitalism may well be the outgrowth of property and trading. Whether it has unlovely or despicable aspects is a matter of taste. Property may well be dependent on the tolerance of society, for this is in the last resort a question of who sets and enforces the rules. But at least let us not teach the young that the dependence on political power is legitimate.

9. THE BOOTSTRAP THEORY OF THE OIL PRICE

It was long believed that only Baron Münchhausen was capable of lifting himself up by his own bootstraps. Strident voices all around us now proclaim that the oil price does it, too. More precisely, speculators buy oil which drives up its price which enables speculators to sell out at a profit. It is easy, simple, and wicked.

Many strange explanations have been floated to persuade us that the brutal rise in the price of crude is not due to excessive consumption or sluggish production. An OPEC (Organization of Petroleum Exporting Countries) minister said recently in all seriousness that because of underinvestment in refining, refinery capacity was short, therefore gasoline and diesel prices went up, which pulled up the price of crude. Plain men would think that if refinery capacity was insufficient, it is refining margins that would go up and crude would go down or stay put, but the price of oil today is decidedly not a subject for plain men. Another OPEC minister, in turn, affirmed that oil producers cannot even sell all their current output. He omitted to add that it is Iran that is trying to sell high-sulphur oil at the price of Arab Light, and not succeeding.

All the world hates a speculator, and it is deeply satisfying to believe that the rising price of oil (and of wheat, corn, and soybeans, not to speak of rice which has no developed futures market) that threatens world prosperity and the very survival of the poor in Asia and Africa is the fault of heartless profiteers.

George Soros, whose nebulous warnings about the perverse effects of financial markets and speculation enjoy the credibility that people lend to a brilliantly successful practitioner of the art, has recently told a subcommittee of Congress that the large positions taken by pension and other investment funds in commodity indices—of the order of $250 billion—were creating a commodity "bubble." As three-quarters

First published by Liberty Fund, Inc., at www.econlib.org on July 7, 2008. Reprinted by permission.

THE BOOTSTRAP THEORY OF THE OIL PRICE

of the main index is accounted for by oil, most of the effect is exerted on the oil price. He did not explain why there is any effect at all and how it is exerted, but maybe all that went without saying.

Lord Desai, who has taught generations of British students the Marxist economics that had benumbed his native India for half a century, recently went public in the *Financial Times*, calling on the authorities to "Act Now to Prick the Oil Bubble." He clearly believes that "pricking" it can substantially reduce the oil price, and he thinks it can be "pricked" by raising futures margin requirements for "speculators" to 50 percent while leaving them at 7 percent for "legitimate" users. Doing that may or may not be feasible in a non-regimented economy, but that is not the real problem. The real problem is that much of this talk is based on a fundamental misunderstanding of "speculation." That "bubble" of confused ideas certainly needs pricking.

For every purchase, there is a sale. When a "speculator" buys ten thousand barrels of Texas Light for delivery in, say, July 2009, because he thinks the price will trend upward between now and then, somebody is selling him ten thousand barrels for the same date. The seller may be a "speculator" who has no oil to deliver, but who thinks the price will trend downward. The buyer who went "long" and the seller who went "short" cancel out and there is no effect on physical stocks of oil. However, if the buyer finds no willing seller at the current futures price, he must bid it up. The futures price must rise above the spot price until the difference is large enough to cover the carrying cost of physical oil for the coming year, namely, interest on the capital tied up in it and storage costs. This difference is called in the trade the *contango*. If more "speculators" tried to buy than to sell future oil, the futures price would tend to rise above the normal contango. It would then be profitable to buy spot oil, store it, and sell it for future delivery. The converse would be the case if backwardation occurred. De-stocking would then be profitable.

In a well-functioning market, *arbitrageurs*, by stocking or de-stocking, see to it that spot and futures prices remain in the normal relation without the future price pulling up the spot price. Indeed, in a speculative equilibrium arbitrage stays on the sidelines, and it pays neither to stock nor to de-stock. "Speculative" buying is matched by "speculative" selling at both the spot and the futures market. Any change in stocks must then be ascribed to refiners' anticipations of demand (e.g., the spring "driving season" or extreme cold or extreme hot weather forecasts) compared to deliveries they have already arranged for. This Lord Desai, the politicians, and the man in the street would have to regard as "legitimate" (though for an economist such management of refinery stocks of crude is no less "speculative," i.e., rationally forward-looking, than the reputedly bootstrap-like variety that generates profits at will).

The long and short of it is that if a speculative "bubble" were responsible for a substantial part of the rocketing oil price since February 2008, we should have seen a very large increase in nongovernmental stocks, for any speculation that was not reflected in a change in stocks would have been self-canceling. But there was no massive increase in stocks. In fact, stocks were low throughout, and their ups and downs were minor and not systematic. Speculators may well have swum with the tide, but they did not make the tide so they may swim with it.

In closing, let us recall from elementary economics that speculators make money only if they buy low and sell high, and thus reduce the amplitude of price changes between trough and peak that would otherwise take place. They act as stabilizers. If, on the contrary, they buy high and sell low, they magnify the amplitude of the changes that would take place without them; they must lose money and if they lose often enough, they must stop destabilizing the markets because they have no money left to "speculate" with. This should suffice to show that "speculators" either stabilize the price or must self-destruct.

PART 7

Better Economic Theory or Not?

1. THANK HEAVEN FOR AN INEFFICIENT MARKET: A TALE OF ZOMBIES AND SPECULATORS

Since the series of banking and stock market mishaps of the last eighteen months, there is an intense revival of interest in the "efficient market" theory of exchange-traded asset prices. The theory proposes that the prices reflect all the available information relevant to them. Various inferences have been drawn from this. One is that since future information is not "available," prices cannot be predicted. It is therefore no use to try and "play" the market. Since there is a random pattern of future prices depending on the unknown future news flow, it cannot be affirmed that present prices are "wrong." From this, the further inference is drawn that they are "right" and—an even less justified inference—that they are a good approximation to the price pattern that will make capital flow into the most efficient uses and out of the least efficient ones. Hence the ambitious name "efficient market."

It is now argued that it was being drilled at university and business school in this theory that misled a whole army of young bankers into trusting the "efficiency" of asset markets and entering into vast commitments that have ended in astronomical losses. Their mathematics were sophisticated and worthy of the schools they graduated from, but their underlying idea was only moderately clever: if asset prices were broadly right, there was a probability distribution that favored the hypothesis of their staying at their present level; i.e., the risk was moderate and seemed to lend itself to calculation. Moreover, future bad news impacting one type of asset would not impact other types; risk was particular and not general.

Misplaced confidence in this reasoning was far from being the only cause of the shambles of 2007–08, but it was an important cause.

First published by Liberty Fund, Inc., at www.econlib.org on September 7, 2009. Reprinted by permission.

Why is the "efficient market" theory a poorly conceived one? When it speaks of "all available information that is relevant," it must mean all information that actually reaches the attention of investors, rather than information they did not bother to notice or have put in the in-tray to be discussed at next week's investment committee meeting. On this definition, there is a fraction of the body of investors who think the news they just received makes the stock they hold worth more than the top of the price range at which they were prepared to just hold it. They should therefore try and buy more of what they have (or buy the stock they previously thought too dear to hold at all). Another fraction of investors may react to the news by concluding that the stock in question is not worth what they have previously believed, and will try to sell it. The balance between the two groups of investors would generate a net buying or net selling interest. The price would instantaneously adjust to it, perhaps on minute additional volume or no additional volume at all, since market-makers would just mark the price up or down to choke off the buying or selling interest. They should do this if they believed in the "efficient market" theory they have heard spoken of. After all, it was the price at which net buying or selling in the wake of the new information was choked off that fully "reflected" that information.

Retreat from the logic of instantaneous adjustment to the new "right" price would allow investors to react to the new information, not when it becomes "available," but next week, next month, or next year. This would render the scenario more realistic, but render the hypothesis of the "right" price and the efficient allocation of capital useless because it would make it unfalsifiable. The actual price will reflect the news one day, but that day may always lie in the future—next week, next month, next year, or whenever—especially as the impact of one piece of news will with the passage of time be overlaid by additional news. Under these circumstances, one could say both that the price is right because it (ultimately) reflects the news, and that it is "wrong" because full adjustment to the news is indefinitely delayed. It is "jam, jam tomorrow, but never have jam today."

For the idea to be worth discussing, we must revert to the version that supposes instantaneous adjustment. Under this version, the immense majority of investors—in the limiting case, all investors—would remain passive. They would buy only index funds for their retirement, never favoring one stock or one industry, for the relative prices of different assets would be just right and nothing could be gained by investing in one rather than another. Nor would they try to "time" the market, buying the index fund when they thought the market was low and postponing the purchase when they thought it was too high. They would sell their index fund to pay the tuition fees of their daughters at an expensive college, but never because they expected it to slump. In short, they would be the model investors populist politicians and leader-writers dream of when they call for "moral capitalism" and call the stock market a "casino" for greedy gamblers.

Where does all this leave the "efficient" asset market? On a rigorous look, it leaves it nowhere at all, because if investors always just blindly accepted any asset price as the right price, they would never influence the allocation of capital between companies, market sectors, asset types, regions, and continents.

This is not to say that, as zombies hypnotized by a false or at least misinterpreted theory, they would be acting irrationally when they just passively accepted a market price as the right price. It is perfectly rational for the average investor to stay passively invested in the index, since if he is average, he can by definition not do better than the average.

However, it must be clear that if he acts in this manner, he is doing nothing whatever to allocate capital, let alone to allocate it "efficiently." The theory tells investors that if they are rational, they must understand that future prices are intrinsically unpredictable, hence it is a mistake to try and anticipate them. But it is only by anticipating them that investors are adjusting the allocation of capital to what they think is going to happen in the future and that will be an efficient allocation if they guessed the future right. If they have guessed wrong, they will sway the flow of funds in the wrong way, allowing ultimately less productive uses to absorb too much capital and more productive ones too little. But in doing so, they will also lose their ammunition that would permit them to make a similar mistake next time.

Those who get it right get rich and with their more ample ammunition can have a greater impact on the market next time, pushing it closer to the price pattern that would best adjust the flow of capital to what future events and developments demanded. This supposes that successful speculators remain mostly successful and unsuccessful ones wither away, a supposition that is more plausible than its opposite would be. Hoping for the best on this score, let us conclude that the efficient market theory promotes zombies, but speculators promote an efficient market.

Available information testifies about the *past efficiency* of capital allocation. Adjusting asset prices to available information may or may not do anything for efficiency now. Only the information that becomes available as the future unfolds will tell whether capital allocation was what it should have been. It was what it should have been if and only if present asset prices leave no room for successful speculation—if semiconductors are never overproduced, if power generating capacity is always just adequate, if shipping freight rates are broadly stable, if no industry is made suddenly obsolescent by the rise of another, if there is no recovery from a slump, and no bubble is ever pricked. The inefficient asset market allows things to happen that should not, and also permits successful speculation to mitigate them by changing the allocation of capital in anticipation of them, and mitigating their ill effects. Perfect foresight would do an even better job, but let the best not be an enemy of the good.

2. CORRUPTION, PARASITISM, AND
THE ABUSE OF AGENCY

Transparency International, a non-profit organization, relies on reports of data and impressions from correspondents the world over to compile a ranking of countries in order of corruptness.[1] The more corrupt the country, the lower it is placed. The ranking is inevitably imperfect and contestable, for corruption is by its very nature hidden and becomes a known fact only if the attempt of its perpetrators to conceal it fails. Besides, different correspondents report on different countries according to the experience or knowledge they have of particular ones. Hence individual bias, depth of familiarity with the local scene, and severity of judgment of the observer will impact the ranking of different countries differently. Nevertheless, the attempt to rank states by their corruptness is definitely worthwhile. Transparency International's report, being the only one, is the best we have.

The list for the year 2010 makes interesting reading. The top ten countries are Denmark, New Zealand, Singapore, Finland, Sweden, Canada, The Netherlands, Australia, Switzerland, and Norway. The ten bottom countries down to 178 are Equatorial Guinea, Burundi, Chad, Sudan, Turkmenistan, Uzbekistan, Iraq, Afghanistan, and Somalia. The first thing that springs to the eye is that the least corrupt countries are all rich and the most corrupt ones all poor, or worse, downright miserable basket cases.

There is, then, an evident correlation between rectitude and wealth as well as between corruption and poverty. But there is no telling whether the correlation signals a causal connection or merely what David Hume would call a "constant conjunction." Nor can we easily

First published by Liberty Fund, Inc., at www.econlib.org on August 1, 2011. Reprinted by permission.

1. Transparency International describes itself as a "global civil society organization leading the fight against corruption."

tell which way the causation runs if there is one. Are countries rich because their people are righteous, demonstrating by their prosperity
that honesty is really the best policy? Or are they righteous because
sheer need does not press them and they can more easily afford self-
respect and clean hands? By the same token, is it corruption that drags
countries into backwardness and misery, or are they corrupt because
poverty has few defenses against corrupt practices just as a weak body
has few defenses against illness?

As is often the case when the direction of causation is not obvious, it
is not obvious because it runs both ways at the same time along a feed-
back loop. Each point and each phase in the loop is both cause and
effect. It looks tempting to think that they reinforce each other in a virtuous cycle for the clean countries and a vicious circle for the corrupt
ones, but I think this would be jumping to conclusions. It would be
ignoring all the other causes at work in a tangle of multiple causation,
including history and its unpredictable turning points.

Italy and Spain are both Latin, Catholic, and Mediterranean countries. Italy is richer than Spain and we might expect it to rank much
higher than Spain. Instead, it is considerably lower in the list, presumably because the history of Naples and Sicily has brought into being
strong organized-crime societies as defenders of the common people
and they have remained, after all these stormy centuries, an integral
yet intensely corrupt thread in the social fabric. No such criminal societies exist in Spain. Another historical twist accounts, at least in part,
for the place of Russia as a very corrupt country in the list. The Soviet
Union was no doubt a thoroughly corrupt place, but it devoted such
an extraordinarily big share of its national income to internal controls
and surveillance of everybody by everybody else that large-scale corruption remained limited (though petty corruption flourished as did
petty crime). With the collapse of the Soviet system, organs of control
turned themselves into organs of corruption. Russia is now corrupt almost beyond belief, much more so than its wealth and education would
lead us to predict.

A few standard types of corruption might be distinguished for a
better understanding of the whole phenomenon. One is simple para-
sitism, where a person or group uses its power to suck up resources that
would otherwise accrue to those under their power. The case of Angola

is a shining example. French and American oil companies discovered vast oil fields offshore Angola in the 1980s and 1990s and obtained concessions to exploit them. An explicit clause in the concessions forbade them ever to publish or otherwise disclose the astronomical royalties and production-sharing profits they paid annually to the government. The latter used some of it to keep the army happy and run the state, and stole the rest; in fact, it is presumably still stealing it while suppressing the evidence that it is doing so. The Angolan people who own the oil remain dirt poor. A similarly parasitic practice on a less spectacular scale is the creation of sinecures and their allocation to friends of the ruling elite and their children.

In another and most widespread type of corruption, officials in some local or central government administrations are supposed to render some service (to pay entitlements; certify facts of birth, death, or property; or award a license permitting some business activity), but will only do so in exchange for bribes at tacitly understood tariffs. Such corruption may be petty, but in unique cases, such as the awarding of a large government contract to a favored insider instead of to the lowest bidder, the excess cost and the misallocation of resources to inefficient uses is doing great damage.

Crowning it all is corruption within the police and the judiciary which are supposed to detect and punish, and hence to scare off, corruption by others. Alliances between corrupt officials (as well as common-law criminals) and the police, the public prosecutor and the judge appear to be standard practice in Russia today, and also occur in countries with heavy involvement in the drug trade.

All or nearly all forms of corruption can be reduced to a basic principal-agent problem. Instead of principals (families, owners of property and business) acting for themselves and dealing with other principals on terms of conventional bargaining equilibria or conventional rules (that may or may not involve payment), principals resort to agents who are supposed to represent and defend them and are better equipped to deal with the agents on the opposite side. The incentives that motivate the agents are never identical with the interests of their principals. The agents are under a constant temptation to abuse the bargaining and dealing powers delegated to them, and in effect to betray their principals.

The greatest agent, overarching them all, is of course the sovereign state acting on behalf of its principal, the people. The great majority of less universal principal-agent relations are created by and derived from the many roles the state as the people's putative agent has been empowered to play. It is the ultimate creator of opportunities for corruption.

If a lesson can be drawn from such reflections, it is that fighting corruption by investing in police and judicial activity is unlikely to yield much of a result even against types of corruption where the perpetrator is not the government itself, but its lower-grade agents. The near-epic war against the drug trade in Mexico and Colombia has shown that as narco-traders are picked off by police and army, they are promptly replaced by others, for the size of the drug industry is dependent almost exclusively on American demand for drugs that, in turn, resists attempts to reduce it by police work. Likewise, corruption fills the scope that is inherent in the principal-agent relationship and its built-in ease of abuse. The reduction of corruption would follow as naturally from a reduction in the scope of government as the decline of the drug trade would follow from a fall in the demand for narcotics.

3. THE DEMISE OF GDP IS PREMATURE

Replacing GDP with more sophisticated yardsticks could prove to be the slippery slope to Daddy-knows-best.

When one messenger keeps bringing bad news, shoot him and find another. This is what France seems about to do. For nearly three decades, the country has been inexorably slipping down the world (and even the European) league tables of income per head. Little by little the sluggishness of GDP growth, and in particular the nationally very sensitive comparison with newly dynamic post-Thatcher Britain, has undermined French pride and arrogance and spread an unwonted sense of humility and self-pity. The presidency of Nicholas Sarkozy was to change all that. He was aiming at GDP rising by a regular 3 percent per annum and said that if growth will not come soon, he will go and get it. Unlike his two predecessors, he is plainly trying hard but seems less and less sure of success. In the new year 2008, he has put forward an alternative that may be easier to realize.

If GDP will not grow as one would wish, use an alternative that will. Referring to the teaching of the communist sociologist Edgar Morin, Mr. Sarkozy reminded public opinion that gross national product was not the same thing as well-being, and that it took many other variables than material production to make a civilization and a high quality of life. On the league tables of these other variables, France ranked much higher than on the GDP table.

To drive home the point, he invited the two most prominent economists of the worldwide Left, Amartya Sen and Joseph Stiglitz, both of impeccable technical credentials and a high political profile, to co-chair a committee to be charged with working out measurements of components of well-being and civilization that would tell us more than plain GDP. That GDP does not tell a complete story of the good life is not news. It has been common knowledge for at least a generation. A

First published by Liberty Fund, Inc., at www.econlib.org on February 4, 2008. Reprinted by permission.

working party of the OECD has been studying the problem for years, but one more committee must surely be a good idea.

The GDP has many venial sins but it has one great virtue. Like any other index number, it suffers from the necessity of adding apples and oranges and subtracting bananas from the sum, operations that are intrinsically meaningless. For operations that are not nonsensical, the apples, oranges, and bananas have all to be artificially converted into numbers on the same scale. Their sum can serve as an index. In most indices, the number assigned to the apples, oranges, and bananas are ultimately matters of opinions and judgments. GDP as an index number, on the contrary, has nothing to do with the opinions of the indexer. It is the "objective" result of the "subjective" choices of billions of consumers and producers who jointly determine world prices. GDP is based on market prices, not on opinions about how apples and oranges ought to be valued from a moral point of view. It would be impossible for a left-leaning statistician to overweigh welfare provisions or public ill-care, and for a right-leaning one to overweigh police services over and above the money spent on these services which, though not sold in a market, employ labor whose price depends to a great extent on the value the market puts on labor of various types. GDP, for all its faults, does not admit ideological massaging. It can hardly be manipulated to favor Left or Right.

Admittedly, GDP can come up with silly results, but those are small-scale. If people start taking in each other's washing instead of doing it themselves, GDP will go up. The Swedish welfare state used to be mocked for mothers looking after the small children of other mothers and grown children taking care of other people's aged parents instead of their own, all of which lifted GDP. In a tiny sheikdom, GDP per head may go sky-high as the oil is pumped out from beneath the desert sand, but no depletion allowance is deducted to account for there being that much less left to pump out in future years. In the northern hemisphere, a mild winter depresses GDP and a hard one boosts it. There is a bit of double counting in most national income accounts, and adding in the "black" economy is educated guesswork. But these vices do not vitiate the concept nor its honesty in conveying good and bad news alike.

What should we expect Sen-Stiglitz amendments to do? For one, they might decide that if money GDP goes up by 2 percent, quality-adjusted GDP is higher if all incomes go up by 2 percent than if all incomes go up by 1.8 percent and the remaining 0.2 percent swells the incomes of a few thousand households by 30 percent. Mr. Sen is intellectually fastidious enough not to say that the former distribution is actually bigger than the latter. But he might say that he likes it better, and that most people do too, and that this should in some way be accounted for. Distribution would in any case affect quality and may be awarded an index number.

It would be no surprise if the Sen-Stiglitz committee also composed an index number out of the several indices that seek to measure the achievements of popular education, perhaps building into it a special allowance for the occupational or income category of parents. Another obvious candidate for an adjustment factor for the quality of life could reflect the state of health of the population and the success of efforts to care for the sick. Questions of equality and inequality might well enter into these calculations too.

A quality-adjusted GDP could very well also reflect the length of time couples living together stay together, the ratio of urban parks to built-up areas, data on rubbish collection and disposal, the average time the gainfully employed population spends traveling to and from work, the rigor of food safety standards, crime statistics, the suicide rate, pub drinking hours, and the regulation of industry and commerce in the public interest.

The list could go on and on, depending on the productivity and ambitions of the Sen-Stiglitz committee and the brief they are given. Some of the potential items on it are trivial or risible, but most do have a serious impact on how people get on with their lives and how propitious are the circumstances for them not to be too discontented even if GDP growth gives them little or nothing from one year to the next.

Nothing much can be done about many of the items on the list; they are facts of life, time, and place. Others, however, can be modulated, pushed back or forth, and generally shaped by public policy.

Precisely here lies the ground for fresh concern. When faced with the choice between the status quo and some potential improvement that it is the legitimate business of government to tackle, at a cost spread so widely and thinly over the entire society that nobody much notices it, the bias of public policy in most societies is to go for the improvement.

The effect can be good in detail but unexpectedly and puzzlingly bad in the aggregate. Welfare states tend to suffer from this syndrome. It is not new, and has been noticeable even before the replacement of bare GDP data by sophisticated adjustments and allowances for quality have come to the center of media attention and political "spin."

Now, however, a new element will redouble the activist bias. When, as in the case of modern France, one welfare provision, one administrative intervention, and one extension of the area of public policy follows another, and each of the several hundred laws and decrees passed each year brings a putative improvement, yet GDP for that very reason grows more and more sluggishly, opinion in the country becomes dubious and may even flirt with some liberal ideas. But if the race for improvement along a hundred fronts produces heartening improvement in the quality-adjusted neo-GDP that is destined to bury the orthodox one, the hand of activist government is incomparably strengthened. Not only does Daddy know better what should be done, but the numbers start saying so too. This looks like the ideal start of a long slippery slope. On the whole, it may be safer to face embarrassing truths and unflattering league table positions, and not hasten the demise of the old and plain GDP.

4. WHEN IS A CHANGE A GOOD THING?

Political economy is much, perhaps most, of the time on the side of the angels. It teaches people that resources are scarce, realities cannot be wished away, the consequences of well-meaning government action are often painfully surprising, and you cannot have it both ways. At times, though, political economy will implant beliefs in the public consciousness that lend legitimacy and moral support to policies that democratic governments are only too inclined to adopt. The "infant industry" argument against free trade is one example, and there are many others. The most important is probably utilitarianism that used to hold the intellectual high ground from the time of Bentham to that of Pigou. It accustomed the public to the strange idea that happiness, satisfaction, or "utility" was a homogenous entity that pervaded society and increased or decreased as desirable goods and services enjoyed by individuals increased or decreased, though not necessarily in the same proportion. As a rule, as an individual's budget of goods (i.e., his income) increased, the "marginal utility" of the income decreased. The marginal dollar given to a poor man generated more "utility" than the same dollar given to the rich man. Simple arithmetic told you that total utility would increase if you gave to the poor and took from the rich, and that total utility reached its maximum when all incomes were equalized. Redistribution enhanced the common good.

The "new welfare economics" of the 1930s and beyond has recognized that adding different individuals' "utilities" was arrant nonsense and subtracting the losses of some from the gains of others was doubly so. As the English philosopher Philippa Foot tellingly put it, "There was only a black hole where the common good used to be."

Following Vilfredo Pareto, a change in the social state of affairs was accepted as unequivocally better only if it was worse for none and better for at least one person (whether "better" and "worse" meant ex

First published by Liberty Fund, Inc., at www.econlib.org on June 2, 2008. Reprinted by permission.

ante preference or ex post satisfaction). Changes that produced some gainers but also some losers were objectively noncomparable. Like any interpersonal comparison, they could be assessed by any observer as matters of his personal value judgment, but could always be challenged by another observer with a different value judgment. Within the wide bounds of grim misery and smiling abundance, which all observers would rank the same way, there could always be legitimate disagreement about the goodness or badness of a change that seemed good for some and bad for others. The common good or the public interest were up for debate and not fit subjects for scientific inquiry and agreement on facts.

It so happened, however, that many or most people who played the role of observer and habitually proffered judgments on matters of welfare carried and still carry in their subconscious a large residue of the old utilitarian tradition and instinctively reason in the marginal dollar yielding a "greater utility" in the hands of the poor than in those of the rich. They thus draw a false conclusion about how to increase "aggregate" utility (instead of saying, quite correctly, that a dollar makes a greater difference to the poor than to the rich—a finding that is then confusedly transformed into a finding about aggregate utility and how to increase it). The upshot is that despite the Paretian logic of the new welfare economics, there is a climate of opinion that not only favors rich-to-poor redistribution on both altruistic and self-interested grounds, or out of envy and spite, but also imagines that its stand is supported by an obvious rational argument.

While a change involving straightforward redistribution in a definite direction can only be taken as good or bad by choosing between rival value judgments (which in turn involves further value judgments), certain other changes lend themselves to fact-finding as well as value judgment. The standard case is reorganization of production—an investment project, a technological innovation, a shift in the terms of trade, excise taxes or other causes impacting relative prices—from which some people or groups gain but others lose. Attempts have been made to determine the net effect of such Pareto-noncomparable changes. All are question-begging, though some more so than others.

Friedrich Hayek, along with his immense learning and magisterial intelligence, is occasionally of an angelic innocence that can be downright startling. In discussing whether the state should produce generally useful goods and services the market could or would not produce, he blandly offers this conclusion: ". . . the only question which arises is whether the benefits are worth the costs."[1]

Discussing the compulsory acquisition of land by the planning authority, his conclusion is no less question-begging: "If they are to be beneficial, the sum of the gains must exceed the sum of the losses."[2]

Of course, if the benefits are worth the cost, or the gains exceed the losses, all that needs to be said has been said; it is a tautology that the change is a good change. But the problem is precisely that the answer to the question that is being begged is so controversial and wickedly complicated. It has tormented some of the sharpest minds in economics. It would be reduced to relatively straightforward cost-benefit analysis if the preferences or satisfactions of taxpayers and beneficiaries, gainers and losers could be taken as adequately reflected by the sums of money they paid or received, and where a cost of $100 paid by one person were exactly offset by a benefit of $100 received by another. However, nothing permits us to suppose this.

The famous Kaldor-Hicks[3] theorem proposed a "test" of whether a change induced by a reorganization of production was a good one. Little, in his equally famous *Critique of Welfare Economics*, rightly pointed out that the theorem formulated is not a "test" but a "definition" of a change being good; but this does not really affect the present argument.

Suppose that in a river valley there are many farms, each tilling some of the valley bottom and grazing sheep on the hillsides. A dam is then built at the valley mouth to produce hydro power for the region's towns and cities. The arable land of the farmers is flooded and they are reduced to the hillside sheep runs. They lose. The townspeople of the region gain. By Kaldor-Hicks, the dam is a good thing if the gainers could overcompensate the losers, pay for the dam, and have something left over.

1. Friedrich A. Hayek, *The Constitution of Liberty* (Chicago: Chicago University Press, 1960), 222.

2. Ibid., 351.

3. Nicholas Kaldor, "Welfare Propositions of Economics and Interpersonal Comparisons of Utility," *Economic Journal* (September 1939): 549, and J. R. Hicks, "The Rehabilitation of Consumer Surplus," *Review of Economic Studies* (1940–41): 108.

One objection made to this definition of goodness was that if the change entails a "bad" distribution of income, it would not be good. It may make rich gainers super-rich and leave the poor losers as poor or nearly as poor as before, even if compensation for their loss was actual and not just hypothetical. This objection, of course, relies on a value judgment about income distribution and represents a subjective element in the assessment of the change.

A perhaps more devastating objection made by Tibor Scitovsky[4] was that under certain conditions the gainers could bribe the losers to accept the change and then the losers could bribe the gainers to undo it, thus reducing the "test" to absurdity.

The more arcane and fragile the theorem turns out to be, the more one feels the absence of an obvious question that it does not ask: Why does a Pareto-noncomparable change, with its gainers and losers, exist at all? Without abnormally high transactions costs and unspecified obstacles, including incomplete information, the prospective profitability of a hydroelectric dam across the valley would attract entrepreneurs, one of whom would contract with the valley farmers for their bottom lands, with electric utilities for the future power supply, and with builders and engineers for the dam. There would be no losers to begin with; all parties would be made as well off as before and most probably better off. Instead of the Pareto-noncomparable situation that must leave us agnostic about its goodness, we would have a clear and simple Pareto-improvement "tested" by the fact that all parties entered their contracts voluntarily.

Believers in the prevalence of "market failure" could invoke transactions costs and the other "usual suspects" to explain why the state should be called upon to reallocate productive resources when gainers could compensate losers as a result. The burden of proof would lie with them to show why transactions costs and the usual suspects obstruct solutions by voluntary exchange but do not obstruct the state, thanks presumably to its proverbial superior competence.

4. Tibor Scitovsky, "A Reconsideration of the Theory of Tariffs," *Review of Economic Studies* 9, no. 2 (1942).

5. THE PRICE OF EVERYTHING

In his new book, *The Price of Inequality*,[1] Professor Joseph E. Stiglitz nearly completes his metamorphosis from left-leaning but serious scholar to severe prosecutor. The reader owes him thanks, for the book carries the germs of interesting conclusions, though they are the very opposite to which Professor Stiglitz seeks to lead him.

The author who, according to the *New York Times*, holds the "commanding position" in the storm troop of unorthodox economists has earned his Nobel Prize for his work on asymmetric information in exchanges between a well-informed seller and a poorly informed buyer on terms that are, on some definition, inefficient and false, and can subjectively be condemned as unjust. In his new book, Professor Stiglitz remains faithful to the asymmetric information that has earned him fame as an observer. He now makes massive use of it, but no longer as an observer. Now he is the seller, bowling the buyer over with an avalanche of arguments supported by eloquent statistics. The statistics are selective and serve the purposes of the selector. If the reader buys the argument, he does so mainly because he is less informed than the author about the existence of masses of alternative statistics that tell a different story but are kept out of the book.

The lead proposition we are invited to buy is that inequality has drastically increased and is still doing so, not because of globalization or labor-saving technologies, but because the rich and powerful used their influence to rig taxation, expenditures, and public policy in general to weaken government, undermine the bargaining power of labor, destroy some of the regulatory framework and bias what was left of it, reduce competition—the heads of the indictment are rolling out in a seemingly endless sequence. The word "inequality" stands for the lot

First published by Liberty Fund, Inc., at www.econlib.org on October 1, 2012. Reprinted by permission.

1. Joseph E. Stiglitz, *The Price of Inequality: How Today's Divided Society Endangers Our Future* (New York: W. W. Norton, 2012).

as a whole. This inequality imposes a huge cost on society—hence the title of the book.

The price of inequality is paid in three ways: in the degradation of the market economy, in the loss of social justice, and in the threat to democracy.

The degradation of the economy manifests itself in the incapacity of the market to generate growth and employment. It is true enough that in much of the Western world, growth is sluggish and unemployment scandalously high. But it is totally arbitrary to claim that lack of growth and inequality are causally linked. South Korea has had more than a half-century of stellar growth accompanied by extreme inequality of income and wealth and what Mr. Stiglitz more vaguely calls "power." Much the same is true, to a lesser extent, of Taiwan, Hong Kong, Singapore, China, India, Chile, and Peru. Western Europe is distinctly more egalitarian than the United States but does not show any convincing capacity for faster growth and seems clearly less able to employ its population usefully. Japan is as close as any developed country to an equal income distribution, and has had near-zero economic growth for the last two decades. Are all these big and small, developed and undeveloped countries exceptions to the rule Professor Stiglitz asks us to believe in, and if so, what is left of the rule? One might more plausibly interpret the statistics as evidence that growth goes with inequality, stagnation with equality. In fact, however, such a reading of the numbers would be just as questionable as its opposite. This is surely one conclusion Mr. Stiglitz did not mean for us to draw. Like it or not, "other things are not equal" and it is "other things" that tell true stories.

Another way in which we are supposed to pay a grievously heavy price for inequality is the lost sense of social justice. In the United States, the income of the lawyers, medical specialists, and hedge fund managers in the top 1 percent of the income spectrum has risen from two hundred to three hundred times the average household income. The latter, at $50,000, has in real terms been stagnant for two decades. This, we are told from all sides, is creating bitter resentment. Dire consequences may follow.

The idea is tricky and must be handled with care. As likely as not, resentment would be no less bitter if top incomes were thirty or only three times the median than it is when they are three hundred times higher. The trigger of resentment may well be the change in inequality rather than its level; and there is little doubt that a large segment of the population resents any inequality, whether the top incomes are three hundred times or merely three times its own. Professor Stiglitz's proposed 70 percent income tax for the top bracket may elicit a grunt of satisfaction on the Left, but no easing of the resentment. It is reasonable to suppose, in addition, that the bitterness felt in the middle- and low-income groups is due as much to the persistent stagnation of their real incomes as to the rich getting richer in a hurry.

Contrary to the author's claim that the rich are getting richer not due to underlying economic trends but by using their power and influence to enrich themselves, I have in this column more than once suggested that the real reason is the enormous expansion of the world supply of unskilled and semi-skilled labor brought about by falling transport costs and trade barriers. With globalization, a billion or more rural people in Asia could be recruited into the urban industrial sector to produce the tradeable goods that undersell the goods hitherto produced in the United States and Europe. Until this new Asian labor is wholly absorbed and its wages rise to Western levels, u.s. and European unskilled wages will remain depressed and the share of profits in value added will rise. Ironically, while this sharpens inequality in the West, it promotes equality on a world scale as Asian and eventually also African peoples are lifted out of misery.

None of this, however, has much of anything to do with justice. Resenting something does not make it unjust. The Stiglitz technique, the same as has been employed by the majority of opinion-makers for the last half-century or more, is to use "equality" as synonymous with "social justice." Once the habit of using either of the two as meaning the other has taken root, inequality has become tautologically the same as a violation of social justice. It became as good as impossible to defend inequality, for you could not possibly argue in favor of injustice. But realizing as we do that Stiglitz, together with the whole soft Left, relies on a linguistic trick to drive home his claims may well lend us the intellectual courage to reject the entire attack on inequality more radically than if the recourse to justice had not been so ambitiously employed.

Finally, we are warned, inequality exacts a heavy price by menacing our cherished form of government, democracy itself. Votes are to a large extent bought for money; with income and wealth distributed un-equally, the rich have much more money than the poor; the rich will buy votes for the Right and pre-empt the votes that would have gone to the Left. Votes for the candidates of the rich make the rich more in-fluential, hence richer, which enables them to buy even more votes the next time round. Their reign becomes unbreakable, self-perpetuating.

Oddly enough the Stiglitz reasoning is once again out of luck. For the 2008 presidential election, $745 million was raised for Barack Obama, twice the $368 million raised for John McCain. The Left duly won, presumably because the so-called fat capitalists raised much less money for vote-buying than minorities, Hollywood actors, labor unions, and students. The Stiglitz theory of the rich buying the votes works a little better for congressional elections, but the buying is not done always for the Right but as often as not for the Left, according to whether it is the Republican or the Democratic candidate who can better serve particular local and special interests. Contrary to Europe, the American legislator may be less ideological and more venal, but his venality serves more to preserve a messy distributional status quo than to make it ever more unequal.

Even if the Stiglitz thesis did not get it wrong too often, it would still be a failure on one fundamental score: it tacitly ignores the rule that you must take the rough with the smooth. Inequality, if he is to be believed, has countless painful consequences that amount to a heavy price. Tacitly and sometimes overtly, he invites the reader to go for re-making it, to smooth out the rough and accept only the smooth with the smooth. This, however, cannot be done. Every alternative social order has built-in consequences, some rough and some smooth, that cannot be sorted out from one another. Equality also has a price like every other system of collective choice rules, and it suffices to think of the late Soviet Union, North Korea, Cuba, and many less acute ex-amples to suspect that its price could be an awesome one, even if im-posed in less exotic countries. It is always tempting for the would-be so-cial engineer to propose reforms that promise to smooth out the rough and reduce the price of the social order. Before yielding to the tempta-tion, it is well to remember that everything has a price, but the price of everything is very hard to recognize, let alone to predict.

6. ENOUGH FOLLY IS ENOUGH

Amateur historians, and even some professional ones, seem to believe that there is such a thing as a theory of history which lifts our sights above the kaleidoscope of events and helps us recognize vast and uniform movements that are to events as tides are to choppy whitecaps. When such movements are looked at in detail, they often turn out to be neither uniform, nor going one way, nor due to a dominant cause. Their uniformity is a subjective impression in the eye of the beholder. They nonetheless remain as parts of the folklore.

The foremost biographers of John Maynard Keynes, Robert (now Lord) Skidelsky and his son Edward, in a recent article in the *Financial Times* headed "Enough Is Enough,"[1] seem to accept the theory that the economic history of the West takes the form of three vast waves or distinct eras of development, starting with production, followed by consumption, and ending in abundance.

So far, the authors do no particular harm—it is done in their subsequent argument—although the three waves they cite are largely imaginary. Production, by which they mean a high share of investment in total output, has sometimes preceded consumption, but occasionally rather followed it. Consumption today is high by historical standards, but even in the prosperous West about one-fifth of the population lives below the official poverty line and has only just started to consume in the sense its critics give to that word. Above all, abundance notoriously lacks a standard meaning. What strikes me as your abundance is mere adequacy of comfort and security to you. Moreover, even these subjective ideas of abundance shift widely with leaps and bounds from one generation to the next and one society to the other. The consumption habits of today's blue-collar family would have looked wildly extrava-

First published by Liberty Fund, Inc., at www.econlib.org on August 6, 2012. Reprinted by permission.

1. The article is a summary of their recently published book. Robert Skidelsky and Edward Skidelsky, *How Much Is Enough? Money and the Good Life* (New York: Other Press, 2012).

gant before World War I. Today's top decile income-receivers do look to be living in abundance in everybody's eyes except their own. Moreover, contrary to the three-waves theory of economic history, there is no noticeable rise in preferences for leisure over work; in fact, higher income continues to stimulate the willingness to work, and the successful and the well-to-do are as often as not "workaholics."

Be all this as it may, the Skidelskys feel authorized to conclude that we have reached a state of abundance where only advertising and the other "usual suspects" drive us to ever higher consumption. They declare that "enough is enough." There is, as opposed to abundance, such a thing as the good life where consumption is not excessive and leisure better appreciated.

If people were bright enough to realize that the good life is better and happiness lies that way, would they not change their working and consuming habits? They could obviously not do it wholly and all at once, but there should be a noticeable migration from what the authors sum up as the "treadmill" towards a life of less work, more leisure, and subdued habits of consumption. No such migration is discernible.

At this point, folly is let loose. People manifestly do not know what makes them happy, and they must be led to the good life. There should be a strict limit on the hours people are allowed to work. This would not only move them nearer to the good life, but would also deal with the scourge of unemployment. Government should guarantee full employment (though only for the permitted number of hours) and should also guarantee a basic income to everyone, whether he worked the permitted number of hours or not. If some people chose not to work at all, that would be all to the good because there would be less output of the merchandise we do not want people to have anyway. Consumption should be taxed at 75 percent, which seems to mean that people are driven to invest rather than consume—a strange objective, given that the greater production the investment would bring about would presumably be unwanted. In fairness, we must allow that the good life these hair-raising measures would be aimed to produce would be better than life in today's North Korea, though perhaps not all that much.

"Enough Is Enough" is impregnated with the ideology that was fashionable a quarter-century ago, and reflects its ideas. It is anti-work, anti-industry, and believes in a vague notion labeled the "good life" which has little to do with the satisfaction of material wants. It is unimpressed by the plain fact that even in the prosperous West, hundreds of millions strive fairly hard to earn more and satisfy more fully their material wants; advertising leads them by the nose and obscures their view of the good life. The authors would keep jobs open for anyone who wanted to work, but are even kinder to the beachcomber who does not, but would still get the basic income everyone is entitled to—a social achievement that used to raise much enthusiasm among the soft Left academia of the latter part of the last century, though it has fallen into disuse more recently. Mercifully, the article invokes neither market socialism nor environmentalism, but even without these two ingredients, enough folly is enough.

What makes this attempt to revive out-of-fashion ideas so untimely and incongruous is the kind of future we seem to be facing. It looks likely that whether or not we recognize the good life, in the foreseeable future we will have to work rather harder and consume a little less than we have expected to do until quite recently. There are two main reasons for that. One is that even without special generosity to the beachcomber, the entitlements of the welfare state have grown to cost more than we were willing to pay for, and the cumulative shortfall has been loaded onto the backs of future taxpayers until no more could safely be loaded. In particular, the spectacular lengthening of life expectancy was making the charge of future pensions a crippling one. The other claim upon our capacity to work harder is the future cost of dealing with such contingencies as a more capricious climate, a rising sea level, and the switch from cheaper sources of energy, such as nuclear and hydrocarbons, to dear ones like windmills and solar panels. None of this may turn out to be as catastrophic as it sounds, but the sum of it all must inevitably require more effort and make the prospect of a beachcomber nirvana recede in the distance of adolescent imagination.

To call for making work purely optional and prohibiting it beyond a strict limited number of hours at this precise juncture of our history is the last thing a responsible thinking man should do. It is sheer raving folly, and of this folly, enough is enough.

7. THE MILLSTONES OF EGALITARIANISM, PART 1: DISTRIBUTIONISM BY FACTS OF LIFE

Western societies are dragging along egalitarian millstones. The ropes that tie these on deserve a close look.

Air traffic controllers must be observant, alert, concentrated, and dependable, but need not be rocket scientists. For what they are and do, they earn salaries way above the average of their peers in the same kind of class. Traders in financial products and commodities in the major investment banks need to be similarly observant, alert, rapid but not rash, and dependable. Except for some specialists who fashion bespoke derivatives, they need no rocket science. For what they are and do, they earn from ten to fifty times more than the air traffic controllers. Stars among them may earn hundreds of times more.

When bank chiefs are castigated about this by their governments and the press, they reply that they can't help it; if they paid much lower bonuses, their best traders would be poached away by their competitors.

This is one of the small mysteries in the theory of income distribution. There are hardly more than about ten investment banks in the world with the capital and the trading volume that can bear the cost of astronomical trader bonuses. The chiefs of these ten or so banks all know each other quite well and are in frequent contact. The setting looks ideal for an oligopsony, a small number of buyers quietly agreeing to reduce the price at which they will all buy. It goes against the textbooks, and against common sense, that these banks do not gradually reduce traders' bonuses in tacit concert with one another.

This anomaly is but a minor incident, but as an irritant under the skin of public opinion it is most potent. It raises to real fury the banker-bashing passion which, understandably enough, has been exciting so many commentators since 2008. Like ever-widening rings in the water,

First published by Liberty Fund, Inc., at www.econlib.org on March 7, 2011. Reprinted by permission.

passionate interest expands to the great questions of distribution. The really burning question facing our societies is that collective demands for welfare entitlements of all sorts, most of them arguably justified on grounds of compassion and solidarity, chronically exceed the resources we produce to meet these demands. We cannot afford the entitlements we have already granted to ourselves, but we refuse to cut them. The only sensible alternative would be to try and induce the economy to grow faster so as to fill in the resource gap. Instead, more attention than ever is paid to the "slicing of the cake," to the distribution of the resources that are actually being produced.

SOME ECONOMIC FACTS OF LIFE

The elementary truth about distribution is that the product accrues to the factors that are producing it, each factor getting the value of its contribution. The cake is not, as popular and populist economics often falsely pretends, baked first and then bargained over who gets how big a slice. Production and distribution are not two distinct phases of a process. In a reasonably competitive market for labor and capital, the slice each gets is determined by their marginal contribution to the cake that is about to be baked. Capital and labor will be devoted to cake-baking as long as the marginal product of each is not less than their price. When marginal products are equal to factor prices and when the number of cakes that it is worthwhile to bake at these prices is equal to the number of cakes the owners of these factors want to buy, all is well. Profit from cake-baking is maximized, greed is satisfied, and "greed is good" because it is the sole incentive known to man that is satisfied by behavior that happens to conform to the optimal allocation of resources.

Factors of production, however, are not homogenous. The labor of one person may be worth many times the labor of another depending on the brains and muscle, various talents or the lack of them, the character or its absence, and the level of education of each. These personal endowments weigh even more heavily in the balance for independent entrepreneurs and heads of enterprises than for those they employ. Economic facts of life generate an unequal distribution for two major reasons. The primary one is that personal endowments are intrinsically different and so are the resulting marginal contributions of members of the labor force. The distribution of the national income would be growing more unequal over time even if, by some sinister miracle, an initial "starting gate" position of the same property and the same income for everybody could be created.

Once the distribution is unequal, a secondary reason kicks in to make it more unequal. Since the proportion saved from high incomes is generally higher than from low ones, capital accumulation from an unequally distributed total is higher than from an equally distributed one. This tends not only to speed up economic growth, but also further promotes inequality due to the unequally distributed ownership of capital.

Evidently, like most other facts of life, the tendency to inequality loses some of its force as it progresses. If capital accumulates faster than the growth of the labor force, and technical progress is not biased in favor of capital, the demand for labor will grow, the marginal product of capital will decline relative to that of labor, and the share of wages in national income will swing in favor of labor. Needless to say, when trade liberalization and the fast advance in transport technology causes four hundred million or so rural Chinese to enter the world industrial labor force, to be followed by as many Indians, basic wages will not rise as they would have done without this massive influx of fresh labor. Inequality will continue to grow instead of slowing down, let alone stopping. This is the actual situation which is, pardonably enough, so much resented. Sooner rather than later, however, the forces equilibrating distribution at a high but steady degree of inequality must gain the upper hand. The underlying tendency of unequal distributions to grow faster than equal ones remains intact, and so does their capacity to rescue the poor from permanent poverty.

EGALITARIAN PROPENSITIES

Three propensities account for many, and probably most, people leaning towards egalitarianism of a vague, ill-defined kind. The simplest and most visceral is envy, the desire to see the "tall poppies" cut down to size and deprived of the good things of which they have such an outrageous excess. The envious is satisfied if the rich are deprived of the good things they do not deserve, but he does not count on these good things to be handed over to him. In this sense, envy is selfless yet demeaning and therefore not openly avowed.

A different propensity, on the other hand, is the selfish one of looking for material gain from an egalitarian move. A society's mean income being above the median signifies unequal distribution. Convergence of the mean toward the median potentially increases all below-average incomes; those with incomes below the median gain in any case, and those with incomes above the median but below the mean benefit if the egalitarian move takes the form of cutting down the excess of incomes above the mean and redistributing this excess only. Intermediate solutions that cut partially into incomes below the mean but above the median, as well as into the ones above the mean, would still leave a majority of gainers and a minority of losers. A majority would naturally tend to be egalitarian, subconsciously convinced that the equalizing move would work to their benefit. A belief that the good of the majority is somehow the same as the "common good," a belief that is no less widespread for being grossly arbitrary, reinforces the egalitarian propensity.

A third egalitarian propensity is less evidently at work, and its very existence is open to dispute. Most evolutionary theorists contend that the conditions of life of wandering hunter-gatherers for at least a hundred thousand years imposed the equal sharing of irregularly obtained food in the extended family or group as the best survival strategy. The wandering life and the unpredictability of finding food, as well as the limited techniques of preserving surpluses for rainy days, promoted the survival of people inclined to share food. Their genes were selected for survival over the genes of the non-sharers. Present-day populations carry the same genes and hence have an egalitarian propensity.

This contention is neither verifiable nor falsifiable, but not wholly convincing. For at least the last ten thousand years, the wandering hunter-gatherer has been mainly replaced by the sedentary peasant who had an adequate technique of storing food as security for his nuclear family. Sharing it more widely would benefit the genes of kinfolk to the detriment of his own. As a genetic survival strategy, this would be an inferior one. Supposing that the peasant persists with share-and-share-alike would mean that he allows himself to be fooled into an obsolete behavior that no longer best serves his genetic survival. We cannot argue that he would not be so fooled, but we can at least doubt that the genetic heritage of hunter-gatherer life makes of him a natural egalitarian today.

SOME POLITICAL FACTS OF LIFE

When state-of-nature society first coagulates into a state and collective choice starts to dominate individual choices, the effect is initially inegalitarian. The leader of the war band, the tribal chief, the king asserts his power by acquiring the support of a minority group that he selects and rewards by large grants of land and serfs, or confirming it in its pre-existing large possessions. Command over the majority is exercised by relying on the organized force of this privileged group. Often the commanding minority selects itself in the course of conquering the land of the majority, as was the case of the Franks in Gaul, the Normans in Britain, and the Scandinavians in Russia. The resulting very unequal distribution of wealth, income, and status may remain fairly stable for centuries, subject only to dynastic and feudal conflicts and the slow erosion that economic forces inflict on political structures.

Political facts of life, inegalitarian at the outset, turned massively egalitarian as the conditions of exercising collective choice underwent accelerating change from the seventeenth century onwards, until they came to take the shape that we know as the democracy typical of the modern Western world. The two key changes were that the important decisions were to be made by the majority imposing them on the minority and not the other way round as in past centuries, and that the tenure of government power was no longer freehold—permanent until terminated by some stochastic event—but leasehold, terminated automatically at intervals imposed by an electoral calendar. The power to govern expired periodically and had to be regained by winning the grace of the majority.

With competition for the majority's grace and favor more or less open, a redistributive auction in order to recruit a majority was the obvious consequence. In its purely logical form, stripped of historical and incidental detail, the conclusion was defined by the median voter

THE MILLSTONES OF EGALITARIANISM, PART 1

theorem. Competitive bidding for votes would, in this pure theory, converge to identical redistributive offers in which half of the electorate plus one would benefit at the expense of the other half of the electorate minus one. In real life, for a multitude of good reasons, the median voter theorem is only quite imperfectly realized. In its stead, we have the irregularly but irrepressibly expanding welfare state. It is the most robust fact of political life. In its effects, it is the diametric opposite of the economic facts of life that act upon distribution. Ostensibly, equalization of income and wealth is not the object of the welfare state. Its specific measures aim at entitling specific groups to specific benefits at the expense of the general public. The groups in question are invariably deserving of help. It takes stony hearts to oppose their entitlements. The raising of the necessary means is achieved in three main ways. One is by sales or value-added taxes that are regressive but are supposed to be largely unnoticed, painless. Another, increasingly important, is the shifting of the cost on to a future generation by deficit financing and unfunded pension liabilities. Only the third source, progressive income capital gains and inheritance taxes, is overtly egalitarian. But compared to the total budget, such direct taxes are not very large. However, they serve as a useful egalitarian fig leaf and play well to the populist galleries.

The overwhelmingly largest part of the egalitarian work done by the welfare state is done not by taxation or borrowing on the revenue side, but by the targeted free or below-cost allocation of public goods and services to low-income groups and by compulsory "social" insurance. It is clear enough to the lucid mind that the phenomenon has little to do with right or left wing convictions and ideas about the common good. It is simply the consequence, or perhaps even the logical corollary, of the political facts of life—no matter how it is disguised and embellished as a moral imperative.

8. THE MILLSTONES OF EGALITARIANISM, PART 2: ROPEMANSHIP, OR THE MORALITY OF DISTRIBUTIONS

A PRESUMPTION OF INEQUALITY

There may be changes in the distribution of status, wealth, and income that are made in heaven in the sense of being better for some and worse for none, but they must be hard to find. Arguably, if they were easy to find, they would have been made before now by those closest to them and best able to benefit from the gain they promise. In any event, the great and never-ending debate about how politics should shape society has its focus on the immense variety of possible distributive changes in which some gain but others lose (including the cases where the losers lose not absolutely, but only relatively to the gainers, though there are good reasons for keeping such changes firmly out of the argument).

The net balance of the gainers' gains over the losers' losses is the product of the now discredited aggregation of individual utilities. For most modern thinkers, it is a meaningless operation and must be avoided. But it is a deeply rooted habit of everyday political discourse, and as such, needs to be met head on.

What sort of distribution promises a greater semblance of a net aggregate gain?

Economic facts of life generate inequalities due mainly to human endowments being unequal. Inequalities cause growth and vice versa because they favor capital accumulation. The conclusion strongly suggests itself that inequality is the best or perhaps the only way out of mass poverty, while an equal distribution would leave everybody permanently in the same poverty they suffer at present.

This line of reasoning used to be opposed by "scientific" socialism

First published by Liberty Fund, Inc., at www.econlib.org on April 4, 2011. Reprinted by permission.

which claimed that a rationally planned economy with "production for needs, not for profit" performs better. This claim is now almost stone dead, but not quite: Mervyn King, the governor of the Bank of England, has confidently declared that the British financial services industry was not "socially useful." All in all, however, the emphasis of egalitarian advocacy has clearly shifted to modern "happiness economics." One strand in the happiness-maximizer recipe is that since the success of others makes the unsuccessful unhappy (and this they say so themselves), success should be discouraged by fiscal means. A similar line, though relying not on the say-so of the unhappy but on empirical data, finds that unequal societies have a worse record on life expectancy, cancer, teenage pregnancy, and other ills than equal ones. Much of the empirical evidence has lately come to be contested. In any case, the symptoms of ill health, short life, and related miseries can be just as well imputed to the victims being poor as to the others being richer than the poor.

In sum, in terms of sheer money and the lifting of great masses out of chronic poverty, unequal distributions probably score better. However, the political facts of life are like millstones hung around their necks, a handicap that irons out the inequalities on which much of their performance depends. Egalitarian distributions, used to the millstones, may or may not score better in terms of "total utility" or happiness, but there is no earthly way of telling by any objective measure whether this is so or not. More unequal societies may resemble live streams with some white water here and there. More equal ones look more like stale, lukewarm ponds. Where the fish are happier depends on the kind of fish. In terms of human happiness, we do not have the answers and must stay agnostic. Failing a judgment on happiness, we can only fall back on a general presumption in favor of unequal distributions that come about when no millstones are hung on them, no deliberate political attempts to change them.

EQUALITY POSING AS A MORAL IMPERATIVE

Happiness-based arguments for equality are defeated by their own inherent subjectivity, their utter lack of objective proof, a lack that provokes an agnostic reaction and is defeated by it. The way out for egalitarianism has been, and to some extent remains, the abandonment of the instrumental idea of equality. Since the latter cannot be proven to be a utility-maximizer, an instrument that best helps to achieve the final end of happiness, well-being, the perfect life, or kindred ideals, a more radical defense must be found for it. It must be raised out of its humble instrumental role and promoted to the rank of moral imperative instead.

Doing so is essentially a matter of saying-so, an assertion that depends for its acceptance on repetition and a measure of plausibility.

Perhaps the most popular of these claims is that God has created all men equal. This is tautologically true in that all men are men (and all women are women), hence in that particular respect they are all equal. However, since (except for identical twins) they are in literally countless other respects unequal, the claim is simply absurd. A somewhat similar assertion is that all men are owed, or have a "right," to equal respect and concern. Since as a matter of an elementary fact of life we all respect some people, are indifferent to many, and feel downright contempt for a few, and since we feel and show more concern for next-of-kin and friends than distant "Hottentots," this assertion is also implausible. Finally, it has been strongly affirmed that since talents and other personal endowments are "morally arbitrary" (to use John Rawls' phrase), it would be unfair to profit from their consequences; unequal consequences, such as unequal success or failure in life, cannot be morally defended. However, such consequences are not in need of being morally defended except perhaps if some moral blame is attached to their causes—a condition that talents and character do not suffer from. The claim that they are unfair is preposterous.

THE INDIAN ROPE TRICK

An assertion or affirmation has no intrinsic credibility except accessorily to the extent that the trustworthiness of the attestant or the nature of the thing affirmed lends it some degree of plausibility. In the preceding section, I briefly reviewed the most prominent affirmations that equality is a moral imperative, and found them wholly devoid of verisimilitude. Though they do have some emotional appeal, they lack the content that would permit their inductive or deductive development into a moral rule. I cannot, of course, be sure that no other hitherto unthought-of or at least to me unknown affirmations of equality exist that, contrary to the examples used above, could serve as moral imperatives. However, this seems to me unlikely. Subject to proof of the opposite, I will treat the rhetorical approach to equality as fruitless.

However, there is an alternative approach that is neither rhetorical nor logical and that has proved to be gloriously fruitful. For easy reference, I will call it "ropemanship." One form of ropemanship might be described as the finding of a fastener by which an object that will not fly is tied to one that will, and that will lift it off into a higher sphere.

There are pairs of conceptually related words where the first word in the pair is self-evidently superior, stronger, better, or otherwise preferable. Good and bad make such a pair, just and unjust another. Any argument that good is indeed better than bad, or just is indeed preferable to unjust, would be fatuous and redundant. Let us call these pairs hierarchical. For purposes of ropemanship, they will fly.

A different type of pairs is non-hierarchical; one member of the pair is superior or inferior to the other, depending entirely on the context. Long and short, warm and cold are such pairs, and so is equal and unequal. It is the merits of the case that determine whether equality is superior, more conducive to aggregate happiness and morally ordained than inequality, or whether the ranking goes the other way round. Intrinsically, however, equality does not rank self-evidently higher than inequality. Trying to show that it does leads to a never-ending argument in which the last word recedes into boundless emptiness.

Justice, of course, always ranks above injustice. It suffices to create the word "social justice" to perform ropemanship. Social justice for some must be like justice, for the words resemble each other, hence it must be self-evidently better than social injustice. However, while justice is precisely defined by existing rules of justice, and injustice by the breach of these rules, "social" justice has no ascertainable rules. Nor can social injustice be easily recognized as a breach of relevant rules. (To substitute "fairness" for "justice" is merely stating the same conundrum at one remove, without solving it.)

This embarrassing vacuity is covered up by the relatively new but widespread linguistic abuse of treating "social justice" and "equality" as practically closely connected, "much the same thing."

Since we do not know what else "social" justice might possibly mean, it is easy enough to accept that it must mean a sort of equality. Inequality, by implication, must mean social injustice.

Perhaps the supreme feat of ropemanship is the Indian Rope Trick in which the fakir throws a rope in the air and climbs up along it to the sky. The social philosopher who fastens equality that will not fly to the rope of "social" justice that will take it to the moral stratosphere is just as good an illusionist as the wonderful fakir.

de Jasay, Anthony (*continued*)
    fare; stability; *specific topics, e.g.*
    global financial crisis
democracy: collective choice and, 66,
    140; critical scrutiny of, 140–41; as
    descriptive versus valuative term,
    137–38, 139; economic success
    and, 222; income inequality and,
    263–64; maximin rule and, 138–
    39; redistribution of income and,
    152; rule of law and, 139; social
    welfare and, 137, 140, 273; tenure
    of power in, 139
Denmark, in corruption rankings, 249
Desai, Lord, 241, 242
descriptive versus valuative terms,
    137–38, 139, 154
dissaving. *See* saving/dissaving
distribution and production, fallacy of
    separateness of, 160–61, 225, 269
distribution of income: advantages of
    inequality in, 274–75; distribution-
    independence, theory of, 237–38;
    executive compensation levels,
    popular disgust at, 89, 91–92, 148,
    199, 268; human egalitarian pro-
    pensities and, 270–72; moral im-
    perative, equality as, 275–77; po-
    litical developments and, 272–73;
    unequal nature, basic economic
    fact of, 269–70
distributive justice, 25, 53
Dodd-Frank Act (US), xii, 113, 228,
    233
Double Dip, 13, 44
drug trade, 252
Dunkirk oil refinery, France, pro-
    posed shutdown and strike at,
    114–15
Dutch disease, 130

ECB (European Central Bank), 99,
    105, 195

Ecofin, 213
economic growth: equality/inequality
    and, 262; GNP, 8, 9, 40, 253; re-
    distribution of income affecting,
    39, 161–62; ways to increase, 38–
    39, 211–15. *See also* gross domestic
    product
economic history, concept of uniform
    movements in, 265–66
economics education, 218, 236–39,
    245
Economist, 46, 86
*The Economist as Preacher and Other
    Essays* (Stigler, 1982), 224
education in economics, 218, 236–39,
    245
efficient market theory, 245–48
elasticity of expectations, 209–10
"Enough is Enough" (Skidelsky and
    Skidelsky, 2012), 265–67
equality/inequality: churning versus,
    147–50; democracy, egalitarian
    ideology in, 139; as descriptive ver-
    sus valuative terms, 137–38, 139,
    154; distribution of income, basic
    economic fact of unequal nature
    of, 269–70; economics textbooks
    on, 237–38; empirical studies of,
    157–58, 275; equal poverty ver-
    sus unequal affluence, 156–59,
    274–75; globalization and, 148,
    173–74, 263, 270; human desire
    for equality, 270–72; moral im-
    perative, equality as, 275–77; of
    opportunity versus outcomes,
    225; reasons for, 154–55; religious
    egalitarianism, 60, 156, 276; social
    justice equated with equality, 277–
    78; Stiglitz on price of inequality,
    261–64
Equatorial Guinea, 249
euro. *See* Eurozone
Eurobonds, 31, 234–35

solvency ratios, xii, 61, 64, 190–200,
    210, 230–31, 233
solvency versus liquidity, 179–83, 189
Somalia, 249
Soros, George, 14, 186–87, 240–41
South Korea, 140, 174, 264
Southstream pipeline project, 132–33
sovereign debt. *See* national debt
Soviet Union. *See* Russia
Spain: "contagion," fears of default by,
    219; corruption ranking of, 250;
    deficit of, 4, 86; Eurozone and,
    100, 104; fiscal austerity in, 29;
    housing price bubble in, 75, 186;
    national debt of, 86, 105; social
    welfare and democracy in, 140; un-
    employment and labor laws in, 38,
    67, 72, 214
speculation: bootstrap theory of oil
    prices and, 240–42; commodity
    prices and, 87–88; demonization
    of, xiv, 14–15, 61–62, 103, 192; effi-
    cient market theory and, 245–48;
    Eurobonds and, 234–35; Volcker
    plan and, 102–5
spending. *See* public spending
stability: capitalism, instability at-
    tributed to, 53–55; foolishness of
    desiring, 85–88; global financial
    crisis attributed to inherent insta-
    bility of free markets, 13–16, 85;
    hybrid system of regulated capi-
    talism, instability of, xii, 5, 18, 49,
    53, 58, 61, 64, 65, 79, 85, 228;
    Maastricht Treaty and, 213; of Rhe-
    nanian versus Anglo-American
    economies, 54–55; schemes for
    achieving, 61–62; social welfare
    and, 43–44; stressless economy,
    search for, 74–77
stakeholder theory, 51, 161–62
Standard & Poor's, 189n2, 193–96

The State (Bastiat, 1848), 166n1
Steinbruck, Peer, 90
Stigler, George, 224
Stiglitz, Joseph: Asian financial crisis
    of 1997 compared to global finan-
    cial crisis by, 179, 180–81; on
    asymmetric information, 261; on
    fiscal fetishism, 105; GDP, French
    efforts to replace, 253, 254–55;
    globalization condemned by, 147;
    on price of inequality, 261–64; on
    public spending versus fiscal aus-
    terity, 29, 211; on 2008 as 1989 of
    capitalism, 59
stimulus packages, 3–7. *See also* public
    spending
Strauss-Kahn, Dominique, 184
stressless economy, search for, 74–77
structured investment vehicles (SIVs),
    182
subprime mortgage crisis in U.S., xii,
    10, 14, 57, 60–61, 74–75, 182, 186,
    189
Sudan, 249
supply-side economics, 5, 165
Sweden: in corruption rankings, 249;
    on Russian invasion of Georgia,
    131; social welfare in, 36, 161, 254
Switzerland: bank secrecy in, 118; cor-
    ruption ranking of, 249; voting
    practices in, 27

Taiwan, 262
taxation: capital gains, 273; consump-
    tion (sales or value-added) taxes,
    32, 42, 60, 149, 220, 273; fiscal
    austerity by raising or curbing eva-
    sion of, 29, 30, 32, 37–38; German
    constitutional amendment to limit
    deficit and, 41–42; government
    lifestyle, choice of, 37–38; income
    taxes, 60, 149, 263, 273; inheri-

tance taxes, 273; justice or abusive-
ness of, 119–21; Stiglitz's 70 percent top income bracket, 263; tax
havens and tax evasion, 118–21;
Tobin tax, 14n2, 90, 219, 229
teachers, left-leaning bias and underpaid status of, 236–37
technological innovation, xi, 172, 261
textbooks, economic, 236–39
Thailand, 173
Thatcher, Margaret, and Thatcherism,
5, 11, 19, 26, 32, 63, 207, 253
thin gruel, human preference for
chocolate cake versus, 211, 215
Third Way (between capitalism and
socialism), 59, 61, 62, 65, 161
time preference, 164–65
TNK BP, 129
Tobin tax, 14n2, 90, 219, 229
Total (French oil company), 106,
114–15
total utility, 147, 257, 258, 275
"toxic" securities, 16, 64, 103, 207
transactions costs, 260
transparency, concept of, 119
Transparency International, 125, 249
transport technology, effects of, xi
Tullock, Gordon, 144
Turkey, 111, 129, 131, 133, 184
Turkmenistan, 131, 249
Turner, Lord, 89–90

UBS, 89
Ukraine: Russian gas pipeline passing
through, 132; as tax haven, 119
unemployment: collective choice and,
66–69; fiscal stimulus and liquidity
trap, 22–24; labor laws, onerous-
ness of, 38–39, 70–73, 108, 214,
216–17; Russia's low level of, 122;
workweek, reduction of, 216–17,
266–67

unilateral promises, of self-denial, 35
unions. See labor and labor laws
United Kingdom: Anglo-American
economy of, 54–55; consumer
credit culture in, 3–4; deficit of, 4,
10–11, 40; euro, efforts to "save,"
232; fiscal austerity in, 19, 25–28;
Golden Rule, refusal to commit to,
34; health care in, 110n1, 165–66;
housing price bubble in, 75, 186;
national debt of, 8, 10–11; nation-
alization in, 121; natural gas production in, 132; slowed growth
during global financial crisis in,
208; social welfare in, 110–11, 161;
stimulus package, 4, 5; subprime
mortgage crisis in U.S., reaction to,
57; tax evasion, moral standing of,
119; Tobin tax, rejection of, 229
United States: Anglo-American
economy of, 54–55; Canada, currency difference and trade with,
95; consumer credit culture in,
3–4; deficit of, 40; Europeanization of economy, 112, 113, 137, 140;
financial reform, Atlantic divide
on, 89–92; foreign capital account
in 1970s, efforts to protect, 9; government bond yield, 190; health
care in, 113, 166; income inequality
in, 262; Latino immigration to,
111; national debt of, 170; OECD
economic forecasts for, 54–55;
regulatory costs in, 39; social welfare in, 95–96; stimulus package,
4; subprime mortgage crisis and
housing bubble in, xii, 10, 14, 57,
60–61, 74–75, 182, 186, 189; Tobin
tax, rejection of, 229; triple-A
rating of debt, 104–5; Volcker
Plan, 100–103
utilitarianism, 257, 258